Contents

FOREWORD

MAJOR GENERAL JULIAN THOMPSON
COMMANDER OF 3 COMMANDO BRIGADE
DURING THE FALKLANDS WAR

Although it is now twenty years since the events so graphically illustrated in David Reynolds's book, sometimes it seems like only yesterday to many of us who took part. One of my most vivid memories is being woken by the telephone at 3.15am on Friday 2 April 1982 to be told by Major General Jeremy Moore that the Falkland Islands were about to be invaded by the Argentinians, and my brigade was to load and go south. As I had been told only the day before that the 3rd Commando Brigade, which I commanded, was 'stood down' from any possible tasks, I was doubly surprised.

Even the youngest of us, and at least one of the marines in my brigade was only seventeen, is now thirty-seven years old, and some are a good deal older than that. But in my mind's eye most of the marines, soldiers and sailors who took part in the campaign are still young, and the youthfulness of those who fought and won down south may strike the reader looking at the pictures in this book.

It is a fact of life that in any combat on land, the majority of those who do the actual fighting are in their late teens and early twenties, and the Falklands War was no different. The sailors in the Task Force ships were similarly youthful. Without the young men, the plans and hopes of politicians and senior commanders would have come to naught. Of course the aircrew, both Fleet Air Arm and Royal Air Force, played an indispensable part, as did the crews of the Royal Fleet Auxiliary and Merchant Navy ships, and the war would not have been won without them. But the job of finishing the business lay with young marines and soldiers closing with the enemy, gunners supporting them, sappers clearing mines, logisticians and medics working under air attack and other fire, sailors manning anti-aircraft guns or on lonely duty in enclosed spaces far below the water line. David Reynolds has done a magnificent job putting this book together as a tribute to the men of the Task Force, and of course the women on *Canberra* and *Uganda*.

Julian Thompson

INTRODUCTION

In 1982 Britain sent a naval Task Force to the South Atlantic in response to Argentina's surprise invasion of British sovereign territory. Ironically, at the time the Royal Navy was bracing itself for a series of cuts to its surface fleet. In addition, there were no plans to replace or enhance the ageing amphibious force, leaving the future of the Royal Marines very much in doubt. The Parachute Regiment was also fighting for survival – the airborne brigade had been disbanded just a few years earlier. The Royal Navy's Gannet long-range early warning aircraft had been retired and not replaced, leaving the Navy's air defence exposed. In addition, basic equipment – even soldiers' boots – left much to be desired.

Sadly, it took a war for the UK government to remind itself that the wheel of history has a habit of turning just when you least expect it and therefore well-trained, well-equipped military forces must always be retained. The Falklands conflict also marked a sea change in public attitude towards the military. In an echo of Rudyard Kipling's 'Tommy', the country had for many years held the military in low esteem, sometimes banning soldiers from public houses just for being soldiers. When the Task Force returned the band played, the beer was free and 'Tommy Atkins' was the pride of the nation. The Task Force sailed 8,000 miles into a hostile environment. It landed, marched into battle and conquered.

Opposite: This famous 'Yomper' picture was taken by Peter Holdgate as 45 Commando made their advance across the Falklands. The man carrying the flag was radio operator Peter Robinson who, along with 40 Commando's Mortar Troop, was attached to 45 for the yomp across the island. The photograph was taken at 1030hrs just after a snowstorm ended. The marines were looking at the ground because they were passing through a minefield. They were heading for Teal Inlet having left Two Sisters and Sapper Hill. *Inset*: This rare picture shows the face of Marine Robinson. After the conflict his image was immortalised in a statue, now outside the Royal Marines Museum in Portsmouth.

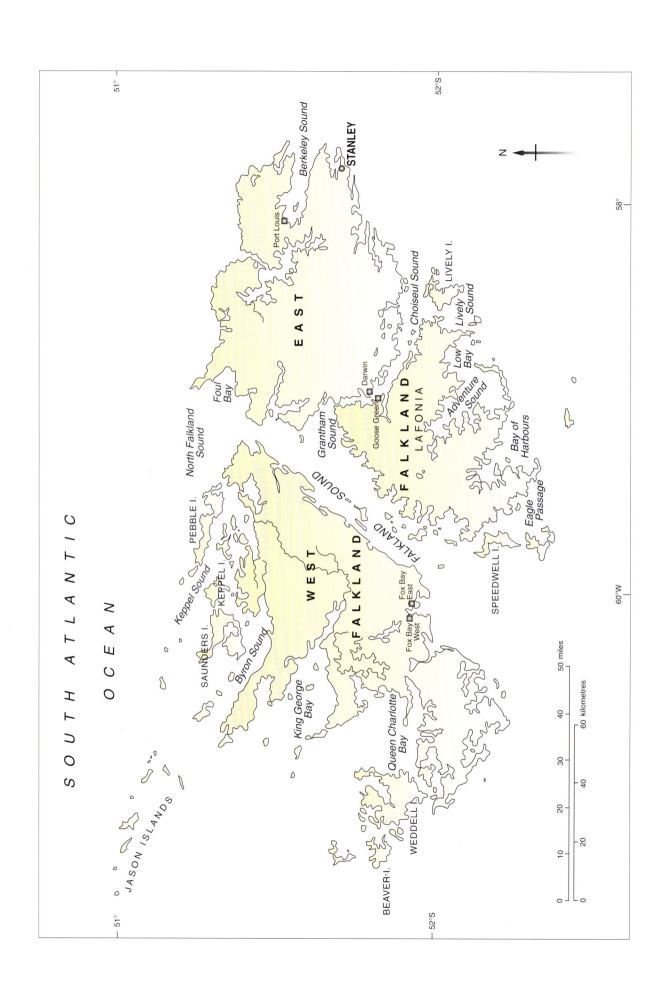

ONE

SOVEREIGNTY DISPUTED

The Argentinian invasion of the Falkland Islands on 2 April 1982 caught Britain and the then Conservative government totally off guard. While repeated intelligence warnings had been passed to politicians in London indicating that Buenos Aires was planning military action to recover the islands, even at the eleventh hour London regarded a full-scale invasion as unthinkable.

In the months prior to the Argentinian occupation there had been a series of worrying incidents indicating that the junta was becoming impatient with the progress of negotiations and that diplomacy could be replaced by direct military action. A scrap dealer had landed on South Georgia on 19 March with a military escort. Repeated warnings to leave issued by the British government were ignored and then Galtieri's naval forces deployed for exercises. Politicians had missed the signals or perhaps had been too preoccupied with matters at home.

When Margaret Thatcher told the Commons she was sure that the House would condemn the unprovoked aggression by Argentina she got its full support. However, many MPs were highly critical of the bungled diplomacy leading up to the crisis, particularly as it was now clear that failure to act in response to the warning signs had left Britain unprepared.

Britain may have misjudged the intelligence reports, but the junta had underestimated the UK's resolve to protect the islanders and fight for the queen's sovereignty. Within hours of the invasion, telephone calls were made by senior officers and troops were put on standby to deploy to the Falklands. This was to be the last colonial war that Britain would fight and for the first time since the Second World War the Royal Navy would engage in open warfare on the high seas.

Government Communications Headquarters (GCHQ) had been monitoring transmissions in the South Atlantic as tension rose, but when it became clear in late March 1982 that an amphibious assault was potentially being planned by Argentina, it was too late for Britain to reinforce the islands. Instead, as ministers slept in their beds a small force of Royal Marines was left on its own to face an initial assault of more than 3,000 Argentinian troops. In what can only be described as one of the most courageous acts by British troops since the Second World War the commandos went into a battle in which they expected to fight to the death.

News of the landings stunned Britain. Within days the country was consumed with patriotic fever as Union flags were hung from office windows and newspapers called

Port Stanley from the air. The majority of Falkland islanders live here. This was the target of the Argentinian force, but only a small number of troops were moved beyond Stanley – a tactical blunder by their commanders.

for military retribution. At the naval bases of Portsmouth and Plymouth dockers worked around the clock to prepare warships for sea. Wives and loved ones then waved a fond farewell, quietly hoping that the conflict would be resolved before the ships hit the South Atlantic.

Few people in Britain had actually ever heard of the Falkland Islands in 1982. Situated 8,000 miles away in the South Atlantic they had for many years been the subject of a sovereignty battle with mainland Argentina. The landscape there is similar to the open countryside of Dartmoor, offering little natural protection from the elements, and in winter the weather is harsh and unforgiving with biting winds, snow and rain making any outdoor activity difficult.

The islanders have always been fiercely proud of their British roots, but as Argentina began to reinforce its claim to sovereignty in the early 1980s they feared the UK government was ignoring their plight. The perception of many Falklanders was that they had been forgotten and that at the first opportunity London would be more than happy to allow Argentina to take control. In 1982 fewer than 1,800 people lived on the islands, with the majority of that number resident in Stanley. Many of the port's buildings were wooden and the quiet town enjoyed the sedate lifestyle of a village community where neighbours knew each other, children played in the streets and crime was unheard of.

Britain's territory in the South Atlantic also included South Georgia, 800 miles to the east of the Falklands. It is extremely mountainous with peaks rising to 9,000 feet and since the closure of the whaling station in 1950 had remained largely uninhabited although members of the British Antarctic Survey were regular visitors. A further 500 miles south-east of South Georgia in the South Sandwich Islands lies Southern Thule, where a small scientific and meteorological base had been located until the 1970s. In 1976 this small island had been occupied by the Argentinians and in 1982 they were still there.

Britain's military presence in the South Atlantic in March 1982 consisted of a small unit of Royal Marines who volunteered to serve in the islands. These men were placed on the ship's detachment drafting list and joined what was called Naval Party 8901. The prospect of serving twelve months in the Falklands where there was little action did not suit all marines. For some it was the opportunity to save money, others would spend the year training before volunteering for special forces duties, while some just wanted to see this wildlife haven. For many, adjusting to the isolation was not easy because even with the luxury of television, radio and numerous bars the islands can be a lonely place, and it is easy to see why some of the earliest settlers did not stay long.

The Falklands were discovered by the Arctic explorer John Davis in August 1592 and two years later Sir John Hawkins, an English adventurer, sighted the islands, but it

South Georgia in 1982, snow-covered and inhospitable. For many years the British Antarctic Survey team had been the island's only guests. The explorer Ernest Shackleton is buried at Grytviken.

was not until 27 January 1690 that the first recorded landing was made by John Strong. For the next 144 years the islands were the subject of sovereignty claim and counter-claim by the French, Spanish, British and Americans. Then in 1834 the Royal Navy warship *Tyne* landed a party of Royal Marines and sailors to help re-establish the British outpost. Since that date the British have always maintained a presence in the islands. A decade later, in 1843, Letters Patent established the colony and Lieutenant Richard Moody of the Royal Engineers was appointed the first Governor and Commander-in-Chief. However, the territorial disputes did not end there. They rumbled on throughout the nineteenth century and into the twentieth. In the post-Second World War upsurge of Argentinian nationalism, Juan Peron became obsessed with his desire to challenge British sovereignty. In 1948 an Argentinian naval task force was assembled ready to sail for the Falklands. In London the Foreign Secretary, Ernest Bevin, defused the potentially dangerous situation and an uneasy calm returned. But in view of the unsettled situation it was decided that British ships would visit the Falklands annually and from 1953 Royal Marine detachments were landed in Stanley on a regular basis. Political relations between the two countries slowly improved, but Argentina's sovereignty claim was not withdrawn. The Falkland islanders were now concerned that the government in London had lost interest in the South Atlantic and feared for the future.

In 1964, after a decade of calm, a pilot landed near Stanley, planted an Argentinian flag and took off again, but sovereignty was not high on the agenda again until September 1966 when a group of Peron supporters calling themselves the New Argentina Movement hijacked a Dakota in what they called Operation Condor and flew to Port Stanley, landing at the racecourse. (The airstrip – later airport – did not exist then.) They detained two British officials at gunpoint, but members of the Royal Marines detachment quickly arrested them and after questioning they were flown back to Argentina.

A year later, in 1967, negotiations over the Falklands took place in New York between British and Argentinian politicians, with the conclusion that the UK government would only consider a concession on sovereignty if it were clear that the Falkland islanders themselves regarded such an agreement as satisfactory. In 1968, after a study and further talks on the subject of sovereignty headed by Lord Chalfont, the Foreign Office minister Michael Stewart announced that 'no transfer could be made against the wishes of the islanders'. The Tory opposition spokesman Sir Alec Douglas Home supported the announcement and added that the Tories would strike 'sovereignty from the agenda' when they returned to office. But in 1968 the British public was unaware that Lord Chalfont had in fact held secret talks with Argentina where he presented a proposal to hand the Falklands over. In November 2001 documents released by the Public Record Office showed that the Cabinet had instructed Chalfont to reach an agreement. Following a six-day trip in November 1968 the junior foreign office minister reported that the Falklands were 'violently anti-Argentine' and their leaders rejected his proposal. The papers released by the Public Record Office after more than thirty years confirmed the claims made by the islanders in the late 1960s that Britain wanted to unload itself of the burden of the Falklands.

In 1973 Juan Peron returned to the presidency of Argentina after a twenty-year exile and nationalistic feeling was stirred up again. The demand for the return of the Falklands to Argentina was taken to the United Nations. By 1975 relations between the two countries were at an all-time low and, concerned at Argentina's possible military intent, Britain responded by saying that any attack on the islands would be met with force. Argentina responded by breaking diplomatic links with the UK.

In 1976, following a military coup, General Videla led a powerful junta in Buenos Aires. Under the direction of the new regime, more than fifty technicians landed at Southern Thule in the South Sandwich Islands in 1976. News of the occupation was suppressed for almost a year until the Callaghan government finally revealed the situation to the Commons in May 1978, but no action was taken to remove the men.

In 1977 British intelligence had indicated that it believed the Argentinians could be planning to mount a further landing after Southern Thule and the government tasked the Ministry of Defence to respond. The Royal Navy deployed the Leander class frigate HMS *Phoebe*, the Type 21 frigate HMS *Alacrity*, the support ships RFA *Resource* and RFA *Olwen* as well as the nuclear submarine HMS *Dreadnought*. Codenamed Operation Journeyman, the mission was planned to provide a significant naval presence in the South Atlantic. It was classified top secret and the operation was only revealed to the Commons in March 1982 at the height of the tension between the UK and Argentina.

By mid-1981 the very mention of the word Falklands was enough to prompt tired yawns from most British politicians. Their reaction was probably not surprising because the dispute over the islands had dragged on for decades with no sign of conclusion. At this time the political temperature between Britain and Argentina appeared to be 'business as usual'. Talks were still on the agenda but were taking a back seat as the junta struggled to resolve its internal problems. In December 1981 General Roberto Viola resigned as president and General Leopoldo Galtieri, who was already commanding the army, took his place. Among Galtieri's supporters was an old friend, Admiral Jorge Anaya, who was a fierce, hard-line member of the junta keen to see the recovery of the Falklands. For Galtieri, capturing the islands would also be an opportunity to generate public support. The two men drew up a plan to get the islands back in Argentina's hands within two years. Anaya's naval forces were to head the invasion.

In early 1982 Argentina was in economic meltdown. A poor administration had created internal chaos, which now threatened the country's future stability. The national debt had soared and banks were preparing to freeze accounts. At the same

The Leander class frigate HMS *Phoebe* (left), Type 21 Amazon class frigate HMS *Alacrity* (above) and support vessel *Resource*. The ships were part of Operation Journeyman in 1977. The mission aimed to increase significantly the Royal Navy's presence in the South Atlantic. The warships were joined by the nuclear submarine HMS *Dreadnought*.

time the UK government made a series of decisions concerning the Falklands which were interpreted by the new dictatorship in Buenos Aires as a clear message that Britain was 'losing interest in the islands'.

Before taking office Galtieri had planned with Anaya to retake the islands. Now he confided in colleagues that the recovery of the Malvinas would solve all their problems. It would divert the nation's eyes from the problems at home. It would also raise national morale and secure his future. The general put his senior planners to work on Operation Rosario – the invasion. Dr Costa Mendes, the Foreign Minister, was given a clear directive to develop the diplomatic environment that would present a sense of legitimate grievance over sovereignty. Mendes's political objective was to win international support for Argentina in any talks with the Falklands Legislative Council.

In contrast, by early 1982 the Falklands were rarely the subject of political debate in Britain. The fact was that the islands were far away and Britain itself was experiencing difficult economic times. For the twelve months before the invasion the government's attention was totally focused on budgetary considerations. All departments were encountering problems with the Treasury as spending reviews were announced. Pressure on the Ministry of Defence was particularly intense and significant savings were demanded. John Nott, the Defence Secretary, suggested, no doubt on advice from senior civil servants, that the Royal Navy's amphibious capability and the ability of warships to provide a naval gunfire support (NGS) role were outdated and irrelevant to the strategic requirement of a future surface fleet. On advice he directed that the Navy should concentrate on submarine operations and countering the Soviet threat.

Nott's White Paper made depressing reading for the First Sea Lord, Admiral Sir Henry Leach, because the senior service was faced with making the biggest reductions. Destroyers and frigates would be axed and it was decided not to replace the entire amphibious fleet. This called into question the seaborne capability of the Royal Marines and potentially put their role, if not their future, in doubt.

The ships listed for the scrapyard included HMS *Endurance*, the visible symbol of the UK's commitment to the Falklands. Painted red and known as the Red Plum, the ship patrolled the South Atlantic and based itself in and around the Falklands every year. The mere presence of *Endurance* around the Falklands and in Port Stanley provided reassurance to the community and sent an important political message to Buenos Aires about the UK's continuing commitment to the islands. Any change in this military deployment could be interpreted as a significant change in British policy.

Opposite: The amphibious assault ship *Fearless*. In 1981 the defence secretary stated the government's intention to focus on the Soviet threat by increasing the sub-surface fleet and made no plans to maintain or replace amphibious vessels. Just twelve months later the Royal Navy showed that seaborne operations were still vital.

THE RED PLUM – HMS ENDURANCE

HMS *Endurance* was one of the Royal Navy's least glamorous ships. She had no big guns or missile silos and was not even painted warship grey. *Endurance* was assigned to the hydrographic department of the fleet, surveying the oceans of the world to produce charts. The ship had been purchased by the Ministry of Defence in 1967 for £300,000 from Denmark where she had started life in 1956 as the *Anita Dan*. She was refitted and painted bright red and white for easy recognition in the Arctic wasteland. The Admiralty then renamed her *Endurance* after Ernest Shackleton's ship and with her unique paint livery the vessel was affectionately known as the Red Plum.

Every year the Naval Drafting Office at Portsmouth would invite Royal Marine volunteers to serve with NP 8901 through the pages of the Corps' journal, the *Globe & Laurel*. After pre-embarkation training at Poole in Dorset the new detachment would join *Endurance* at Portsmouth in the autumn and the vessel would return with the old detachment on board in the spring of the following year. The detachment was normally forty-three strong, commanded by a major, with a lieutenant second-in-command and a colour sergeant in the post of detachment sergeant major. The team also included a signal sergeant and a platoon weapons sergeant as well as corporals representing key SQs (specialist qualifications), those being PW (platoon weapons), HW (heavy weapons), AE (assault engineer), VM (vehicle mechanic), a driver and chef. The remainder were marines drawn from across the Commando units and some direct from training. Marines who served aboard HMS *Endurance* recall amazing sights from their experience in the South Atlantic, including icebergs bigger than the ship and polar bears chasing across the open ice to tear open rubbish bags dumped from the vessel – this of course was before the days of environmental prudence and special regulations which ensure all waste is now returned to port.

Endurance bore the pennant number A171 and at 3,600 tons she had the capacity to carry a ship's company of 116 and two Wasp helicopters which operated from a large helideck at the aft of the ship.

The Red Plum sailing out of Portsmouth naval base. The ship usually sailed from Britain in the autumn carrying the new Royal Marine detachment for the Falklands and returned the following spring. In 1982 her return was to be delayed.

The junta quickly received news of the British Defence White Paper. The withdrawal of HMS *Endurance* was questioned by many and when Lord Tregarne announced the decision to dispose of the ice patrol ship an Argentinian official rang Lord Shackleton to ask if Britain was backing down over sovereignty. The Labour peer, whose father the explorer Sir Ernest Shackleton is buried on South Georgia, had a personal interest in the Falklands. He replied of course not. The islanders themselves were furious at the announcement and sent a message to Lord Carrington on 26 June 1981 which stated: 'The people of the Falklands islands deplore in the strongest terms the decision to withdraw HMS *Endurance* from service. They express extreme concern that Britain appears to be abandoning its defence of British interest in the South Atlantic at a time when other powers are strengthening their position in these areas.' In addition, 1981 brought problems over British citizenship for some islanders and it was announced that the British Antarctic Survey station on South Georgia was about to close for lack of funds.

The junta and Foreign Minister Costa Mendes had now convinced themselves that Britain had changed its policy regarding the Falklands. In February 1982 rumours of potential military action against the Malvinas were leaked to the country's national press and at the end of the month Argentina's national newspaper *La Presna* ran the story. The paper claimed that the military government was to submit a number of conditions to the British and that if the negotiations failed Buenos Aires would take the islands by force. The newspaper claim fuelled belief at the British Embassy that Argentina might try to mount a 'spectacular event' in order to generate international interest and sympathy for its claim to sovereignty. The defence attaché had made a personal visit to the Falklands and wrote a detailed report to the Governor, Rex Hunt.

Colonel Stephen Love, an experienced Royal Artillery officer, sent his secret report to Hunt in Port Stanley on 2 March 1982. It was copied to the Foreign Office and was headed 'The Argentinian Military Threat to the Falklands'. In the paper he clearly highlighted the threat of invasion in six detailed paragraphs, stating that in his opinion if talks did not go their way the Argentinians might see a straight seizure of the islands as an obvious alternative. He also identified the Royal Marines

The Governor of the Falkland Islands, Rex Hunt, who was knighted after the conflict. He warned London about intelligence reports which indicated that Argentina might use force to retake the islands.

detachment as being a key target for Argentina to neutralise. Meanwhile the commanding officer of HMS *Endurance*, Captain Nick Barker, was enjoying his second year in charge of the vessel and in early 1982 reported to the Admiralty a significant increase in Argentinian military radio traffic, but his reports were not acted upon. As the tension between Britain and Argentina mounted the sudden arrival of a scrap dealer in South Georgia was to change events. His appearance may have been a deliberate challenge or an innocent business contract. Constantino Davidoff claimed that he applied in early March 1982 for permission from the UK to implement a contract which he had signed in 1978 giving him an option to buy redundant machinery from the old whaling station in Leith harbour. The contract stated he must dismantle and remove the scrap to Argentina. He claimed permission was granted, although later the British Ambassador in Buenos Aires would deny this. Davidoff had informed the British Embassy that he was planning to sail for South Georgia on 11 March aboard the *Bahia Buen Suceso*, an Argentinian naval support vessel.

On 20 March the base commander of the British Antarctic Survey (BAS) in Grytviken reported that a large party of civilians and military personnel had landed the day before at Leith harbour and raised the Argentinian flag. In addition a notice warning against unauthorised landings had been destroyed by the visitors. Told by the BAS that they should report to the base commander in Grytviken, the Argentinians claimed they had permission from the British Embassy in Buenos Aires to land.

On receiving the reports from South Georgia, Governor Hunt told London he believed the scrap contract was a front for the establishment of an Argentinian presence on the islands and suggested that the party should be ordered to leave if it did not report to Grytviken. Having consulted the commander of HMS *Endurance* he further suggested that the ice patrol ship should sail to South Georgia to enforce the eviction.

Endurance had been scheduled to sail home on 16 March, stopping off at Port Stanley, Montevideo, Buenos Aires, Barbados and the Azores. Instead she had embarked her helicopter and an extra nine marines, then headed for South Georgia on 21 March. After a series of diplomatic exchanges Argentina stated that its ship had left Leith and added that all personnel had left aboard the vessel.

On 22 March the political temperature increased again when minor incidents took place at the offices of the Argentinian Air Force airline in Port Stanley – the Argentinian flag had been replaced with the Union flag and the words 'UK OK'

Opposite: The Royal Navy's ice patrol ship was named after explorer Ernest Shackleton's vessel. News that Britain was to withdraw her from service gave Argentina the impression that the UK was pulling out of the South Atlantic. In March *Endurance* was scheduled to begin her journey home but instead she was redirected to South Georgia to monitor Argentinian military personnel there and await orders to enforce an eviction.

The underground bunker at Northwood where planners directed warships and co-ordinated the operation.

written on windows. On the same day the base commander at Grytviken reported that some Argentinians were still in South Georgia, adding that a French yacht had ignored instructions not to go into Leith and was making contact with them. At this point HMS *Endurance* was 'officially' directed to steam for South Georgia and direction was given for the ship's Royal Marines to remove the Argentinians.

On 23 March Costa Mendez made it clear that 'harsh action by the British would precipitate a harsh response'. The British Ambassador suggested that the *Bahia Buen Suceso* might return to remove the men and Mendez said after the meeting that he was confident he could arrange for the ship to collect the men. Two days later information was received that Argentinian warships were being dispatched to prevent HMS *Endurance* from evacuating the personnel at Leith. On the same day (25 March) *Endurance* reported that another vessel had arrived at Leith, the *Bahia Paraiso*. More alarming was the report that a helicopter and three landing craft had been sighted at Leith.

Lieutenant Keith Mills headed the small Royal Marine force aboard *Endurance* and with Sergeant Pete Leach made plans to recapture Leith. The pair made several reconnaissance trips ashore to monitor the movement of the Argentinian force. Lord Carrington reported to the Cabinet that HMS *Endurance* could remove the remaining Argentinians but added that public opinion in Argentina was in a highly charged state over the incident and warned there was a real risk that if the UK made the eviction warships might intercept *Endurance* or carry out some other military action, possibly against the Falkland Islands themselves.

As the crisis developed in South Georgia conflicting and confusing statements were made in London. Nott seemed to dismiss the threat in the South Atlantic during a debate in the House of Commons on 29 March concerning the procurement of the Trident missile system, when former Navy Minister Keith Speed asked why £3 million could not be spent refitting *Endurance*. The reply that the issues of Trident 'are too important to be diverted into a discussion on *Endurance*' did not please Speed, who had resigned following Nott's damaging cuts in the 1981 defence review.

However, on the same day Britain deployed a nuclear submarine to the South Atlantic following persistent Argentinian refusals to remove the troops from South Georgia. Then on 31 March the Joint Operations Commander at Northwood, the UK's underground control bunker, ordered Captain Barker to land his entire Royal Marine detachment at King Edward Point where they could provide protection for the British Antarctic Survey team. HMS *Endurance* was ordered to remain in the region; the RFA *Fort Austin* was directed to sail from Gibraltar to resupply her.

The junta now had its naval forces ready as naval commanders issued orders to prepare for military action. A secret signal was sent to an Argentinian task force to mount a seaborne landing in the Falklands on 1 April, but the weather was to force a delay.

TWO

OPERATION AZUL

THE ARGENTINIAN INVASION

The final decision to proceed with the seizure of the Falkland Islands had been taken by the Argentinian military junta at a meeting headed by General Galtieri at the presidential palace, the Casa Rosada, on 25 March 1982. The amphibious force was already on exercise; now the Navy increased its readiness and waited for the signal to mount a seaborne assault.

On the following day two Argentinian Navy corvettes, bearing the British-sounding names *Drummond* and *Granville*, were withdrawn from joint exercises with Uruguay and ordered to head south to join a flotilla of six vessels, designated Task Force 40, which were to carry out amphibious landings supported by a further six warships of another flotilla, Task Force 20. The entire fleet was under the command of Rear Admiral Gualter Allara, whose flagship was the British-built Type 42 destroyer *Santisima Trinidad*. He would report to the overall naval commander, Admiral Jorge Anaya.

Codenamed Operation Azul (Blue), the invasion comprised two phases. The first was to be an amphibious landing and the seizure of Government House, Governor Rex Hunt's official residence. The landing would be carried out by the 900-strong 2nd Marine Infantry Battalion reinforced by a platoon of C Company 25th Infantry Regiment, the entire landing force being under the command of Rear Admiral Carlos Busser. The main force would be preceded by a reconnaissance team of Argentinian amphibious commandos, who would be landed at Mullett Creek by the submarine *Sante Fe*. The second phase of Azul would consist of an airlift of reinforcements comprising elements of the 9th Brigade. The objectives of the first phase were to reinforce Moody Brook (the marines' base) and Government House after they had been seized by special forces, and secure the airport in Stanley. Once a firm foothold had been established the second phase of reinforcements from mainland Argentina would be flown in aboard Hercules transport aircraft.

A year earlier the Argentinians had placed an agent in Port Stanley in the form of an Argentinian Air Force intelligence officer, Vice Commodore Hector Gilobert. His cover was that of the local manager of Lineas Aéreas del Estado (LADE), Argentina's domestic airline, which provided the air link with the mainland and retained an office in Port Stanley. Gilobert had recently been replaced by another manager but reappeared on 31 March 1982, apparently to carry out an audit but in fact to check on

The British-built Type 42 destroyer which had been procured by Argentina and named *Santisima Trinidad*. It was the key command vessel for Operation Azul and the flagship of Rear Admiral Gualter Allara.

the latest situation in Port Stanley and report on the dispositions of the garrison. It was easy for him to communicate with Buenos Aires because LADE had a radio link with its headquarters in Argentina.

On his return, Gilobert had discovered that there was not one but two Royal Marine detachments, totalling eighty men, in the islands' capital. One of these, commanded by Major Gary Nott, had almost completed its twelve-month stint on the islands and was in the process of handing over to the relieving detachment under Major Mike Norman. Gilobert reported the presence of the additional marines, twenty-four of whom had been dispatched to the island of South Georgia aboard HMS *Endurance*, and said that measures had been taken to block the runway at Stanley airport. However, he failed to notice the defensive positions being established at Government House. In his briefing he advised there would no threat at the Governor's residence and added that the assault force would have no problems deploying into Stanley. His assessment later proved to be very wrong.

The Argentinians had decided to launch Operation Azul on 1 April but were forced to postpone for twenty-four hours because of bad weather. By this time, however, the British government was well aware that an invasion was imminent.

On 26 March the GCHQ had been monitoring Argentinian Navy radio traffic and had intercepted transmissions ordering *Drummond* and *Granville* to head south to join Task Force 40. It had also picked up the transmission ordering the submarine *Santa Fe* to land the commando reconnaissance team at Mullett Creek. These intercepts had been relayed swiftly by secure means to the Joint Intelligence Committee (JIC) in

London and shortly afterwards to 10 Downing Street and Prime Minister Margaret Thatcher. Later Governor Hunt received a warning that an Argentinian invasion fleet was at sea. At 4.30am on 2 April he broadcast a warning to the islands' population over the local radio station, as islander John Smith later recalled:

> There was a report on local radio that the governor was to make an important announcement. Then we listened as Governor Hunt said there was mounting evidence that an Argentinian invasion was imminent. Everyone was stunned. The Falklands Islands Defence Force were ordered to report to the drill hall, then Mike Smallwood, the radio announcer, said, 'Don't panic, folks. We will now continue with record requests. The show must go on.'

Corporal George 'Geordie' Gill, one of the longest-serving NCOs in the Royal Marines, had already joined the NP 8901 detachment and was a member of Major Gary Nott's outgoing detachment which had been preparing to return to Britain. A sniper who had served with numerous Royal Marine reconnaissance troops, he remembers very clearly the events leading up to the invasion:

> There had been a lot of signals, then on the Tuesday before the landings a group of oil workers arrived in Stanley on holiday. They had short hair and a military bearing and we were convinced they were Argies. They were rounded up and detained by the Falklands Islands Defence Force just before the invasion.

At 5.40am on 2 April Governor Hunt announced that Argentinian landing craft were entering the narrows of Stanley harbour. By this time the combined force of the two Royal Marines detachments, under the overall command of Major Mike Norman, had evacuated its barracks at Moody Brook and dispersed in small groups to various locations in and around Port Stanley, Norman establishing a small headquarters in Government House. With his force comprising fifty-six marines and the twenty-three civilians who were members of the Falkland Islands Territorial Defence Force, Norman's plan was to ambush the invaders before they got into Stanley and slow down their advance. If the situation became really grim, those at Government House would escape to the hills with Hunt himself.

Meanwhile 150 men of the Argentinian Navy's Amphibious Commando Company had landed at Mullett Creek at 4.30am and headed for the Royal Marines barracks at Moody Brook which they reached at 6am. Launching their attack, they raked the buildings with fire from automatic weapons and threw phosphorous grenades through the windows. Finding the barracks deserted, they quickly made for Government House which they attacked shortly after 6am.

Corporal Gill, who had married a Falklands girl and had two daughters, takes up the story:

> We heard the first explosions at around 0555hrs and they were on our position about five or ten minutes later. They came very close, possibly about 30 metres, before the firefight with us started. Suddenly six of them [Amphibious Commando Company] came over the back wall at Government House where three of the lads were waiting.
>
> Three of them were dropped straight away, and the three others ran away in the morning darkness. They were about 10 feet away from each other and it was a case of just pull the trigger. Two of us searched the rooms and we could hear them upstairs in the maid's accommodation so we sprayed the ceiling and heard them shout something in Spanish. We found all three of them and took them prisoner.

It is difficult for anyone who was not there to imagine the thoughts that were going through the minds of the marines at Government House on that morning in April 1982. They faced an overwhelming force which was equipped with massive firepower and could easily overrun their position. Corporal Gill continues:

> Quite honestly we were threaders [Royal Marine slang for fed up]. We just wanted to get on with it. We were prepared for the fact that by midday we could be dead. It wasn't something we accepted in any sense, but when you compared the size of their force to us it was a real possibility. We had no intention of giving up, quite the opposite. We wanted to fight to the last man. They had torn our flag down and I personally had two daughters just down the road. I wasn't ready to give up.
>
> Their first wave was probably about 200 strong and consisted of their special forces. It was pitch black and we couldn't see a thing, but we fired every time we saw a target. The fighting was very close, you are talking eyeball to eyeball at just 100 to 200 yards.

At 8am, as the battle raged around Government House, troops of the 2nd Marine Infantry Regiment disembarked from the landing ship *Cabo San Antonio* and landed at Yorke Bay in twenty LVTP-7 Amtrac amphibious tracked armoured personnel carriers (APCs) to link up with the amphibious commandos. Heading south-east, they passed Stanley airport and advanced southwards towards Port Stanley itself. As they reached the edge of the town, however, they encountered a section of eight Royal Marines under Lieutenant Bill Trollope, who engaged the leading two vehicles,

Argentinian soldiers patrol the streets of Stanley. It is unclear exactly when this picture was taken. The photographer, Graham Bound, was trying to ensure he was not seen.

An Argentinian Panhard drives along the main road towards Port Stanley. The Argentinians had good equipment, but were not as well trained and motivated as the small force of Royal Marines based in the islands.

successfully knocking one out with a Carl Gustav 84mm medium anti-tank weapon (MAW) and two 66mm light anti-tank weapons (LAW). The Argentinian advance was halted temporarily as the remaining APCs disgorged their troops and a fierce action ensued during which more than thirty-two Argentinians are believed to have been killed.

Having received reports of the attack on Moody Brook and the landing at Yorke Bay, Major Mike Norman decided to concentrate his 56-strong force at Government House. Lieutenant Trollope and his men broke contact and withdrew without loss or injury, joining the remainder of the force at the Governor's residence where a fierce battle was raging.

An experienced marine who had been awarded a distinguished pass on the Corps' highly respected sniper course at Lympstone (it is also attended by the SAS and police marksmen), Corporal George Gill patiently waited with his L42A1 7.62mm sniper rifle, which he proceeded to put to good use whenever Argentinian marines and members of the Buzos Tacticos came within range. As he later said:

> No one said anything. We dropped a number of Argentinians as they approached and I had a couple in my sights and made sure they were taken out of the game. It was initially estimated that we had killed five and injured seventeen, but we only counted the bodies that we saw drop in front of us. We know there were many others killed who were not accounted for. By 0900hrs they had landed the rest of their forces, about 3,000 in total, including armoured personnel carriers which were now heading for Government House.

Naval Party 8901 was now fighting against overwhelming odds and yet it had crippled the Argentinians' initial advance (albeit for a short time), taken prisoners and forced the enemy to bring in a second wave of armour to launch a final assault on Government House. Governor Hunt realised, however, that there was no possibility of attempting a breakout and that any further resistance was

George Gill, one of the Royal Marines who took up position at Government House and expected to be overrun and possibly killed in the Argentinian assault. He continued his military career after the Falklands and wrote himself into the history books as the longest-serving NCO in the Corps.

futile. Moreover, the Argentinians had lost no time in seizing the radio station and the Cable & Wireless office in Port Stanley, thus cutting off any communication with the outside world. Hunt decided to surrender and at 9.25am ordered Major Norman and his men to lay down their arms.

The Governor's decision to call a truce was not what the Royal Marines wanted, and Corporal Gill and others were frustrated at the order. Gill said: 'At around 0930hrs the Governor made the decision to stop firing. He told us that the situation was hopeless. We were devastated. We could never have won, but we were damaging them. Suddenly it was all over. We were kept in the paddock; several of the lads were very angry and were snarling at the Argentinians.'

Following the surrender, the commander of the Argentinian forces, General Oswaldo Garcia, appeared at Government House. Determined to leave in style, Hunt changed into his formal gubernatorial regalia, complete with cocked hat adorned with feathers, and shortly afterwards left for the airport in his official staff car, a black London taxicab. Later he was flown in an Argentinian Air Force C-130 Hercules transport to the Uruguayan capital Montevideo, from where he returned to Britain. He was followed soon afterwards by Major Mike Norman and Naval Party 8901. Corporal Gill later described the journey home:

> In the afternoon we were shipped off in a C-130 to an Argentinian air base on the mainland. We were then put on to a Boeing 707 and flown, we thought, to Buenos Aires, where we had been told we would be paraded through the streets. We were all tired but several of the lads made it clear they would rather die than be paraded like goons though the streets of the capital and prepared themselves mentally for a confrontation. When we got off the plane there were crowds cheering us and we just snarled back, unaware that we were not in Argentina.
>
> We had been flown to Uruguay and the people were in fact cheering us with their support. Later we flew back to the UK and the Commandant General, Lieutenant-General Sir Steuart Pringle, was there to meet us. He told us what a good job we had done and added that we were all due some leave. Many of us weren't interested in leave and went to the CG to tell him that we wanted to get back south as soon as possible. He personally guaranteed that we would go back.

Following the battle at Port Stanley, further action took place on South Georgia where Lieutenant Keith Mills and his detachment of two dozen Royal Marines had deployed in positions at King Edward Point, the base location of the British Antarctic Survey team stationed on the island. On the morning of 3 April the Argentinian corvette *Guerrico* and the ice patrol ship *Bahia Paraiso* appeared in King Edward Cove. Lieutenant Mills made radio contact with the two vessels and informed them that British troops were on South Georgia and that any landing would meet resistance. The two vessels withdrew, but shortly afterwards a Puma helicopter landed and disembarked some Argentinian marines who opened fire on Mills and his men. As the firefight continued the Royal Marines hit the Puma and destroyed it. Morale in the small British force rose.

The *Guerrico* now sailed back into King Edward Cove and opened fire on the Royal Marine positions with its 40mm gun. Waiting until it had closed to within close range, Mills and his men responded with their 84mm Carl Gustav, hitting the vessel on the waterline. A second round hit the vessel's gun and damaged it, while a fusillade of small-arms fire and 66mm LAW rockets scored further hits on its hull and superstructure, forcing it to withdraw. However, the Argentinians succeeded in landing more marines, and after a battle lasting two hours the Royal Marine detachment was surrounded and fast running out of ammunition. Lieutenant Mills and his small team had delivered a punch out of all proportion to their size. Mills had fulfilled his brief – to put up a token resistance – while also achieving his own aim of causing the Argentinians as much damage as possible. Accordingly, he ordered his men to lay down their arms. A few days later the entire detachment was repatriated via Uruguay to Britain where they received a heroes' welcome. Lieutenant Mills was subsequently awarded the Distinguished Service Cross.

Following the Argentinians' successful operation at Port Stanley, C-130 transports began flying in units of the 9th Brigade from Comodoro Rivadavia. The brigade's commander, Brigadier General Americo Daher, relieved General Oswaldo Garcia. First to arrive was the 25th Infantry Regiment, followed by the 8th Infantry Regiment and a battalion of marines. The latter and the 25th Regiment, less C Company which was dispatched to Goose Green, remained at Port Stanley while the 8th Regiment was deployed to Fox Bay on West Falkland.

Within hours of the seizure of the Falkland Islands, Argentina was trumpeting the news worldwide. In Buenos Aires General Galtieri addressed jubilant crowds in the Plaza de Mayo outside the Casa Rosada and basked in their acclaim. In London, meanwhile, there was an atmosphere of shock as Prime Minister Margaret Thatcher and her Cabinet held an emergency meeting.

The lack of communications with the islands meant that the Foreign Office was unable to ascertain the truth of the Argentinian claims for several hours as politicians and service chiefs gathered to consider the options open to them. The decision was quickly taken by the Cabinet to dispatch a force to recover the Falkland Islands. As a result of the events leading up to the week of the invasion, the Royal Navy was already well advanced with its plans for assembling a Task Force. Orders had been given on 29 March for the dispatch of an advance force of three nuclear attack submarines (SSN), HMS *Spartan*, *Splendid* and *Conqueror*. *Spartan* sailed from Gibraltar for the South

Phoenix
Assurance
Bicentenary

AGENTS
SUD ATLANTICA
FLORIDA 142 2° PISO   TEL 49-6676

Buenos Aires Herald

EL HERALDO DE BUENOS AIRES

1782~1982

Founded 1876
106th Year — 2005 (new series)

BUENOS AIRES, SATURDAY, APRIL 3, 1982

16 Pages · Price: $ 5,000.-
Air mail $ 100.- surcharge

• A group of soldiers raise the Argentine flag at dawn yesterday on the Malvinas islands. (DYN photo supplied by the Argentine Navy)

Thatcher pressured to fight

Argentina recovers Malvinas by force

ARGENTINA yesterday unilaterally put an end to a century and a half of vain negotiations to establish its right to govern the Malvinas islands by sending in a 4,000-man invasion force to take them over from their British administrators.

The pre-dawn landing included members of the three Argentine armed forces who easily overcame the handful of British troops stationed at Port Stanley, the Malvinas capital.

There was, however, armed resistance to the occupation, in which one Argentine officer died and another officer and an enlisted man were injured.

The Argentine Navy High Command reported yesterday afternoon that during the landing of the first wave of Argentine Marines, there was a firefight with the British Royal Marines. During the fighting, Captain Pedro Giachino, "who advanced heroically at the head of his men" on the British positions, was shot dead. Wounded were Navy Lieutenant Diego Garcia Quiroga and Petty Officer Ernesto Urbina.

The operation was termed a complete success by the Argentine military who announced that the islands with their 1,900 inhabitants were under complete Argentine control following the surrender of British Governor Rex Hunt, who was earlier reported to have ordered the Royal Marines to cease resistance.

Argentine naval sources indicated last night that military protocol had been observed to the utmost, with the British personnel and island residents being treated with total consideration by the occupation force. The sources said that orders were also strict for the treatment of the British flag which was reportedly granted upon its removal the same respect given the Argentine colours which were run up.

On securing the islands the junta put out a communique in which it stated that "a long period of fruitless negotiations has come to an end" and added that the "Argentine people ...feel the happiness of having obtained just recourse on their demands for (recognition of) their legitimate rights."

The communique then went on to say that the junta, "as the supreme organ of state, informs the people of the Argentine nation that today the republic, through the armed forces, (which) carried out a successful joint operation, has regained the Malvinas, the South Georgia and Sandwich islands for the national patrimony".

The junta later in the day announced that it was ordering the evacuation of British military and adminstrative personnel which had been serving in the Malvinas. These people were expected to be flown to a British diplomatic mission elsewhere in Latin America. The Argentine Air Force would, the junta indicated, take care · of the evacuation, shipping the British subjects out of Comodoro Rivadavia.

In London, British Prime Minister Margaret Thatcher called an emergency session of her cabinet as the British Royal Navy began feverish work to muster a naval task force to send to the south Atlantic, but last night at press time, she had apparently still not taken a definite decision as to whether or not to fight to regain control of the islands.

Sources in London made it clear that some British ships were already on their way to the islands while London worked at preparing a bigger more powerful strike force.

Meanwhile Mrs Thatcher faced a political storm which was brewing in parliament as the morning newspapers were last night preparing editions which would call on her to make the decision to go to war to wrest the islands from Argentine control.

The rightwing Daily Express published a frontpage photo of a group of islanders with the caption: "Our loyal subjects—we must defend them".

The Sun, a conservative tabloid, said simply, "It's war!" in an exclamation which covered most of the front page.

The Daily Mail opted for "Shamed" as its main headline, while The Times, the voice of the British establishment, urged that further efforts to resolve the conflict by diplomacy should be made "only as a prelude to taking action".

The Times added: "We still have one of the world's most powerful navies, including a number of nuclear-powered submarines, one at least of which is almost certainly now close to the scene."

President Galtieri and the military junta made it clear in their statements yesterday after the successful occupation of the Malvinas that Argentina would answer with force any attempt by the British at a counterattack to retake the islands. (UP, Reuters, NA, DYN, and own sources).

Britain demands immediate withdrawal from islands

United Nations
BRITAIN asked the UN Security Council yesterday to demand the immediate withdrawal of all Argentine forces from the Malvinas islands following what it called a massive invasion.

Submitting a resolution and appealing for its unanimous adoption, Sir Anthony Parsons, Britain's chief delegate, said: "I cannot find words strong enough to express my government's condemnation of this wanton act of armed force."

The Argentine delegate, Eduardo Roca, replied that his government has recovered for its national sovereignty the Malvinas which Britain had wained since 1833.

He said there were no civilian casualties in the Argentine military action that ended "a situation of tension and injustice."

Argentina was prepared to negotiate its differences with Britain, but sovereignty over the Malvinas, off South America, was not negotiable, he said.

The 15-nation Security Council deferred a scheduled debate on Nicaraguan charges against the United States to take up the Malvinas crisis.

After hearing the British and Argentine statements, members adjourned. They were expected to meet later yesterday to consider the British resolution.

The resolution would have the Security Council demand an immediate cessation of hostilities, demand the immediate withdrawal of all Argentine forces and call on the Argentine and British governments to seek a diplomatic solution and respect the purposes and principles of the UN charter.

Through a statement by its president, the Security Council on Thursday night called on both sides to observe the utmost restraint and refrain from the use or threat of force.

Sir Anthony accepted that appeal, but Roca did not respond.

When the Security Council met yesterday Sir Anthony said Argentina had ignored the appeal by the council president, Kamanda Wa Kamanda of Zaire, and two appeals by UN Secretary General Javier Perez de Cuellar.

Sir Anthony yesterday called the Argentine action a blatant violation of the UN charter and of international law.

"It is an attempt to impose by force a foreign and unwanted control over 1,900 peaceful agricultural people who have chosen in free and fair elections to maintain their links with Britain and the British way of life," he said. (Reuters)

Thousands gather at plaza

PRESIDENT Leopoldo Galtieri, spoke to a crowd of about 10,000 people gathered yesterday afternoon opposite Government House in the historic Plaza de Mayo square.

He received an enthusiastic ovation as he appeared on one of the balconies of the Casa Rosada and spoke for several minutes.

The President's improvised speech was interrupted several times as the crowd clapped and cheered as he announced the country's recovery of the disputed islands.

Galtieri said his government and the Argentine people would accept talks with the British government following Argentina's forcible takeover of the islands, but "dignity and national pride will be maintained at all costs."

(Continued on page 7)

Front page of the *Buenos Aires Herald* for Saturday 3 April 1982.

An Argentinian Amtrac, an amphibious armoured personnel carrier. The invaders had twenty of these vehicles, which could wade ashore from landing ships and offered armoured protection for infantry soldiers. The Royal Marines fired an anti-tank missile into the back of one such vehicle, crippling the carrier and its crew.

Atlantic within 48 hours, followed by *Splendid* from her base at Faslane in western Scotland on 1 April. *Conqueror* would follow on 4 April. The RFA vessel *Fort Austin* had already sailed on 29 March with the task of providing support for HMS *Endurance*.

Meanwhile preparations were already under way for assembling the remainder of the naval task group. It would be spearheaded by the twenty warships of the First Flotilla which, under its flag officer Rear Admiral John 'Sandy' Woodward, was deployed in mid-Atlantic on a major exercise. On the night of 29 March the Commander-in-Chief Fleet, Admiral Sir John Fieldhouse, who was aboard the destroyer HMS *Glamorgan* observing the exercise, had been advised by his headquarters at Northwood in north-west London of the deteriorating situation. Following a meeting with Rear Admiral Woodward aboard *Glamorgan* in the early hours of Tuesday 30 March, Fieldhouse had been ferried by helicopter to Gibraltar from where he had flown to London. With intelligence now confirming an increase in Argentinian warships in the South Atlantic the invasion which the British thought would never happen was all too evident.

After the first assault, thousands more troops were flown to Stanley, but the majority could not wait to get home.

As the news was passed to Prime Minister Margaret Thatcher she summoned her Defence Secretary, John Nott, for advice and an appreciation of what the military could do in response. He was clear that there was very little that could be done and the distance – 8,000 miles – was too far to mount a military operation. But the First Sea Lord, Admiral Sir Henry Leach, was furious at the minister's response and sought a meeting with the Prime Minister himself. He advised her that he could mobilise a full Task Force and that he believed action should be taken, even though he later confessed that he should perhaps not have expressed his own opinion. The Prime Minister agreed and the decision was later confirmed by the War Cabinet.

As the Argentinians stepped ashore in the early hours of 2 April, the planning required to deploy the biggest Task Force since Suez was under way. Rear Admiral Woodward was to head the naval force and was given the directive: 'The Task Force is to be made ready and sailed.'

Argentinian soldiers in Stanley. When the initial invasion was launched on 2 April Argentinian press reports indicated that just two of their soldiers died in the assault but the true figure was much higher.

In London the Secret Intelligence Service (SIS) was assembling all available data on the Argentinian forces, and in particular their naval assets. Much of this had been supplied by the United States Central Intelligence Agency (CIA) whose Latin American Division of its Directorate of Operations (DDO) had compiled a detailed overview of the Argentinian order of battle. This was delivered by the CIA station chief in London in exchange for intelligence from SIS on the Soviet Union, the latter having been supplied by Oleg Gordievsky, an officer in the First Chief Directorate of the KGB. The CIA-supplied intelligence formed the basis for four papers produced by SIS's Latin American Current Intelligence Group (LACIG) for submission to the War Cabinet. One significant point raised by the LACIG was the Argentinian Navy's possession of the French-manufactured AM-39 Exocet surface-to-surface (SSM) missile.

Enquiries to the manufacturer, Aerospatiale, revealed that the Argentinians had taken delivery of five missiles out of a total order of fourteen due for delivery by September

1982. However, the European Community's recently imposed ban on all military exports to Argentina had come into force before modifications could be carried out to the Argentinian Navy's Super Etendard carrier-based attack aircraft, which would enable them to carry the Exocet. Meanwhile the RAF produced an intelligence assessment stating that the Super Etendard had a range of only 425 nautical miles at low level and that the Argentinian Air Force would be unwilling to risk its two KC-130 tankers for aerial refuelling to enable the Super Etendards to return to their base. The combined result of all this information led to the conclusion that the Task Force would be safe from air-launched Exocet attacks in the area to the east of the Falkland Islands. In fact, these intelligence assessments were to prove disastrously incorrect.

Although small, the Argentinian Navy posed a not inconsiderable threat to the Task Force. Foremost among its assets was the 20,000-ton aircraft carrier *Veintecinco de Mayo*, formerly the British Colossus class HMS *Venerable*. The *Veintecinco* carried up to fourteen A-4 Skyhawk attack aircraft, a number of Super Etendards and Sea King anti-submarine helicopters. She was escorted by three Type 42 destroyers, the *Santisima Trinidad* and *Hercules*. Next came the heavy cruiser *General Belgrano*, formerly the Brooklyn class USS *Phoenix*, which was armed with fifteen newly fitted 6-inch and eight 5-inch guns, and featured heavy armour on her hull, decks and much of her superstructure. The *Belgrano's* escorts were two destroyers, the *Hipolito Bouchard* and *Piedra Buena*, both of which were equipped with the sea-launched variant of the Exocet. Other vessels included the two corvettes *Drummond* and *Granville*, along with a third vessel of the same Type A-69 class, *Guerrico*, which had been encountered by Lieutenant Keith Mills and his Royal Marine detachment on South Georgia.

The Argentinians also possessed six submarines. Two of these, the *Santa Fe* and *Santara del Estero*, formerly the USS *Catfish* and *Chivo* respectively, were elderly boats of 1945 vintage, while a second pair, the *San Luis* and *Salta*, were both Type 209 boats commissioned in 1974. The most recent additions were two West German-designed boats, the *Santa Cruz* and *San Juan*. To oppose the small Argentinian fleet, Britain assembled a powerful force comprising: the Royal Navy's two aircraft carriers, *Hermes* and *Invincible*, carrying a total of twenty Sea Harriers and thirty-three Sea King helicopters; the Type 82 destroyer HMS *Bristol*; two County class destroyers, HMS *Antrim* and *Glamorgan*; five Type 42 destroyers, HMS *Cardiff, Coventry, Exeter, Glasgow* and *Sheffield*; two Type 22 Broadsword class frigates, HMS *Broadsword* and *Brilliant*; seven Type 21 Amazon class frigates, HMS *Active, Alacrity, Ambuscade, Antelope, Ardent, Arrow* and *Avenge*; four Type 12 Leander class frigates, HMS *Andromeda, Argonaut, Minerva* and *Penelope*; two Rothesay class frigates, HMS *Plymouth* and *Yarmouth*; the Oberon class patrol submarine HMS *Onyx*; and two amphibious warfare vessels – the landing platform docks (LPD) HMS *Fearless* and *Intrepid*. Last but not least were two minesweepers, HMS *Brecon* and *Ledbury*, and five Humberside trawlers converted for minesweeping and renamed HMS *Cordella*, *Farnella*, *Junella*, *Northella* and *Pict* respectively. In addition to all these vessels there was a force of five SSNs comprising the Swiftsure class HMS *Spartan* and *Splendid*, the Valiant class HMS *Valiant* and *Courageous* and the Churchill class HMS *Conqueror*. These brought the fleet to a total of forty-one warships, forming the largest that the Royal Navy had deployed since the Second World War.

A large number of vessels of the Royal Fleet Auxiliary (RFA) and merchant ships taken up from trade (STUFT) were to accompany the fleet to transport the military element of the Task Force and the entire logistical support it would require for the campaign. The RFA vessels comprised: the six landing ship logistics (LSL) *Sir Bedivere*, *Sir Galahad*, *Sir Geraint*, *Sir Lancelot*, *Sir Percivale* and *Sir Tristram*; the replenishment ships *Fort Austin*, *Fort Grange*, *Regent* and *Resource*; the stores support ship *Stromness*; and the tankers *Bayleaf*, *Blue Rover*, *Olmeda*, *Olna*, *Pearleaf*, *Plumleaf*, *Tidepool* and *Tidespring*. The STUFT vessels included the *Canberra* and North Sea ferry MV *Norland*, which would transport troops while others, such as the container ships *Atlantic Causeway*, *Atlantic Conveyor* and MV *Europic Ferry*, would carry cargo, including helicopters, vehicles, guns, ammunition and stores.

Among a number of specialist support vessels were the Royal Navy's hydrographic vessels, HMS *Hecla*, *Herald* and *Hydra*, all of which had been converted into hospital

The Argentinians aimed to use Stanley airfield as a launch pad for attacks on the British fleet, but they failed to achieve this objective and instead air attacks were mounted from the mainland. This A4 Skyhawk is taking off from Rio Gallegos.

The Type 21 frigate HMS *Ardent* sails out of Devonport in the sunshine for the wild seas of the South Atlantic. *Ardent* would later be hit during an Argentinian air raid; she subsequently sank.

HMS *Antelope*, *Ardent*'s sister ship, leaves Devonport for the South Atlantic.

transports for ferrying casualties to the Task Force's hospital ship, the SS *Uganda*. Others included the *Stena Seaspread*, a diving support vessel normally employed in the offshore oil industry but now adapted as a heavy repair vessel.

The leading element of the fleet would be provided by the Royal Navy's First Flotilla which was already at sea on exercise. The remaining warships had to be assembled, along with the RFA and merchant vessels. Some of the latter had to be adapted or converted for their new roles.

The day after the invasion Britain's ambassador to the United Nations, Sir Anthony Parsons, made representation at the UN Council calling for the immediate removal of all Argentinian forces from the Falklands. The UN voted in support of the UK and passed Resolution 502 demanding Argentinian withdrawal. However, it was clear that the Argentinians were not going anywhere and military force would be needed to retake the islands.

The nuclear-powered submarines *Spartan*, *Splendid*, *Valiant*, *Courageous* and *Conqueror* were dispatched to the South Atlantic, but there was little these boats could do as the Argentinians established their base at Stanley.

THREE

OPERATION CORPORATE BEGINS

PREPARING BRITAIN'S MILITARY MACHINE

It was 3.15am on Friday 2 April when Brigadier Julian Thompson, the commander of 3 Commando Brigade RM, received a telephone call at his home near Plymouth from Major General Jeremy Moore, the Major General Commanding Commando Forces RM. Using guarded language, Moore informed Thompson that the Falkland Islands were about to be invaded and ordered him to bring his brigade to seventy-two hours' notice ready to move south.

The task of wresting the Falkland Islands back from the Argentinian invaders was being given to 3 Commando Brigade, the only formation within the British armed forces capable of carrying out an amphibious operation at such short notice. Comprising 40, 42 and 45 Commandos RM, its supporting arms consisted of 29 Commando Regiment RA, 59 Independent Commando Squadron RE, and the Commando Logistics Regiment. In addition, it also possessed specialist units in the form of the Mountain & Arctic Warfare Cadre (whose role was to go forward as the reconnaissance 'eyes and ears' of the Brigade), the 1st Raiding Squadron RM and an air defence troop equipped with twelve Blowpipe man-portable surface-to-air missile (SAM) launchers.

Most of the members of Thompson's brigade headquarters staff were in the process of returning from Denmark where they had been conducting reconnaissance for a NATO exercise later that year, while the remainder were in Plymouth, the brigade's home, preparing to go on Easter leave. Of the three commando units, 40 Commando was in the process of returning to Plymouth from training in the north of England and 42 Commando was on leave, while 45 Commando, based at Arbroath in Scotland was due to depart on leave that day.

Accompanied by the three members of his staff, Brigadier Thompson moved on the morning of 2 April to Moore's headquarters at Hamoaze House, Devonport. At 10.30am confirmation was received that the Falkland Islands had been invaded. Thompson's first task was to recall all units of the brigade to their base locations to begin preparations for deployment. By the evening of 2 April he had been joined by the remainder of his staff who set about the considerable task of preparing to move the entire brigade and its war maintenance reserve – comprising 4,500 tons of ammunition, food, stores and spares – to the ports for loading.

Brigadier Julian Thompson briefs his staff at his Plymouth headquarters just days after getting the word to prepare his formation for deployment to the South Atlantic. One of the first concerns was that only one assault ship was available for service; the second would join the fleet later.

Planners at the MoD had decided that the brigade would need to be reinforced with a number of additional units. These initially comprised: the 3rd Battalion The Parachute Regiment (3 PARA), commanded by Lieutenant Colonel Hew Pike; T Battery (Shah Sujah's Troop) RA equipped with the Rapier SAM; two troops of the Blues & Royals equipped with four Scorpion and four Scimitar CVR-T armoured reconnaissance vehicles, and a Samson recovery vehicle; and the Band of the Commando Forces whose members would be employed in their secondary role of medics and stretcher-bearers. In addition to the reinforced 3 Commando Brigade,

The Oberon class submarine HMS *Onyx* deployed with members of the Special Boat Squadron (later named Special Boat Service) and would take part in operations to land SBS teams ashore.

special forces were also to play a key role in Corporate, the codename for the operation to recover the Falkland Islands. D and G Squadrons of 22nd Special Air Service Regiment (22 SAS), together with a small tactical headquarters element, would be deployed separately, as would Nos 2, 3 and 6 Special Boat Sections (SBS).

A major problem facing Brigadier Thompson and his staff was the initially limited amount of shipping allocated to transport his brigade, the bulk of which would be carried by the Royal Fleet Auxiliary ships. LSLs would be available but it was clear to the brigade that more shipping was needed. Only one amphibious warfare vessel, the LPD HMS *Fearless*, was initially available because her sister ship, *Intrepid*, was laid up and out of commission. A request for the carrier HMS *Hermes* was refused because she would be embarking twenty Sea Harriers and Sea King helicopters. She would, however, carry a company of 40 Commando in case a force was required ashore prior to the arrival of 3 Commando Brigade.

Thompson's staff turned to the Red Book, a manual listing all Merchant Navy vessels which could be requisitioned or chartered in the event of war, but the problem was solved with the announcement that the Ministry of Defence would requisition the P&O liner SS *Canberra* which could accommodate approximately 2,000 troops. Homeward bound from the Mediterranean, she would dock at Southampton in two days time. A team of Royal Navy and Royal Marine personnel was flown to Gibraltar.

There, dressed in civilian clothes, they boarded her and spent the following two days selecting locations for accommodating units, medical facilities and helicopter landing platforms.

Sunday 4 April saw a briefing for all commanding officers who were given what little intelligence was available at the time. Of particular value was the information on the Falklands themselves passed on by Major Ewen Southby-Tailyour, a Royal Marine officer who in 1978 had carried out a year's tour of duty in the islands during which, as a keen yachtsman, he had carried out his own personal surveys. These were to be published as part of a guide for the Royal Cruising Club and Royal Yacht Squadron, of which he was a member. Southby-Tailyour was a trained landing craft officer and had been able to study various locations with a view to their suitability as landing beaches. His briefing covered life and conditions on the Falklands, the shores, climate, wildlife, ecology, economy and local politics, and was illustrated with charts and a selection of the 1,000 or so photographs that he had taken four years earlier.

Other elements of the briefing were given by Captain Vivian Rowe, the brigade's intelligence officer, a tall quietly spoken Welshman who had seen operational service in

SBS troops were among the first to land on the Falklands, several weeks before the Task Force arrived. They had with them artillery officers from 148 Forward Observation Battery who would be ready to direct naval gunfire when the ships arrived.

Oman and had commanded Recce Troop at 40 Commando. He was very much respected by his colleagues, but had little information on the Argentinian armed forces beyond what was printed in reference works such as the *Military Balance*, published annually by the International Institute for Strategic Studies. It appears that the information provided by the CIA to the SIS had not permeated down to those who would need it the most.

Brigadier Thompson was the last to speak. He outlined the shape of Operation Corporate. Naval superiority and control of the seas would have to be won before any landings could take place, and so the brigade had to be prepared for a lengthy period at sea. During this period reconnaissance missions would be carried out by elements of 22 SAS and the SBS. Due to limited resources, a direct assault on Port Stanley had been discounted and instead a beachhead would have to be established where reinforcements would be landed subsequently. Finally, Thompson emphasised to those present that they should not make the error of underestimating the Argentinians whose operation to seize the islands had been a model of efficiency.

Following the briefing, Brigadier Thompson and Commodore Michael Clapp, the Commodore Amphibious Warfare, who would command all the vessels which would transport 3 Commando Brigade, travelled by helicopter to Northwood and the headquarters of the Commander-in-Chief Fleet, Admiral Sir John Fieldhouse. As Thompson later recounted in his book *No Picnic*:

> Nobody seemed to know why we had come. We explained that, as the commanders intimately involved with executing Britain's response to the Argentinian invasion, we were trying to find out what was required of us.
>
> We sat down with some of the staff and, after listening to administrative details, which concerned the carriers, but appeared to have no bearing on the amphibious operations, we were asked for our views on how amphibious operations might be conducted. As at this stage we had not been given a mission, or any other direction other than to get the Brigade loaded and to sea as quickly as possible, this came as a surprise.
>
> At one stage we were taken to see Admiral Fieldhouse. We both made two points. First, that a head-on assault in the vicinity of Port Stanley, or anywhere else that was strongly held, should be avoided. The British did not possess the equipment to make this possible. This was agreed. Second, it was vital that air

Opposite: Mountain & Arctic Warfare Cadre members were among the specialists that Thompson could call upon. Commanded by Captain Rod Boswell they were the Brigadier's reconnaissance 'eyes and ears'. Selection for the cadre involved a ten-month course and attracted some of the best marines in the Corps.

superiority, at least over the beachhead area, was achieved before any landing was attempted. This we were promised.

We followed up by asking if HMS *Intrepid*, sister ship to *Fearless*, could be made available as we might need more landing craft. We stressed the need for more assault helicopters. We were given little hope that these requests would be met, and were given the impression that we must cope with what was available at the time. We felt we would be at a severe disadvantage.

Present at the meeting was Rear Admiral Reffell, the Flag Officer Third Flotilla, normally the commander of all the amphibious ships and the carriers. He had commanded the commando helicopter carrier HMS *Albion*, had been the Commodore Amphibious Warfare, and was now Clapp's immediate superior.

He was the Flag Officer with the most amphibious experience in the Navy, and probably the most training for the type of conventional maritime warfare we expected. His staff consisted of the right mix of specialists for joint operations, including aviators. He wholeheartedly supported both the points we made at this meagre briefing.

Both Clapp and I hoped that his presence at Northwood meant that his experience would be called on while we prepared our forces for whatever was required. With luck, he would be appointed the overall commander. We climbed back into our helicopter. It was some time before we voiced what was in our minds. We were not impressed.

Meanwhile those units allocated for reinforcement of 3 Commando Brigade had been preparing for war. The Army had opened its war maintenance reserve stocks of arms, ammunition and equipment, which were loaded aboard convoys of vehicles and moved to the embarkation ports of Portsmouth and Southampton. Other units had been recalled from leave or training, returning to their respective bases to be met by a deluge of equipment normally denied them by the economies of peacetime. In the words of Lieutenant Colonel Hew Pike, the commanding officer of 3 PARA: 'It was like Christmas.' At Plymouth support vessels of the Royal Fleet Auxiliary were being loaded for sea, frigates were leaving to join the Task Force and plans were being drawn up to modify any STUFT shipping that might be sent to Devonport dockyard prior to sailing south.

Monday 5 April found units moving to their points of embarkation. At RAF Brize Norton in Oxfordshire, Lieutenant Colonel Michael Rose, the commanding officer of 22 SAS, bade farewell to D Squadron, commanded by Major Cedric Delves, and a group of signallers and support personnel as they embarked on an aircraft bound for

Royal Navy Leander class frigates at a naval dockyard as they stored ship throughout the night in preparation for their journey to the South Atlantic.

In the weeks before they joined the carrier Group RAF Harrier crews underwent additional training in Scotland and took part in live-firing exercises to prepare them for battle in the South Atlantic.

Ascension Island. Deep in the Atlantic, Ascension would be a midway base for the Task Force prior to sailing further south.

Back in Portsmouth ships had been loaded and Sea Harriers and Sea King helicopters had been landing aboard the two carriers, *Invincible* and *Hermes*. That afternoon, Rear Admiral Sandy Woodward's Task Force sailed, the warships' crews lining the decks as crowds waved them farewell from the quaysides and bands played in scenes reminiscent of the Victorian era.

The following day Brigadier Thompson and his staff were making final preparations for departure from their headquarters at Stonehouse Barracks at Plymouth. That afternoon, together with Lieutenant Colonel Michael Rose and his small SAS tactical headquarters, they assembled on the football pitch and embarked in three Sea King helicopters which flew them out into the Channel to rendezvous with *Fearless*, which had sailed from Portsmouth a few hours earlier. Then on Friday the 9th 3 Commando

Families wave goodbye to the *Atlantic Conveyor*, which departed for the South Atlantic with Chinook helicopters and Harrier jump jets packed aboard. The ship was to fall victim to an Argentinian Exocet.

Brigade embarked aboard the SS *Canberra* and sailed from Southampton amid scenes similar to those witnessed at Portsmouth. Seven days after the Argentinian invasion, Britain dispatched its Task Force to recover the Falkland Islands.

◆   ◆   ◆

The first element of 3 Commando Brigade to arrive at Ascension Island was X Company 45 Commando which arrived by air on 13 April, followed by Y Company. The eleven ships carrying the remainder of the brigade arrived during the second week in April. The first to appear was HMS *Fearless*. Carrying Brigadier Thompson, Commodore Clapp and their respective staffs, *Fearless* had steamed ahead of the rest of the Task Force to rendezvous with the overall commander, Admiral John Fieldhouse, who was due to fly out from Britain with his Air and Land Deputy Commanders, Air Marshal Sir John Curtiss and Major General Jeremy Moore.

On 16 April Thompson and Clapp attended a meeting with Woodward to brief him on the progress of planning. This proved to be an unfortunate affair, as Thompson later recounted:

> Neither Clapp nor I had had a chance to talk to Woodward earlier. Indeed I had never met him. Before he arrived on *Fearless*, he was described in enthusiastic terms by Captain Larken, a fellow submariner. I now know that he is an intelligent and sensitive man, calm in the face of danger and unflappable in a crisis. He was, and is, highly regarded by some within his own service. Unfortunately, his style at that first meeting was totally at odds with mine, and Clapp's. By training and experience in command, I always tried, from first acquaintance, to imbue those around me, and in subordinate positions, with confidence in me as a commander. By the end of the day my feelings for Woodward were the opposite.
>
> Now I know why. Unknown to us at the time, he arrived on board having been told by Northwood to examine the feasibility of landing on West Falkland and establishing an air strip capable of operating Phantom air-defence fighters there. The rationale behind this grotesque notion being that having established a foothold, negotiations could then be carried out with Argentina on the future of the islands. That my engineers had neither the plant nor the numbers to carry out such an ambitious project, which would have taken a large force of contractors months, all within easy range of the Argentinian Air Force, was dismissed. Landing on West Falkland would also necessitate another amphibious operation on East Falkland. This in itself was reason enough not to

contemplate such a move. Fortunately, the notion was killed at the Council of War the following day.

The 'Council of War' to which Thompson refers took place on 17 April and was attended by Admiral Fieldhouse, Air Marshal Curtiss and Major General Moore. Thompson and Clapp expressed their concern that air superiority should be won before any landing took place; they were met by a promise that this would indeed be the case. As Thompson later admitted: 'With hindsight, I was naïve not to question such a bland statement, which a few moments' analysis would have exposed as being a fabrication, unless the Argentinian Air Force was stupid, or we were to interdict Argentinian mainland airfields.'

By this time it had been decided that further reinforcement of 3 Commando Brigade would be necessary and Brigadier Thompson was informed that further units had been allocated to him. These comprised: the 2nd Battalion The Parachute Regiment (2 PARA); 29 (Corunna) Battery of 4th Field Regiment RA, like 29 Commando Regiment equipped with 105mm light guns; a troop of sappers from 9th Independent Parachute Squadron RE; two sections of 32 Guided Weapons Regiment RA, equipped with Blowpipe SAM; a flight from 656 Squadron AAC, equipped with Westland Scout light helicopters; and a troop of 16 Field Ambulance RAMC. Even these additional resources, however, would not be sufficient to take on a force of Argentinian troops believed to number some 10,000 and it was suggested that 5 Infantry Brigade, comprising the 2nd Battalion Scots Guards (2SG), 1st Battalion Welsh Guards (1WG) and the 1st Battalion 7th Duke of Edinburgh's Own Gurkha Rifles (7GR), together with supporting arm units, should be dispatched to join 3 Commando.

Brigadier Thompson pointed out that five battalions or commandos was the maximum he could handle effectively in battle and that, in the event of 5 Infantry Brigade becoming part of the Task Force, a divisional headquarters would be required to command both brigades, bringing the ground forces to a total of 8,000 men. As he noted at the time, however, even that number would not meet the normally required superiority ratio of 3:1.

One of Thompson's principal concerns was securing intelligence about the Argentinian forces on the Falkland Islands because this would be a vital ingredient for planning a successful landing. Intelligence would have to be obtained by the SAS and SBS. Their patrols could be landed from warships of the Carrier Battle Group under Rear Admiral Sandy Woodward, which would be in the process of establishing air and sea superiority over an area of 200 nautical miles around the islands. The initial task of such patrols would be to reconnoitre and report on enemy strengths and dispositions.

Royal Marines aboard *Canberra* keep fit on their way to Ascension Island. Wombat anti-tank guns are parked in the foreground, but they were not used in the Falklands.

Meanwhile Thompson's and Clapp's staffs had two priority tasks on their hands: restowing the ships, and carrying out trials and work-ups of the two task groups. As Thompson later explained:

The normal sequence for an amphibious operation is: identify the tasks (the mission), find out all you can about the enemy (intelligence), make the plan, stow your ships so that men and loads will come off in the sequence you want to meet your plan; then land. There had not been the time or intelligence to make a plan or stow properly before the ships left the United Kingdom, so a massive restow of loads was necessary. Some of the LSLs arrived at Ascension over eighteen inches over their loading marks. An additional LSL arriving empty from Belize provided the opportunity to redistribute loads. It was also found that *Canberra* and other ships could take many more men than they had sailed with from Britain.

Concurrently with the restow of ships, there was a need to test and work up the various parts of the amphibious and landing force task groups. How, for example, could men be loaded into landing craft utilities (LCUs) from *Canberra*? Only trials by day and by night would establish a drill to get heavily laden men, possibly in choppy seas and almost certainly in the dark, quickly into an LCU. Should the ship be at anchor, lying still or steaming slowly forward? Could Scorpions and Scimitars be loaded into the bow of the LCU and fire over the lowered ramp on the run-in to the beach to provide a poor man's version of the landing craft gun that had been found so essential in the Second World War to suppress enemy fire in the critical stage after naval gunfire has to lift? How long would it take ten helicopters arriving two at a time, one on each of the two helicopter decks on *Canberra*, to lift a rifle company, form up into a wave and land them? All these and many other questions could only be answered by trials with helicopters and landing craft, both of which were also needed for restowing ships.

Matters were made all the more difficult by the fact that HMS *Fearless*'s fuel stocks were low as a result of her having steamed at speed from Portsmouth to Ascension Island in time for the Council of War; this had resulted in a lack of fuel for use as the ballast that was necessary when she 'docked down'. During this process the dock in the rear half of her hull was flooded to allow her to deploy her four LCUs and four landing craft vehicle and personnel (LCVPs). It was not until two days after she reached Ascension that a tanker arrived and refuelling could take place. This resulted in each unit being allocated one day for training with helicopters, and a day and a night for exercising with landing craft. Moreover, each unit also received only one day ashore on Ascension Island to carry out live firing. The two troops of the Blues & Royals deployed their Scorpion and Scimitar CVR-Ts aboard landing craft and practised firing their 76mm guns and 30mm Rarden cannon over lowered ramps, accurate gunnery proving difficult from the craft heaving in a swell.

In the meantime planning for the landing on the Falkland Islands continued aboard HMS *Fearless*, the headquarters vessel of the Amphibious and Landing Force Task Groups. The choice of landing site was governed by a large number of factors, as Major Ewen Southby-Tailyour, who had been appointed to command the Task Force's landing craft squadron, later explained:

The landing force required as short an approach to the objective as possible. At the same time, a frontal assault on landing beaches was not even considered, that not being the British way. The Argentinians, influenced by American doctrine and believing us to follow the same philosophy, expected us to land on the east of East Falkland. In so doing, they underestimated our military thinking as well as our subtlety, physical fitness and endurance. Landing close to Stanley would have made us vulnerable to easterly gales and to attack by Exocet and submarine. It would also have resulted in heavy casualties among the civilian population, a further unacceptable factor in our planning.

Fortunately, the enemy had positioned his defences according to US military doctrine and, even following our landings, was reluctant to redeploy in strength, fearing that they were a diversion. As our knowledge and understanding of the enemy's defensive positions improved, we began looking at beaches and options further away from Stanley and the enemy's heavy

The Royal Navy assault ship *Fearless*. The floating dock at her stern allowed landing craft to sail inside the warship and pick up troops. There was now an urgent need for her sister ship, *Intrepid*, to be pulled out of mothballs and deployed. Two assault ships were vital in case one was hit.

3 COMMANDO BRIGADE ROYAL MARINES

All three Royal Marine Commando units of 3 Commando Brigade deployed to the Falklands in 1982. Their specialist training and experience in mountain warfare gave them the pedigree which ensured commanders selected them as the key force for Operation Corporate.

In 1982 each commando was organised as three rifle or fighting companies, a support company and a headquarters company. The marines' trickle drafting system had resulted in the majority of men having served with either 42 or 45, the main mountain and arctic warfare units at the time. 40 Commando did not have the unit experience of the other two.

Specialists from the brigade, including Raiding Squadron, Medical Squadron, Mountain & Arctic Warfare Cadre, signallers and military police, also deployed to the South Atlantic. It was the Corps' biggest deployment since Suez in 1956 when the entire brigade landed at Port Said.

The Royal Marines who 'yomped' across the Falklands carried bergens (back packs), weighing more than 90lb, which contained ammunition, rations, spare clothing, radio batteries, grenades and sleeping bags. However, when the opportunity arose their packs were ferried by tractor.

The rifle companies carried additional support weapons in the form of the Carl Gustav 84mm anti-tank weapon, the Milan anti-tank missile system, the general purpose machine-gun (GPMG), and where available the 66mm light anti-tank rocket. The standard issue weapon was the 7.62mm SLR, while radio operators were issued with the 9mm SMG.

artillery. North of Stanley, we studied the areas of Volunteer and Cow Bay, and the entire Macbride Head peninsula.

The land approaches to Stanley, however, were not good and there was a bottleneck between Salvador Waters and Berkeley Sound which we believed was certain to be heavily reinforced. If we had landed in that area, we would have had to fight a fixed battle at Green Patch, an area which would have taken the place of Goose Green in British military history. However, unlike Goose Green, we would have been forced into battle.

To the south of Stanley there was little that presented itself as sensible from either the military or the naval point of view. The beaches were all small and far apart, and the approaches were difficult, with numerous kelp reefs. The enemy would still have a clear run at the amphibious ships, the ground was low and not good for establishing Rapier air defence, and the enemy would have been able to observe everything from the Wickham Heights. Lafonia was discounted for the same reasons, an added factor being a terrible 'yomp' across low country. Moreover, there was again the disadvantage of a bottleneck – Goose Green. The Brigadier was well aware that a march towards Stanley would be arduous enough without any unnecessary actions en route.

At one point, we [the planning staff] were tasked with looking at Stevelly Bay in Port North as, for a few miles behind the beachhead, there was an ideal area to build an airstrip from which Harriers, and ultimately Hercules transports, could operate. It would have taken a long time to construct, however, and was significantly closer to the Argentinian air bases. It was not an option that met with the approval of the amphibious forces. The San Carlos option formed slowly as we looked away from Stanley. It had both advantages and disadvantages for both the landing force and the amphibious ships.

The Royal Navy approved of the location because it would be clear of Exocet attacks and any submarine threat could be contained by blocking off each end of Falkland Sound. The anchorages were sheltered from wind and swell from all quarters, which meant that the offloading of the landing force could take place uninterrupted by nature. The latter could establish a circular Rapier air defence system to defend the ships and the beachhead.

The choice of San Carlos would, however, mean a considerably longer transit of the Total Exclusion Zone [TEZ], much of which would have to be undertaken in daylight. There was also concern over the possibility of mines having been laid by the enemy in the entrances to Falkland Sound and San Carlos Water.

While enemy aircraft which avoided the Task Force's Sea Harriers and the Rapier air defences would have less than three seconds to select and engage a target after flying over the surrounding hills, the ships likewise would have a correspondingly short time to bring their defensive systems to bear. This would force the Navy to deploy ships out in the Sound and to the north and west of the islands to provide early warning.

The Royal Marine element of the landing force liked San Carlos as it possessed four beaches suitable for use by landing craft, each below a high feature. This would ensure good all-round defence of the anchorage. The complicated off-load and the establishment of our initial supply base could be undertaken with some degree of security from ground attacks.

San Carlos was not, however, without its drawbacks. It was as far from Stanley as was possible on East Falkland (with the exception of Low Bay which, for some reason still unexplained, seemed to be the preferred choice of the Battle Group staff) and this would mean a lengthy approach march during which the enemy could redeploy their forces. Moreover, San Carlos, lying to the west, was closer to the Argentinian mainland and thus enemy aircraft, while close to their maximum range, would be able to attack opportunity targets. It was also some distance from the ships of the Battle Group and its Sea Harriers to the east of Stanley. The latter would thus have a very limited time over target when providing air defence for the landing force.

The preferred option of San Carlos as the most suitable location was reinforced by the results of a reconnaissance mission carried out by the SBS on 30 April. Under cover of darkness, patrols were flown 100 miles in Sea King helicopters from HMS *Hermes* to the Falkland Islands. Flying low to avoid detection by radar, the aircraft inserted the SBS men in locations well away from known enemy positions. From there the patrols began the long and arduous approach marches to locations where they established observation posts (OP). One patrol set up its hide and OP in a position from which it could observe Ajax Bay, which was the planned location for 3 Commando Brigade's brigade maintenance area (BMA).

Situated in the bay was a mutton factory which a subsequent close reconnaissance, conducted at night, revealed to be unoccupied and a perfect site for a landing. However, another patrol reconnoitring the area of Fanning Head, a short distance away across the entrance to San Carlos Water, reported the presence of an enemy OP; this would have to be eliminated just prior to the landing in order to prevent it giving a warning and enabling the Argentinians to deploy reinforcements in the area.

Meanwhile the Carrier Battle Group, under Rear Admiral Woodward aboard his flagship HMS *Glamorgan*, had sailed south from Ascension Island on 18 April, preceded by the SSN HMS *Spartan*. On her arrival off the Falkland Islands on 12 April *Spartan* had begun enforcing the maritime element of the Total Exclusion Zone which came into effect that day and extended the 'no-go' area for the Argentinians to 300 miles around the Falklands. *Spartan* observed the Argentinian Navy landing ship *Carlo San Antonio* laying mines off the entrance to Port Stanley harbour. This information was flashed to Northwood and subsequently to the War Cabinet which decided that the vessel was not a warship and was already inside the TEZ rather than attempting to penetrate it. Despite the fact that the *Carlo San Antonio* was carrying out a hostile act, the decision was taken not to attack her. While it has been said that there was reluctance to reveal the submarine's presence, the War Cabinet's refusal to sink an Argentinian vessel at such an early stage in the conflict has been given as the real reason for the vessel's being allowed to proceed.

Ten days later, however, the War Cabinet agreed to allow the submarine force to patrol outside the Maritime Exclusion Zone (MEZ – a 200-mile 'no-go' area for any shipping other than British) towards the coast of Argentina. The freedom of submarines and surface warships to open fire was governed by a set of rules of engagement drawn up by the Chief of Defence Staff, Admiral Sir Terence Lewin, in collaboration with officials from the Cabinet Office. Once the War Cabinet's initial hesitancy had been overcome, Lewin was able to give Rear Admiral Woodward and his captains the widest possible latitude, and this earned him much respect among them.

By now a force of three Type 42 destroyers and the frigates *Brilliant* and *Arrow* had been dispatched to a holding position 1,000 miles equidistant from Port Stanley, South

The Royal Navy's nuclear submarine force presented a powerful psychological threat to the Argentinian Navy.

Georgia and Buenos Aires, maintaining complete radio and radar silence en route. The force, which reached its position on 15 April, was under the command of Captain John Coward, who commanded *Brilliant*.

The principal threat to the Carrier Battle Group was the Argentinian Navy's destroyers and frigates which were armed with the Exocet SSM. Woodward and his captains were well aware that their vessels were woefully ill-equipped to cope with Exocet because only two of them, the Type 22 frigates HMS *Brilliant* and *Broadsword*, were equipped with the Sea Wolf close air defence SAM, the only effective counter to the Exocet. The sole defence the remainder possessed against missiles was 'chaff', aluminium strips cut to precise lengths and fired from dispensers to act as decoys which could confuse missile guidance systems, and helicopters which trailed radar decoys behind them when airborne. Both, however, required sufficient warning to be launched in time to be effective. Much thought was devoted to the best method of countering the Exocet threat, the general opinion eventually forming that a missile should be engaged with all armament and chaff, a target vessel leaving its chaff decoy pattern as swiftly as possible rather than remaining within it as had been laid down previously in procedures for dealing with Soviet missiles fired from high altitude.

The two major targets for Exocets would be the carriers and as a result, in the event of a real threat from the Argentinian Navy, these would be withdrawn out of range to the east. Woodward's principal counter to the enemy surface fleet was his submarine force but in the event of any Argentinian warships succeeding in entering the TEZ they would be engaged by two attack groups, one consisting of three Type 42 destroyers and the other of *Glamorgan* and two Type 21 frigates.

Responsibility for the first line of air defence would fall on the Sea Harrier force, a total of twenty aircraft embarked on *Invincible* and *Hermes*. The next layer would be provided by the Sea Dart SAM carried by the Type 42 destroyers, but this was designed originally to counter the threat of high-flying Soviet aircraft and could not engage targets at low level – only the Sea Wolf SAM, fitted to *Brilliant* and *Broadsword*, was capable of doing so. All other vessels would have to rely on their 20mm Oerlikon and 40mm Bofors anti-aircraft guns. The most glaring deficiency in the battle group's defensive systems was the lack of an airborne early warning system. The Type 965 surveillance radar, fitted to the majority of the vessels in the group, was obsolete and infamous for its poor reliability and lack of effectiveness in heavy seas.

On 24 April the Carrier Battle Group reached a rendezvous with Captain John Coward's force which was holding station in mid-Atlantic. Three days earlier the entire force had moved into battle formation with the Sea Wolf-equipped HMS *Broadsword* and *Brilliant* taking up station as close escorts for the two carriers. The Type 42 destroyers were deployed as advanced radar pickets to the west, covering the battle group's flank nearest to the enemy.

THE PARACHUTE REGIMENT

The 2nd and 3rd Battalions of The Parachute Regiment deployed to the Falklands while the 1st remained on duty in Northern Ireland. The Regiment was selected for its combat capability, and while it did not have the cold weather experience of the Royal Marines it had tremendous aggression and determination to succeed, born from a gruelling recruitment and selection process.

Formed during the Second World War on the instructions of Prime Minister Winston Churchill, the Paras had served alongside their green beret colleagues at Suez, Aden and in Northern Ireland. Organised in a similar structure to the Marines, the PARA battalion was approximately 450 strong. In the rush to be issued with new arctic warfare smocks for the Falklands campaign many soldiers did not have time to sew wings and DZ flashes into their jackets.

In 1982 the Paras were based at Aldershot, Hampshire, and deployed to the Falklands with the standard section and support weapons. The first and bloodiest battle of the war was fought by 2 PARA at Goose Green. Later 3 PARA was engaged in bitter fighting at Mount Longdon. The actions resulted in the Regiment being awarded two Victoria Crosses for the gallant actions of Lieutenant Colonel H. Jones at Goose Green and Sergeant Ian McKay at Longdon.

In Britain 2 PARA, together with 29 (Corunna) Battery RA, the troop of 9 Parachute Squadron RE, the two Blowpipe sections of 32 Guided Weapons Regiment RA, the flight from 656 Squadron AAC, and the troop of 16 Field Ambulance RAMC, had boarded vessels at Portsmouth and sailed on 26 April. 2 PARA travelled aboard the North Sea ferry MV *Norland* under the battalion's second-in-command Major Chris Keeble, as the commanding officer – Lieutenant Colonel H. Jones – had flown ahead to Ascension Island with a small advance party.

The routine aboard *Norland* soon settled down to training and recreation. 2 PARA had its own Royal Marine Liaison Officer, Captain David Constance, who had joined the battalion at Aldershot and now busied himself with training the battalion in helicopter embarkation and disembarkation from the two flight decks now fitted to *Norland*. The men also practised disembarkation into landing craft from the vessel's rear doors. However, not until the ship reached Ascension Island would it be possible to carry out a full-scale practice with landing craft.

Like the other units in 3 Commando Brigade, the men of 2 PARA devoted much effort to maintaining their physical fitness, which would otherwise have declined during the voyage south. The battalion's physical training instructors took on the task and the *Norland*'s decks resounded daily to the pounding of booted feet as members of

Opposite: Paratroopers carry out drills with an RN Sea King helicopter. They had been more used to working with RAF Puma, Chinook and Wessex aircraft.

the battalion ran circuits around the vessel. Inter-company and inter-platoon events, including tug-of-war competitions, were organised and a battalion sports day took the place of the usual crossing-the-line ceremony as the ship sailed over the Equator. Much attention and time was also devoted to command and control, signals and skill at arms, the latter including live firing from the stern of the ship at targets dropped overboard. Each member of the battalion also underwent training in first aid, in particular the application of life-saving drips.

Eventually, *Norland* and her accompanying vessels reached the port of Freetown in Sierra Leone. There she refuelled and took on board some of 2 PARA's equipment from the container ship *Atlantic Conveyor* – a process known as 'cross-decking'. The voyage resumed and on 6 May *Norland* and the rest of the convoy anchored off Ascension Island. Early on the following day Lieutenant Colonel H. Jones rejoined his battalion.

In the meantime, in his headquarters aboard HMS *Fearless* off Ascension Island, Brigadier Thompson had been informed that 5 Infantry Brigade would be added to the Task Force and dispatched from Britain as soon as possible with a divisional headquarters under the command of Major General Jeremy Moore. In addition, he learned that his and Commodore Clapp's earlier request for HMS *Intrepid* had been granted: she would be recommissioned as a matter of urgency and dispatched to Ascension Island to join the Amphibious and Landing Force Task Groups. This was welcome news for Thompson as, like her sister vessel *Fearless*, *Intrepid* was equipped with purpose-built headquarters facilities and operations rooms, as well as flight decks and accommodation for up to five helicopters. *Intrepid* would also boost the assault capability. She, like *Fearless*, carried four LCUs and four LCVPs in a large floodable dock in her rear hull. Moreover, she could accommodate a unit of up to 700 fully equipped troops for a limited period of time.

By now it had become apparent that in order to permit the reinforced amphibious forces time to concentrate prior to a landing, the proposed 'window' for the operation would have to be postponed from the intended date in early May. Accordingly, it was rescheduled to between 19 May and 5 June. Nevertheless, by 7 May Brigadier Thompson was under considerable pressure for the amphibious forces to leave Ascension Island and head south. The five RFA LSLs, which were slower than the rest of the vessels in the amphibious task group, had already been sent ahead on 30 April. However, 2 PARA had only arrived on 6 May and Thompson was anxious that the battalion should be given time to practise disembarkation from the *Norland* into landing craft. His request for such to Northwood was met with an extension of his sailing deadline by just a few hours. On 8 May Commodore Clapp received the order to depart for the South Atlantic and at 10pm the amphibious task group sailed for the Falkland Islands.

As the military machine prepared for battle the initial prospect of support from America did not look promising. The US Ambassador to the United Nations, Jeanne

During the passage south many stores were repositioned between ships so that they would be in the right location for the role assigned to them. Helicopters ferried the supplies from one deck to another in a system known as VIRTREP.

Kirkpatrick, seemed to favour Argentina. And on the very day the Falklands was invaded she dined at the Argentinian embassy. Despite pressure from Britain the US was reluctant to take sides and instead offered to act as a mediator. This resulted in Secretary of State Alexander Haig flying between Buenos Aires, London and New York to try to broker a peace deal. But Haig's shuttle diplomacy failed to break the deadlock: neither side was prepared to budge on the key issue of sovereignty.

On 17 April Haig, after visiting Prime Minister Thatcher, presented a five-point plan to resolve the situation. This was ignored by the Argentinian junta. In the UK ministers were now concerned that the US might condemn any British action as it had in 1956 when troops landed at Suez. However, the US remained impartial and behind the scenes it supplied Britain with crucial intelligence and military weapons systems, which would be a major benefit to those fighting the air war. American Sidewinder missile systems were given to the UK and fitted to the Harriers: their performance was fundamental to success against Argentinian naval aircraft. But it was not until 30 April that America bowed to public opinion at home and finally blamed Argentina for both the failure of the negotiations and the invasion. By then Britain's military forces had already started the operation to recover the Falklands.

Four

Operation Paraquet*

THE RECOVERY OF SOUTH GEORGIA

Military history has often noted that the commander who strikes early scores both a psychological and a tactical victory over his enemy. It was to be no different in 1982. Planning focused on the logistics of getting the Task Force to the Falklands, but the recapture of South Georgia had not been forgotten. Neither had the importance of an early success.

On 6 April, as Brigadier Thompson, Commodore Clapp and their staffs left Britain aboard HMS *Fearless*, the Task Force headquarters at Northwood was examining the recovery of South Georgia as an operation independent of the campaign to be mounted against the Falkland Islands. As Thompson later recalled:

> The Argentinian garrison in South Georgia was estimated to consist of about sixty marines and the island was beyond the range of Argentinian land-based air cover. Because of the severity of the terrain and climate it was highly likely that the Argentinians would be located at the British Antarctic Survey base at King Edward Point, Grytviken or at the old whaling station at Leith.
>
> Climate and terrain were the overriding factors in deciding the composition of the force to retake South Georgia – it must be mountain and arctic warfare trained and equipped. Therefore it was decided that it should come from 42 Commando, the only commando to deploy to Norway for winter training in 1982.

There was now also a need to push advance forces south to support the Brigadier's planning. Both D and G Squadrons 22 SAS and sections of the Special Boat Squadron comprised the special forces deployed as part of the Task Force. The first element of the SBS to head south from Ascension Island was 2 Special Boat Section (2 SBS) which, together with an SBS command team, was originally destined to be flown out and

---

* The official title of the operation was Paraquet, a strange spelling of parakeet. The men on *Fearless* nicknamed it Paraquat – the powerful weedkiller. Brigadier Thompson said: 'We sent a signal back through SAS channels saying, 'Kill Paraquat before it kills us.'' This did not make us popular at Northwood!'

Special forces troops wait to board a Wessex helicopter. The operation to retake South Georgia involved a joint SAS/SBS and Royal Marine assault. The marines were drawn from M Company 42 Commando.

dropped to a mid-ocean rendezvous with an SSN, either HMS *Spartan* or *Splendid*, in which the men would continue their journey to the Falkland Islands. This plan was changed by Northwood and on 5/6 April 2 SBS flew out to Ascension Island instead. In the meantime, 6 SBS travelled from the squadron's base at Poole in Dorset to the Royal Navy nuclear submarine base at Faslane. There it embarked on the SSN HMS *Conqueror*, which departed on 4 April for the South Atlantic. 3 SBS sailed for Ascension Island on the RFA *Stromness*. The remaining section, 1 SBS, stayed at Poole to provide the maritime counter-terrorist force covering shipping and offshore oil installations in the North Sea.

Elements of the special forces assigned to the Task Force were to play a key role in the plan to retake South Georgia, as were the Royal Marines who would fly south for the mission. The force selected for the operation was M Company, commanded by Captain Chris Nunn. Added to it was a section of 42 Commando's mortar troop, a section of the reconnaissance troop, a small party of medics and logistics personnel, two naval gunfire observer parties from 148 (Meiktila) Forward Observation Battery and 2 SBS. Major Guy Sheridan, second-in-command of 42 Commando and a very experienced mountaineer, commanded the force.

On 7 April Sheridan and the M Company group flew from Britain to Ascension Island where they joined D Squadron 22 SAS under Major Cedric Delves. The entire force, numbering some 230 men, then embarked. D Squadron and 2 SBS left on the RFA fleet replenishment ship *Fort Austin* while the M Company group, together with two Wessex helicopters of 845 Squadron, embarked on the RFA tanker *Tidespring* which had arrived from Malta carrying urgently needed supplies for HMS *Endurance*. Both vessels were to form part of a task group comprising HMS *Antrim*, *Brilliant* and *Plymouth* with Captain Brian Young RN, commanding *Antrim*, appointed Commander Task Group. *Fort Austin* left Ascension Island on 9 April and the remainder of the task group followed on the next day.

HMS *Conqueror*, with 6 SBS still aboard, had been carrying out an inshore survey of South Georgia, reporting that there were no signs of any Argentinian vessels. Thereafter, she departed north-west for a location from which she could enforce the MEZ, act in support of Paraquet or engage the enemy aircraft carrier *Veintecinco de Mayo* in the event that she emerged from port.

On 14 April *Fort Austin* rendezvoused with HMS *Endurance* north of South Georgia. During the following twenty-four hours D Squadron and 2 SBS were cross-decked by helicopter from the replenishment vessel to *Endurance*, together with their boats, weapons and equipment. The other vessels in the task group appeared shortly afterwards and the entire force headed south.

The plan for Paraquet was to land D Squadron and 2 SBS patrols from *Endurance*. The latter would be put ashore at Hound Bay to the east and would move across Sorling Valley to Cumberland Bay, thereafter approaching Grytviken from the south and reconnoitring Grytviken and King Edward Point. Meanwhile D Squadron would reconnoitre the areas around Leith and Stromness. Five days would be devoted to these reconnaissance tasks, with subsequent operations to retake South Georgia being based on the information gained from them.

On 17 April D Squadron's 19 Troop – mountaineering and climbing specialists commanded by Captain John Hamilton – were cross-decked to *Antrim*. The squadron was under the operational command of the Commander Task Group and not Major Guy Sheridan. Against his advice the squadron commander, Major Cedric Delves, had decided to insert his patrols by helicopter on the Fortuna Glacier.

Final clearance for Paraquet was given by the War Cabinet on 20 April. It was now more than two weeks since the Task Force had set sail from Britain and public opinion was demanding action. Moreover, it was felt that a successful military action resulting in the recovery of South Georgia would give an added edge to British diplomatic efforts to obtain a peaceful resolution to the conflict.

On the morning of 21 April *Antrim* and *Tidespring* positioned themselves north of Antarctic Bay while *Endurance* and *Plymouth* headed for Hound Bay with 2 SBS.

Film-makers Cindy Buxton and Annie Price were trapped at St Andrew's Bay in South Georgia, where they had been guests of the British Antarctic Survey team. They were filming king penguins and elephant seals.

Shortly afterwards, *Antrim*'s Wessex helicopter, flown by Lieutenant Commander Ian Stanley RN, took off to carry out an inspection of weather conditions close to the shore. Winds were gusting at half-gale strength with snow squalls; visibility was poor with the cloud base at around 400 feet. Nevertheless, Stanley reckoned that an insertion was possible. Within an hour of his return to *Antrim* he was airborne again, along with two other Wessex helicopters from *Tidespring*, flying towards Possession Bay with four four-man SAS patrols aboard.

As his aircraft was the only one fitted with a computerised flight control system, Stanley led the way. The other two aircraft followed him as he twisted his way between steep mountains towards the Fortuna Glacier. As the helicopters approached the coast, however, the weather deteriorated considerably and the aircraft encountered heavy snow. The attempt was aborted and the helicopters returned to their parent vessels. At midday they made a second attempt and this proved successful, despite poor visibility and winds gusting at up to 80mph.

Conditions on the glacier were appalling and the four patrols made little progress as they waded through thick snow which concealed deep crevasses. With the men of each patrol roped together, they pulled three heavily loaded pulks (sleds) carrying up to 200lb each. They had travelled only half a mile before they were forced to halt for the night. The rock-hard surface of the glacier made it impossible for the patrols to hack anything more than shallow trenches for shelter and some of their two-man tents were blown away by winds that reached speeds of almost 100mph.

The morning of 22 April brought no improvement in the weather. Temperatures were so low that the oil on the patrols' weapons had frozen, rendering them inoperable. At 10am the commander decided to abort the mission and radioed *Antrim* with a request for extraction. That afternoon, despite the appalling conditions, the three helicopters took off from *Antrim* and *Tidespring* and headed for the glacier, where the patrols had switched on their radio beacons to guide in the aircraft. First to land was a Wessex from *Tidespring* flown by Lieutenant Mike Tidd RN. Taking off with six SAS soldiers aboard, he headed north but within minutes flew into a white-out, a maelstrom of snow which completely blinded him. Seconds later, the aircraft crashed on to the glacier at a speed of some 30 knots. Unbelievably, all aboard escaped serious injury and were loaded on to the other two aircraft which landed beside the crashed Wessex shortly afterwards.

A few minutes later the helicopters took off and once again began to head for the coast and their parent vessels, Lieutenant Commander Stanley in the lead with Lieutenant Ian Georgeson RN flying behind. Within three minutes, however, they met another white-out. Stanley succeeded in flying through it unscathed, successfully negotiating a high ridge on the edge of the glacier. Georgeson lost sight of Stanley's aircraft as it dipped over the far side of the ridge. Blinded but realising from a glance at his altimeter that the ground was coming up fast to meet him, Georgeson reduced his speed and prepared for a hard landing. No sooner had the aircraft touched down than a massive gust of wind travelling at some 50 knots caught the aircraft and sent it hurtling across the ice, its rotor blades crumpling and becoming entangled with the fuselage. Once again, all escaped serious injury.

Stanley, his aircraft already fully loaded, flew on to *Antrim*, leaving behind the sixteen crew and passengers of the wrecked aircraft. They lost little time in extricating themselves and building a shelter from some of their inflatable boats rescued from the site of the first crash. That afternoon Stanley twice attempted to take off and return to the second crash site to rescue the survivors but on both occasions was forced to abort because of the severe weather. At 4pm conditions improved sufficiently for him to take off but deteriorated again as he crossed the coast and flew inland.

With sixteen men and their equipment to be flown out to *Antrim* Stanley was intending to make two flights but as he approached the crash site he realised that the weather was rapidly getting much worse and that he would be unable to make two trips before darkness fell. There was no option but to abandon all the equipment and just fly out the men. With the four crew of the two crashed helicopters and twelve SAS crammed aboard, Stanley's Wessex took off and headed back towards *Antrim*. The state of the sea was such that the destroyer's flight deck was pitching heavily as he made his final approach to the ship. Hovering above the flight deck, he brought his aircraft down heavily but firmly. The first stage of the attempt to recapture South Georgia had ended at the cost of two helicopters wrecked and a large amount of equipment lost.

Meanwhile only one SBS patrol had been landed at Hound Bay on the north of South Georgia. It had been planned to land three patrols with their equipment using the two Wasp light helicopters carried by HMS *Endurance*. The SBS men's task was to locate the Argentinian forces in the area and report on their strength and dispositions prior to a landing by the M Company group. However, the weather began to deteriorate rapidly for them too and it quickly became apparent that the other two patrols could not be inserted. The men ashore set off alone on their reconnaissance task. By midnight conditions at sea were atrocious and a further attempt to fly in the other two patrols at 3am on 22 April had to be aborted because of heavy snow and thick ice. Undaunted, the two patrols decided to attempt an insertion by sea. HMS *Endurance* moved as close as possible to the shore and two Gemini inflatable assault craft were launched over her side. At 3.30am, the two six-man patrols, their craft heavily laden with equipment, headed inshore. Despite a huge swell and ferocious winds they succeeded in landing in Hound Bay and forty minutes later they had made contact with the first patrol which was in a lying-up place (LUP) on the other side of the bay.

All three patrols now set off to establish an OP above King Edward Point where the Argentinians were believed to be building up their forces on South Georgia. To reach the desired location 8 miles across Cumberland Bay they would need two Gemini craft. Via the radio link with *Endurance*, they arranged for a helicopter to bring in the two boats to a rendezvous on the following morning.

Before dawn on 23 April the three patrols set off. Heavily burdened with packs weighing over 80lb, they crossed the Sorling Valley and by midday had reached the Nordenskjold Glacier, which had been proposed as a possible landing place but turned out to be totally unsuitable. It comprised a gigantic mass of ice in a bay filled with floes – sharp ice which would have made short work of Gemini inflatables. That afternoon the patrols reached the prearranged rendezvous with the helicopter from *Endurance*. A member of one of the patrols later recalled:

The helicopter arrived in mid-afternoon with the two boats and their engines slung in a net beneath the undercarriage. We saw him coming in low so as to avoid being seen by the Argentinian troops over the other side of the bay. In doing so, he probably hit the front tube of one of them on the ice. When we blew it up to full strength, it leaked badly and could not be used. We decided that we would have to split up, half remaining where they were, the others taking the second Gemini across the bay.

We laid up until nightfall, making ourselves as comfortable as possible in freezing winds, with half of us still wet from the journey across. We loaded the boat and made ready for the crossing under darkness. In those couple of hours, the weather had changed dramatically. A force seven was blowing and pack ice was on the move – you could hear it crunching and banging. The change of wind direction was blowing it back into the bay, and it was hitting the shore-line and just stacking up.

By the time we came to launch the Gemini, there was just one small channel free of ice, less than 50 yards wide and closing. Well, the others decided to make a dash for it before the ice closed up completely and headed out in pitch darkness; you couldn't see a bloody thing, and the waters were grey and impossible. Within 800 yards, they were in trouble. You could hear the motor was overworking and hitting chunks of ice; it was like a food mixer with too much to tackle. It faded and stopped several times.

The ice was piling towards them – huge chunks of the bloody stuff – and they needed engine power to avoid being hit and sunk. They had to run back and rejoin the rest of us on the shore. It was decided we would lay up for the night and make another attempt the next day.

Dawn on the following day, 24 April, brought no improvement in the weather and by then there was so much ice in the bay that a crossing was out of the question. The patrols attempted to establish radio contact with the Paraquet command element aboard *Antrim* but failed to do so. Unknown to them, all vessels in the task group had been ordered to withdraw from South Georgia's waters following the sighting of the Argentinian submarine *Sante Fe* in the area. In her haste to leave, *Antrim* had omitted to inform the SBS patrols ashore.

Later that night, however, radio contact was re-established. By then the patrols had decided that they were unable to complete their tasks because of the adverse weather and conditions ashore, and requested that their mission be aborted. Initially, there was some hesitation among the command element aboard *Antrim*: they were of the opinion that another attempt should be made. Eventually, however, sense prevailed and the patrols were extracted by helicopter to *Endurance*.

Meanwhile D Squadron's 17 (Boat) Troop had set off in five Geminis for Grass Island on the night of 23 April. Shortly after leaving *Antrim*, however, one outboard engine failed and the inflatable was whirled away by the howling gale into the night, its three occupants clinging helplessly to their craft. Not long afterwards, a similar fate befell a second Gemini which drifted for several hours in darkness until the signals from its radio beacon were picked up by a Wessex helicopter which rescued the crew. The remaining three boats rafted up and succeeded in reaching Grass Island but by the early afternoon of 24 April it was reported that all three craft had been punctured by ice. They were subsequently recovered by helicopter. At this stage the captain of *Endurance* made a comment to the effect that, in military terms, the operation had become 'a monumental cock-up'.

M Company's landing on South Georgia had been scheduled for 25 April but the presence of the *Santa Fe* had forced a delay. At 8.55am on the 25th Lieutenant Commander Ian Stanley was airborne in his Wessex helicopter when he spotted the *Santa Fe* on the surface at the edge of Cumberland Bay. Radioing a contact report, Stanley immediately pressed home an attack with two depth-charges and succeeded in causing sufficient damage to the vessel's fin (conning tower) and stern to prevent it from submerging.

In the meantime the frigate *Brilliant* launched her Lynx helicopter armed with a Mk46 torpedo. The aircraft sped towards the reported location of the submarine, which by this

A Royal Navy Lynx helicopter is armed for action. A Wessex from *Antrim* and a Lynx from *Brilliant* took part in the attack on the Argentinian submarine *Santa Fe*.

Santa Fe, crippled after the attack at Grytviken. She limped into port under her own steam and remained alongside for the rest of the conflict. The submarine had been making for the open sea when she was spotted and attacked.

time was heading quickly into Cumberland East Bay towards Grytviken, oil leaking from its stern. Above hovered Stanley's Wessex, awaiting the arrival of the Lynx. The pilot of the Lynx carried out a visual attack, the torpedo being released from the helicopter and dropping under its parachute nose-first into the sea. The Mk46 is, however, an underwater weapon which has a minimum operating depth of 30 feet and the *Santa Fe* continued heading for Grytviken with the torpedo circling harmlessly below it.

The Lynx then resorted to machine-gunning the submarine with its pintle-mounted GPMG, operated by the observer and located in one of the doorways of the aircraft's rear cabin. The helicopter carried out three passes before it came under fire from a machine-gun mounted on the fin. It nevertheless continued to strafe the submarine from a range of 100 yards and at a height of 30 feet, concentrating its fire on the fin. At this stage, other helicopters joined the fray. First to arrive was a Wasp which scored a direct hit on the submarine's fin with an As12 wire-guided missile. Shortly afterwards *Brilliant*'s second Lynx arrived and joined in machine-gunning the *Santa Fe* which was leaking more oil and streaming smoke as she limped towards Grytviken. The helicopters continued to press home further missile and machine-gun attacks until forced to withdraw by fire from enemy troops in positions on King Edward Point. The *Santa Fe* finally succeeded in limping into Grytviken harbour where she berthed, badly damaged and listing heavily.

By this time it was believed that the Argentinian force on South Georgia numbered some 140 marines. Although the main body of M Company was still aboard *Tidespring*, some 200 miles away, Major Guy Sheridan, aboard *Antrim*, proposed to the Commander Task Group, Captain Brian Young, that an attack should be launched on Grytviken without delay. Young agreed and Sheridan set about forming an *ad hoc* assault force of seventy-five men comprising 2 SBS, D Squadron, M Company's headquarters personnel, the 42 Commando reconnaissance troop section and the Royal Marines detachments belonging to *Antrim* and *Plymouth*. This force was landed at 1430hrs in three groups on the lower slopes of the Hestesletten by *Antrim*'s, *Brilliant*'s and *Plymouth*'s Lynx anti-submarine helicopters. From there the men fanned out and headed for Grytviken. *Antrim* and *Plymouth* provided covering fire from their 4.5-inch guns in the form of a creeping bombardment of airburst shells which began several hundred yards from the enemy positions and then moved closer. When the bombardment was just a few hundred yards from them, the Argentinians ran up the white flag and surrendered.

That same afternoon a weak signal from a radio beacon was picked up by a helicopter. The pilot followed it to Stromness Bay at the southernmost tip of South Georgia where it found the three missing members of D Squadron. After their Gemini

Royal Marines of M Company 42 Commando establish themselves on South Georgia. The operation to recapture the islands was a total success and an important early step forward in the campaign.

An Argentinian Puma helicopter shot down by Lieutenant Keith Mills and his marines on South Georgia in early April. They ambushed the aircraft and fired anti-tank missiles at a warship before being outnumbered by enemy infantry.

had been swept away when its outboard engine had failed en route to Grass Island in the early hours of 23 April, they had succeeded in paddling ashore on to the last strip of land between them and Antarctica.

South Georgia had been recovered almost without loss of life. The only casualties were members of the *Santa Fe*'s crew: one lost a leg during the helicopter missile attacks while another was shot by a Royal Marine who thought he was attempting to scuttle the submarine.

Royal Marine Jerry 'Rocky' Rowe was one of the 120 commandos of M Company who flew ahead of the Task Force to recapture South Georgia. A tough man who was an excellent boxer and outstanding soldier, he was assigned to guard the submarine after South Georgia had been recaptured, with strict instructions to ensure that the Argentinian crew left aboard to maintain the submarine did not have the chance to destroy it.

When an Argentinian sailor tried to scuttle the *Santa Fe*, Rowe, who was in charge of a party of marines guarding the vessel, shot the man dead. If the boat had been scuttled it would have caused considerable problems: the vessel had not been searched and may have contained sensitive military documents. Rowe later said: 'Anyone who was in my position would have done the same thing. As far as I was concerned he was trying to scuttle the submarine, so I shot.'

In Britain, news of the island's recapture was met with jubilation by the public and overwhelming relief by Margaret Thatcher and her government, who were in sore need of a victory.

Above: The Argentinian commander on South Georgia, Captain Alfredo Astiz, signs the surrender document aboard HMS *Endurance*. It was clear to those who took part that the Argentinians were stunned at the arrival of the British force. *Below*: After the successful assault on South Georgia a small element of M Company, including the unit's Mountain Leaders Sergeants John Napier and David Cunnington, went to South Thule. This island had been in Argentinian hands since 1976 but the Royal Marines restored British rule and raised the Union flag.

Above: Royal Marines from 42 Commando patrol Grytviken after their assault. Damage caused to the stricken submarine *Santa Fe* is clear. A small team of Argentinian engineers were allowed to remain aboard, guarded by Royal Marines in case they tried to scuttle the boat. *Below*: Royal Marines patrol among the elephant seals of South Georgia. After the war British troops were again based here before being pulled out in the late 1990s.

FIVE

THE TASK FORCE ARRIVES

THE FIRST CASUALTIES

A week after the recapture of South Georgia, Britain carried out her first strike against the Argentinian forces on the Falkland Islands. At 4.23am on 1 May an RAF Vulcan bomber of 101 Squadron carried out an attack on the airfield at Port Stanley. Having refuelled at Ascension Island, the aircraft, piloted by Flight Lieutenant Martin Withers, flew south, refuelling in mid-air eight times on the outward flight before carrying out the attack, during which twenty-one 1,000lb bombs were dropped from an altitude of 10,000 feet. The aim of the operation was to damage the runway, rendering it unusable by enemy jet fighters which would then be forced to operate from their bases on the Argentinian mainland. Unfortunately, only one bomb hit the target, blowing a crater in the runway, while the remainder exploded in a line beyond it.

In the early hours of 1 May Rear Admiral Sandy Woodward's Carrier Battle Group entered the Total Exclusion Zone which had been declared by Britain on 30 April. (The Maritime Exclusion Zone was declared on 12 April.) The two carriers and their aircraft had been assigned specific roles: *Invincible*'s air group would provide air defence, providing combat air patrols (CAP) to protect the fleet, while *Hermes*'s would take on a strike role. At dawn the latter's twelve Sea Harriers, led by Lieutenant Commander Andy Auld of 800 Squadron, took off from the carrier and headed for the Falkland Islands, 70 miles away. Flying at low level to avoid detection by enemy radar, the force split into three groups as it reached the islands.

Three aircraft peeled off to launch a strike on the enemy base at Goose Green, while four headed for Port Stanley to attack the radar installations and air defences there. The latter were followed by the remaining five aircraft whose targets were the airfield's runway and installations. Anti-aircraft guns opened fire as the Harriers hurtled over the airfield, releasing their bombs before flying away to rendezvous with the remainder of the squadron before returning to *Hermes*. All landed safely, the only damage being to one aircraft which had been hit by a cannon shell in the tail. No sooner had the Harriers returned than the carrier group turned west to put itself out of range of air attacks which Rear Admiral Woodward expected the Argentinians to mount in response to the raid.

In the meantime a task group of three warships – HMS *Glamorgan*, *Arrow* and *Alacrity* – had been dispatched to bombard enemy positions around Port Stanley.

On 1 May an RAF Vulcan dropped bombs as part of an operation to deny the Argentinians the use of Stanley airfield. However, initial intelligence pictures showed that while the bombs had reached the target, more attacks would be needed. When the Task Force arrived Harriers joined the attack.

A mixed force of Sea Harriers und RAF GR3 aircraft formed the carrier airgroup deployed with the Task Force. As the carrier group arrived within range of the Falklands the Harriers carried out low-level attacks on Argentinian forces. According to the records, six Sea Harriers and four GR3s were lost. Four pilots were killed.

Together with the air strikes on Goose Green and Stanley's airfield, it was a deliberate move to provoke the Argentinian Navy into responding with air and surface counter-attacks. Twelve miles off the coast, the three ships took up position and opened fire with their 4.5-inch guns as they sailed back and forth. The ploy worked. At 1.25pm four enemy aircraft, identified as Mirage IVs, were detected approaching from the west. *Invincible*'s CAP flew to meet the threat, diving to intercept the faster-flying Argentinian jets. The latter, however, closed swiftly with the three warships, which opened fire with their anti-aircraft guns and launched their chaff decoys. One aircraft scored a near miss with two 1,000lb bombs. They straddled HMS *Glamorgan*'s quarterdeck and exploded near the stern, lifting the destroyer's twin screws clear of the water.

As the three vessels withdrew eastwards, *Arrow* having suffered only superficial damage from cannon fire and *Alacrity*'s helicopter having been hit by machine-gun fire from the shore, the CAP pounced on the Mirages, shooting down two of them. (A third was mistakenly downed by Argentinian air defences.) Shortly afterwards two Canberra bombers approaching at high altitude from the west were detected by HMS *Yarmouth* and *Brilliant*. These aircraft were intercepted by the CAP which shot one of them down; the other turned and fled back to the Argentinian mainland. There was no further response from the enemy that day and at 8.40pm HMS *Glamorgan* returned to resume bombardment of the enemy positions around Port Stanley.

The Argentinian *General Belgrano*, formerly the USS *Phoenix,* was identified as a clear threat to the Task Force.

Meanwhile some 300 miles to the west, the Task Force submarines were busy shadowing elements of the Argentinian Navy's surface fleet. While HMS *Spartan* remained within the MEZ, *Conqueror* had been moved to a position south-west of the Falkland Islands, outside the zone. *Splendid* was tasked with patrolling to the north of her. The primary task of the SSNs was to intercept and destroy the enemy's Type 209 submarines, one of which was still believed to be within the MEZ and thus was a considerable source of anxiety.

On 26 April *Splendid* reported sighting a force of two Type 42 destroyers and frigates, the latter armed with Exocet SSMs, moving south along the Argentinian coastline. Initially, she was ordered to shadow them but the main cause for concern at this time was the whereabouts of the Argentinian Navy's carrier *Veintecinco de Mayo* and cruiser *General Belgrano*. Twenty-four hours later *Splendid* was ordered to move north in search of the carrier while *Conqueror* was tasked with searching to the south.

On the afternoon of 1 May *Conqueror* reported sighting the *General Belgrano*; she was escorted by two Type 42 destroyers, which had sailed on 26 April from the port of Ushaia. Like the other SSNs, *Conqueror* was under the direct control of the Task Force headquarters at Northwood, and not Rear Admiral Woodward. Woodward was extremely concerned at the threat posed to the Task Force by the cruiser and her escorts, which he feared were part of a pincer attack being mounted in conjunction with the *Veintecinco de Mayo* and a carrier battle group which had yet to be located. To get the quickest possible reaction from Northwood Woodward sent a signal to *Conqueror*, copied to Northwood, ordering her captain, Commander Christopher Wreford-Brown, to sink *Belgrano*. He was not allowed to give this order but his action had the desired effect of electrifying Northwood. Admiral Sir Terence Lewin, the Chief of Defence Staff, was at Chequers when Woodward's order signal arrived. *Belgrano* was now outside the Total Exclusion Zone but still inside the General Warning Area announced in April (all enemy warships outside the Argentinian 12-mile territorial limit were liable to be attacked without warning). Lewin asked the Prime Minister to change the rules of engagement to allow *Conqueror* to attack *Belgrano*. Permission was granted in a few minutes. The signal giving clearance for the assault was duly transmitted from Northwood and at 3pm *Conqueror* began her attack. Her captain, Commander Christopher Wreford-Brown, later recalled: 'It took us a while to unscramble the signal from Northwood. Rather than being told "attack the *Belgrano*" we were told by our controllers that we were now permitted to attack any Argentinian vessel which posed a threat even if it was outside the TEZ.'

Raising his periscope, Wreford-Brown took a quick look at the enemy vessels before starting to plan his attack. At this stage the Argentinians were not bothering to use their sonar to sweep the surrounding waters for submarines, assuming that they were safe outside the TEZ. This lackadaisical attitude allowed *Conqueror* to move into a position to attack from a range of some 5,000 yards, as Wreford-Brown recalled:

> We positioned ourselves at a right angle to the cruiser. There were two types of torpedo we could have used for the job – World War Two vintage Mark 8s or the new wire-guided Tigerfish. The Mark 8s were free-running and old but they were well tested and packed a punch big enough to get through the cruiser's thick armour. We opted for them.
>
> I decided to pop the periscope back up for a look as the first one hit the *Belgrano* and saw a big flash. When the crew heard the bangs, there was a subdued cheer throughout the sub. My next reaction was to ensure that *Conqueror* could evade any retaliation by the *Belgrano*'s escorting destroyers, so I ordered the sub to dive away deeper towards the east at speed.

The *Belgrano* had been hit by two torpedoes, the first impacting on her port bow, the second on her stern. All power was lost, rendering the cruiser's communications systems useless. Listing heavily to starboard, she began to sink as her crew abandoned ship with haste, scrambling into large yellow liferafts. Wreford-Brown watched through his periscope.

> As the *Belgrano* went down we could hear her breaking up. It has been alleged that we could also hear the screams of her drowning sailors but that is absolute rubbish. Over the next three or four days we heard widely varying accounts about the number of Argentinian sailors who had been killed. When we heard

The submarine HMS *Conqueror* attacked the *General Belgrano* on 2 May and she sank with the loss of hundreds of lives.

The escort ships with the *Belgrano* returned to port, not even stopping to rescue survivors. The Argentinian fleet remained in port for the rest of the war.

it was more than 300, there was a sense of regret aboard the *Conqueror*. They were, after all, sailors just like us and we certainly didn't bear any grudge against the Argentinians.

The surviving members of the *General Belgrano*'s crew were left to their fate by the two escorting destroyers which swiftly abandoned the scene of the attack. Whether they did so to hunt down the *Conqueror* or avoid attack themselves has never been established. By the time rescuers arrived, 368 of the cruiser's crew had died. The sinking of the *General Belgrano* generated considerable controversy. Prime Minister Margaret Thatcher was to be pursued on the issue for some time to come, not least by the Labour opposition, in particular MP Tam Dalyell. The reaction within the Carrier Battle Group was generally one of satisfaction that a major threat had been eliminated, tempered with regret at the large loss of life.

On the afternoon of 3 May the Carrier Battle Group was attacked by two Argentinian fast attack craft, the *Alferez Sobral* and the *Comodoro Somerella*, which were engaged by two Lynx helicopters launched by HMS *Coventry* and *Glasgow*. Armed with Sea Skua SSMs, the aircraft closed with the two swiftly approaching targets. The leading aircraft, flown by Lieutenant Commander Alan Rich, launched its missile which headed for the *Comodoro Somerella*, impacting with a huge flash and explosion. Within a few seconds, the craft began to sink. Meanwhile the second Lynx had attacked the *Alferez Sobral*, damaging her seriously.

In the early hours of the following day the airfield at Port Stanley was subjected to another bombing attack by an RAF Vulcan, which missed the runway completely. Later that morning Sea Harriers from the strike force aboard HMS *Hermes* carried out another attack on Goose Green; on this occasion enemy air defences proved more effective and one of the Argentinian radar-controlled guns hit a Harrier flown by Lieutenant Nick Taylor. He did not eject and his aircraft crashed seconds later.

Meanwhile the Argentinians had been preparing to deliver a major blow to the Carrier Battle Group. Four SPO-2H Neptunes – Second World War vintage twin-engined anti-submarine aircraft from the Navy's Escuadrilla de Exploración (maritime reconnaissance squadron) – had been deployed from Bahia Blanca naval shore base, flying at low level and only climbing briefly at intervals to detect the battle group's radar emissions and thus locate its position. At the same time two Super Etendards of the Argentinian Navy's 2nd Fighter & Attack Squadron had been moved from the squadron's base at Bahia Blanca to the island of Tierra del Fuego. Flown by Lieutenant Commander Augusto Bedacarratz and Sub-Lieutenant Armando Mayoro, both were armed with the Exocet AM-39 missile and were among the five aircraft which the Navy had succeeded in modifying to carry the weapon.

Exocet, the French-built anti-ship missile codenamed AM-39. The Argentinians had only five at the start of the war but they were used with devastating effect against warships of the Task Force.

On 3 May one of the Neptunes, flown by Lieutenant Commander Ernesto Leston, had located the battle group but by the time his information had reached the base on Tierra del Fuego it was too late to arrange for a KC-130 tanker to rendezvous with the two Super Etendards and refuel them so that they could head east of the Falkland Islands to launch their attack. On 4 May it was Leston again who picked up images on his search radar. This time he had located the Type 42 destroyers HMS *Glasgow*, *Coventry* and *Sheffield* which had been deployed as a forward picket line, scanning for enemy aircraft with their long-range radars. HMS *Glamorgan* and three frigates were 18 miles further east while behind them steamed three RFA vessels which would act as expendable decoys in the event that the Argentinians succeeded in penetrating the first two lines of defence. Last came the Type 22 frigates HMS *Brilliant* and *Broadsword*, each escorting a carrier. They were equipped with 997/998 dual-band doppler radars and Sea Wolf anti-missile systems.

Leston's information was flashed to Tierra del Fuego. Within minutes the two Super Etendards had taken off and were heading for a rendezvous with the KC-130 tanker which was positioned 260 miles from their targets. Having refuelled, they made their final approach, flying at low level to avoid the Carrier Battle Group's radars and Sea Dart SAM systems.

It was HMS *Glasgow* that detected the threat first, her radar picking up both aircraft as they climbed to 2,000 feet at maximum speed in order to conduct a brief radar search before diving to low level again. The threat was identified as two incoming Super Etendards approaching at a speed of 450 knots. The destroyer's air warfare officer immediately transmitted the codeword 'Handbrake', signifying an Exocet attack, and gave the bearing 238 degrees. These details were flashed immediately to the rest of the battle group. *Glasgow* turned sharply to face the incoming threat, reducing her profile to the attacking aircraft and their missiles, and began firing her chaff decoys.

Meanwhile the two Super Etendards, flying at 500 knots, climbed briefly to 120 feet to enable their missiles to acquire their targets and lock on. At a range of 40 miles Lieutenant Commander Bedacarratz launched his missile, Sub-Lieutenant Mayoro following suit seconds later. No sooner were both Exocets streaking away at a speed of 680mph than both aircraft peeled off and headed with all speed for the mainland. Hurtling along at just 6 feet above the waves, the two Exocets sped past *Glasgow* – her Sea Dart system, designed to engage incoming aircraft, was unable to lock on to missiles skimming over the sea at low level. As *Glasgow*'s crew watched, one of the missiles headed unerringly for HMS *Sheffield* and seconds later slammed into her amidships on the starboard side, tearing a hole 14 feet wide in her hull.

Opinions vary as to whether the missile's 363lb warhead detonated on impact; the captain of *Sheffield*, Captain Sam Salt, and some members of his ship's company maintain that it did. Others are of the opinion that it was the remaining propellant which exploded. Whatever the case, the missile pierced the auxiliary machinery space and continued into the forward engine room, setting fire to the fuel feeds. The explosion tore open watertight doors and blasted upwards towards the bridge. Within minutes the interior of the destroyer was an inferno and thick black smoke engulfed the vessel, suffocating the crew in the computer room below the operations centre. Damage control parties found themselves hampered by the smoke (spread to all parts of the ship by the

Inside the operations room of a Type 42 destroyer. Aboard HMS *Sheffield* air warfare officers used radar to monitor the skies for enemy aircraft.

vessel's pressurised ventilation system) and by a fractured water main which prevented them from fighting the blaze. The flames continued to spread, heading for the Sea Dart magazine. The heat was so intense that the destroyer's hull became red hot. After four and a half hours, realising that there was nothing that could be done to save *Sheffield*, Captain Salt gave the order to abandon ship. He and his crew were taken off by HMS *Yarmouth* and *Arrow*. Twenty-one men had died and another forty had been injured by the explosion and ensuing blaze; heavier casualties were only prevented by the fact that the ship had been at action stations. A smoking hulk, *Sheffield* drifted for three days before she was reboarded. On 9 May she was taken in tow by *Yarmouth* and it was intended that she would be taken to South Georgia. However, on the morning of the following day she turned over and sank.

On 6 May the Carrier Battle Group suffered further casualties when two Sea Harriers disappeared from the radar screens; it was subsequently assumed that they

Sheffield caught fire after she was hit by an Exocet. Twenty-one members of the crew were killed. Survivors were rescued by the *Yarmouth* and *Arrow*. Later the warship sank while under tow.

The aircraft carrier HMS *Hermes* in the South Atlantic. The Harrier force aboard Hermes was tasked to attack the airport and enemy radar installations before the Task Force landed.

had collided in conditions of poor visibility and crashed into the sea. On the 7th the TEZ was extended to 12 miles off the Argentinian coast. It was enforced by the SSNs *Spartan* and *Splendid* which lay offshore, reporting the take-offs of aircraft departing on sorties against the Task Force.

Hermes's Sea Harrier strike force continued to launch attacks on airfields and enemy radar installations on the Falkland Islands. However, instead of carrying out low-level assaults they switched to the tactic of 'toss bombing' whereby they released their bombs while climbing at distances well short of their targets before peeling away out of range of enemy air defences.

Rear Admiral Woodward now adopted a new tactic to intercept enemy aircraft flying to and from Port Stanley. He deployed HMS *Coventry* and *Broadsword* 12 miles offshore. While *Broadsword* would be able to provide low-level defence against any air threat with her Sea Wolf missiles and could detect any targets close to land with her very effective 997/998 doppler radar, *Coventry* could engage and destroy any enemy aircraft which came within range of her Sea Dart missiles. This new arrangement appeared to work well. Early on the morning of 9 May a C-130 Hercules transport and its escort of two Skyhawks were detected approaching Stanley airfield. *Coventry* launched Sea Dart at a range of 38 miles and succeeded in shooting down both Skyhawks but missed the C-130. Shortly afterwards, she scored another 'kill', shooting down a Puma helicopter at a range of 13 miles.

On the same morning the pilot of a Sea Harrier of 800 Squadron, Lieutenant David Morgan, spotted an Argentinian trawler, the *Narwhal*, close to the Carrier Battle Group. A few days earlier the vessel had been warned to leave the area but had remained, undoubtedly gathering intelligence. Morgan proceeded to attack, strafing and bombing the trawler before a boarding party of Royal Marines was flown aboard by two helicopters. Among the *Narwhal*'s thirty-strong crew, one of whom had been killed and twelve wounded, was an Argentinian Navy lieutenant commander.

Another ship, the *Islas de los Estados*, was detected by HMS *Alacrity* on 10 May. *Alacrity* opened fire and her first shell ignited the vessel's cargo which exploded (and was subsequently assumed to have been fuel).

A Royal Navy Type 21 Amazon class frigate heading through rough seas for the Falklands. This picture was taken on 9 May and shows the vessel (believed to be HMS *Antelope*) test-firing her 4.5-inch gun. Her sister ship HMS *Ardent* was also in the Task Group and both were to come under Argentinian attack.

Like many of the warships in the Task Force, *Antrim* suffered damage in the early days of the naval war.

HMS *Broadsword* escorts the aircraft carrier *Invincible* on the journey south. A frigate always escorted the carrier and, before the Argentinian fleet pulled back to port, a submarine was always nearby protecting the carrier group from sub-surface attack.

HMS *Glasgow* and HMS *Brilliant* replaced *Coventry* and *Broadsword* off Port Stanley on 12 May. *Glasgow* bombarded enemy positions ashore while *Brilliant* kept a wary eye out for enemy aircraft. Suddenly two pairs of Skyhawks appeared, flying towards the two vessels. *Brilliant* engaged them immediately with Sea Wolf, shooting down two, which blew up, and hitting a third, which crashed into the sea. The fourth Skyhawk peeled away and fled back to the mainland. An hour later more aircraft appeared, flying too low to be engaged by Sea Dart. *Brilliant* attempted to bring Sea Wolf to bear but the system refused to respond, its radar apparently confused by the simultaneous approach of four targets. It was left to both vessels' Bofors and Oerlikon anti-aircraft guns to engage the approaching aircraft. The Skyhawks dropped three bombs, which hit the water and ricocheted off, passing over *Brilliant*. A fourth hit *Glasgow* just above her waterline. Piercing her hull without exploding, it hurtled through the ship to exit on the other side. Although shipping water, the destroyer was able to retire east for temporary repairs before subsequently setting course for Britain.

Throughout this period all elements of the Carrier Battle Group were actively involved in either enforcing the TEZ or harassing enemy forces on the islands through bombardment ashore. By this time, however, the strategy of attempting to interdict enemy air movements to and from the Falkland Islands by sea and air was proving costly and air superiority, so essential for a successful landing, had not been achieved. Despite having sunk a small number of supply vessels and an intelligence trawler, and having shot down seven enemy aircraft, the battle group had lost two of its vital air defence vessels, *Sheffield* and *Coventry*, and three of its Sea Harriers.

In conjunction with Northwood, Rear Admiral Woodward considered the alternatives open to him, including the idea of moving the Carrier Battle Group to the west of the Falkland Islands to confront the Argentinian Navy while at the same time enforcing a complete air blockade on the islands. This course of action was rejected because of the increased risk it presented to the carriers and the rest of the battle group from further Exocet and bomb attacks. As described in chapter nine, another option being given serious consideration was a series of attacks by the SAS on enemy air bases on the Argentinian mainland. The rationale behind this idea was that if the Exocet-carrying Super Etendards, together with a number of Mirages and Skyhawks, could be destroyed on the ground, this would do much towards achieving air superiority and thus swing the odds considerably in favour of the Task Force.

However, for the moment it had to be accepted that the Carrier Battle Group had been unable to achieve the air superiority previously promised to 3 Commando Brigade. At the same time it was recognised that any idea of withdrawing and abandoning all efforts to recover the Falkland Islands was politically completely out of the question. There was no alternative but to proceed with the landing and to meet the air threat head-on.

SIX

D-DAY

ASHORE AT SAN CARLOS

Aboard the Amphibious Task Group preparations for the landing at San Carlos by 3 Commando Brigade were proceeding apace but new intelligence was needed to fuel the planning process taking place aboard the assault ship *Fearless*. Of prime importance was topographical information relating to the proposed landing beaches: gradients, amount of surf, approaches, the number of landing craft which could be accommodated at any one time, and the availability of exits suitable for use by wheeled and tracked vehicles. While much of this data had been provided by Major Ewen Southby-Tailyour's surveys, further intelligence was needed on the potential landing beaches under final consideration. Of equal importance was up-to-date information on Argentinian dispositions. Brigadier Thompson and his planning staff needed to know if there were any units on or near the selected beaches, the location of reserves which could be deployed to counter any landing, current activity, the degree of alertness of enemy troops and the state of their morale.

The task of providing both types of intelligence was given to the SAS and SBS, the latter carrying out beach reconnaissance tasks as well as intelligence-gathering missions. In order to reduce to the minimum the risk of being compromised, patrols were landed up to four nights' march from their intended OP locations. The open terrain meant movement was only possible at night, while the going was so bad in some areas that patrols found themselves covering up to only 250 yards in an hour.

Moreover, the lack of vegetation to provide cover for the OPs resulted in their having to conceal themselves in caves or among rocks, or more often digging small hides, which they covered with wire netting and camouflaged with turf. The men remained in these hides for up to four or five days at a time, observing enemy positions and reporting back to the Task Force by radio. The Argentinians had assumed that British special forces were deployed on the islands, and enemy troops and helicopters were observed searching for them. Withdrawal from a target area therefore had to be carried out with as much care as an approach march and took just as long.

Another limiting factor was the requirement for patrols to be landed at night and the small number of helicopters capable of carrying out such a task. Only four Sea Kings were equipped with passive night vision goggle systems which enabled their pilots to fly in darkness at low level to avoid detection by enemy radar and to locate the

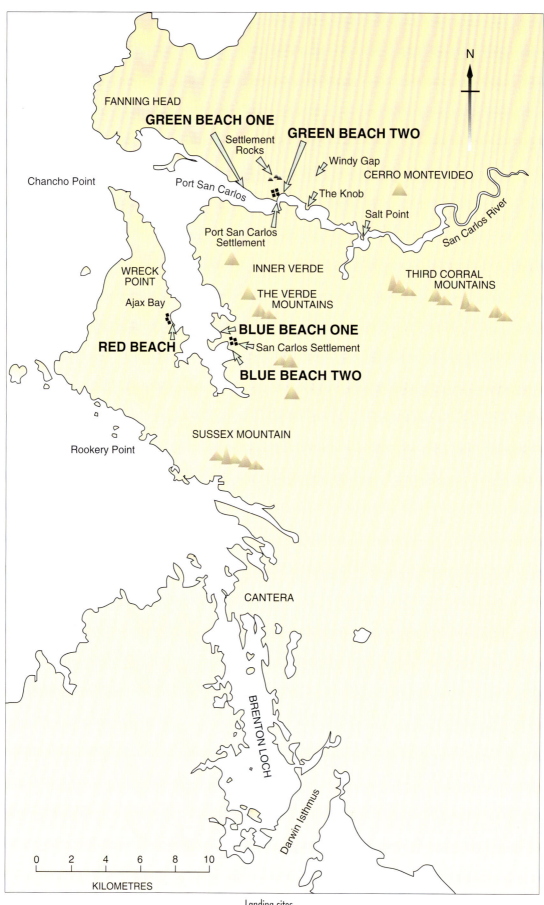

FANNING HEAD

GREEN BEACH ONE

GREEN BEACH TWO

Settlement
Rocks

Windy Gap

CERRO MONTEVIDEO

Chancho Point

Port San Carlos

The Knob

Salt Point

San Carlos River

Port San Carlos
Settlement

INNER VERDE

THIRD CORRAL
MOUNTAINS

WRECK
POINT

THE VERDE
MOUNTAINS

Ajax Bay

BLUE BEACH ONE

RED BEACH

San Carlos Settlement

BLUE BEACH TWO

SUSSEX MOUNTAIN

Rookery Point

CANTERA

BRENTON LOCH

Darwin Isthmus

0   2   4   6   8   10

KILOMETRES

Landing sites.

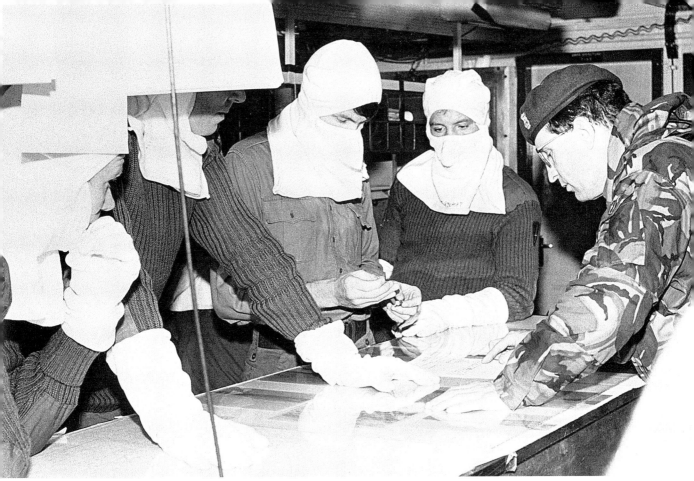

Brigadier Thompson briefs his staff aboard the assault ship HMS *Fearless* about the final details of the landings. Before the landings soldiers would be cross-decked to ensure that they were on the right ship for their part in the assault.

predetermined point where a patrol was to be inserted or extracted. This was complicated by the weather conditions which on occasions prevented insertions or extractions. The only alternative was to land patrols by sea and on a number of occasions warships of the Task Force were employed to deploy men by boat.

Tasks for the SAS and SBS patrols were allocated by Brigadier Thompson and Commodore Clapp in close consultation with Lieutenant Colonel Michael Rose, the commanding officer of 22 SAS, and Major Jonathan Thomson RM, the commanding officer of the Special Boat Squadron. Requests for helicopters and warships to support such tasks were transmitted to Rear Admiral Woodward's Carrier Battle Group, which assigned aircraft and vessels accordingly.

By the end of the second week in May a considerable amount of intelligence had been accumulated about the Argentinian forces on the Falkland Islands. They totalled some 13,000 men, under the command of Major General Mario Menendez. On East Falkland the Argentinian Army's 10th Brigade, commanded by Brigadier General Oscar Jofre, was deployed around Port Stanley, and reinforced with the 4th Infantry Regiment and a marine battalion. The marine battalion comprised a headquarters, five infantry regiments (each of battalion strength) including the 8th and 25th, logistics units and supporting arms. The latter included one and half battalions of artillery equipped with thirty-eight 105mm pack howitzers, engineers and armour consisting of the 10th Armoured Car Squadron and a number of armoured personnel carriers. In addition, the brigade possessed considerable air defence assets comprising: radars; Tiger Cat, Roland and Blowpipe SAMs; and 30mm and 35mm Oerlikon anti-aircraft guns. Finally, it was supported by sufficient helicopters to move a force of 200 troops in one lift.

Also based at Stanley was 601 Company, a 64-strong Argentinian Army commando unit operating under the direct command of Major General Menendez. Along with the Buzos Tacticos, the company formed part of Menendez's mobile reserve, one of its platoons being detached to Pebble Island to the north of West Falkland.

Goose Green and Darwin were garrisoned by troops of the 12th Infantry Regiment which formed part of the 3rd Infantry Brigade, commanded by Brigadier General Omar Parada, whose other two units, the 4th and 5th Infantry Regiments, were based at Port Stanley and at Port Howard on West Falkland respectively. Commanded by Lieutenant Colonel Italo Piaggi, the 12th Infantry Regiment was minus its B Company which had been detached to the 10th Brigade. It had been replaced by C Company 25th Infantry Regiment which in turn was detached to Port San Carlos where it formed a composite force with elements of A Company 12th Infantry Regiment.

The Argentinian Air Force had a number of aircraft and a sizeable contingent of personnel based at Goose Green. Its airstrip, designated 'Air Base Condor', was one of the larger ones outside Port Stanley. The aircraft comprised a squadron of twelve IA-58 Pucaras, a slow-flying but highly manoeuvrable twin-turboprop aircraft originally designed for the counter-insurgency role. Capable of operating off rough airstrips, its powerful armament comprised two 20mm cannon and four 7.62mm machine-guns, plus external ordnance of air-to-ground missiles, rockets and bombs. In addition, there were several helicopters at Goose Green, while the large number of Air Force personnel included anti-aircraft gunners equipped with two Oerlikon twin-barrelled 135mm guns, and logistics personnel who apparently operated a staging post for supplies being transported by helicopter or boat to West Falkland. Also based there, to provide further air defence, was B Battery 601st Anti-Aircraft Artillery Regiment, equipped with Skyguard radar and six Rheinmetall radar-controlled 20mm guns.

Further enemy forces had been observed at Port Louis, Green Patch and North Arm Settlement, and it was believed that an air mobile reserve, comprising an infantry battalion group, some artillery and a company of special forces, was located in the area of Fitzroy.

Close air support for the Argentinian forces on the Falkland Islands was provided by fixed-wing aircraft and helicopters. In addition to Pucaras, these comprised Aermacchi M339s (training aircraft converted to ground attack) and Agusta A-109A attack helicopters. They operated from a number of the thirty-four airstrips located throughout the islands, including the one on Pebble Island to the north of West Falkland, which was occupied by an Argentinian Navy air arm detachment equipped with Pucaras and Shorts Skyvan STOL (short take-off and landing) transports. It was known that a radar detachment was also located at the airstrip, which was defended by No. 2 Platoon of 601 Company. Some of the airstrips on the islands were considered usable by C-130 Hercules transports, a number of which were observed flying regularly between the Argentinian mainland and Port Stanley.

While the Task Force's special forces were principally committed to reconnaissance and intelligence-gathering missions, one direct action operation was carried out some three weeks after the recapture of South Georgia. In mid-May a raid was mounted against the airstrip on Pebble Island, which dominates the northern approach to Falkland Sound and the entrance to San Carlos Water. The Argentinian force there had to be eliminated prior to a British landing and the task was given to D Squadron 22 SAS.

Before the raid members of 17 (Boat) Troop were landed on the island and spent three days reconnoitring the airstrip. On the night of the 14th the remainder of D Squadron was landed by helicopter from HMS *Hermes*. The operation had to be completed and the squadron extracted before dawn at 5am so that *Hermes* could withdraw east beyond the range of enemy aircraft under cover of darkness. The squadron was inserted late, however, as the Sea King helicopters did not land until midnight. Time was of the essence. Major Cedric Delves and his men had to carry out a forced march in order to be on their predetermined start line in time for the attack which was scheduled to begin at 2.45am.

The assault group comprised Captain John Hamilton's 19 (Mountain) Troop while covering fire was provided by a support group armed with GPMGs. HMS *Glamorgan*, her 4.5-inch guns directed by a party of 148 Commando Forward Observation Battery, brought down fire on the enemy while D Squadron's mortar team provided light by firing parachute illuminating flares. Led by Captain Hamilton, 19 Troop succeeded in reaching the Pucaras parked on the side of the airstrip, placing demolition charges on all of them before withdrawing at 3.30am as the explosions began. At that point the Argentinian 601 Company platoon attempted a somewhat half-hearted counter-attack but this petered out after its commander was shot dead, his men pulling back into the darkness.

Withdrawing to a prearranged LZ under covering fire from HMS *Glamorgan*, which should have left the gunline at 3am to withdraw east but had remained to provide support, D Squadron was extracted and flown back to *Hermes*. The operation had been a total success and had been carried out without loss to the SAS.

Two days earlier, on 13 May, Brigadier Thompson had summoned the commanding officers of his units to his headquarters aboard HMS *Fearless* to give them his orders for the forthcoming landing. As he later recalled:

The Argentinians had air superiority over land with a strong force of Pucaras, Aermacchi M339s and Agusta A-109 attack helicopters. It was vital that these were attacked by British Harriers and special forces.

What was clear when I gave my orders to my Brigade on 13 May was that the 11,000 or so Argentinian troops on the islands outnumbered 3 Commando Brigade by more than two to one. The enemy had more helicopters, had air superiority and the added bonus of Pucaras, Aermacchi M339s and Agusta A-109 attack helicopters positioned at various points, many unidentified, throughout the islands. They had more guns, at least as good a helicopter lift as the British and by D-day would have been in position for seven weeks, only 350 miles from home. If the enemy had their wits about them and used the time to good effect, their positions would be well-sited and prepared; counter-attack plans, with well-recced routes and landing sites, would have been made and rehearsed; a quick reaction force, including artillery, would be ready to at least harass the beachhead to delay the break-out and then, having identified the British route or routes to Stanley, establish blocking positions to further delay the advance. Finally, with six regiments around Stanley in prepared defence positions the break-in battle and subsequent fighting for the British would be 'something else'.

The landing was to take place at San Carlos on D-day, a date to be confirmed. It would be a three-phase operation. During the first phase 40 and 45 Commandos

The landings at San Carlos. Landing craft still bearing camouflage from the Commando Brigade's recent exercises in Norway head for the shore. The assault included landing craft utility (LCUs), which could carry almost a company of men (120), and landing craft vehicle platform (LCVPs), which were smaller and carried some 40 troops as well as light tanks.

would be put ashore by landing craft at night at San Carlos Settlement and Ajax Bay respectively. In the second phase 2 and 3 PARA would also land under cover of darkness and secure Sussex Mountain and Port San Carlos. 42 Commando would meanwhile remain at sea as the brigade reserve. As soon as this phase was complete, the offloading of ammunition, fuel, rations, water and other first-line stores not already taken ashore by units would commence. The third phase, beginning at dawn, would comprise the Rapier SAM battery and artillery being brought ashore by helicopter.

Thompson's orders detailed the task of every unit in the brigade and he was followed by his chief of staff, Major Chester, who gave coordinating instructions. Chester was followed by Commodore Clapp's staff officer operations (SOO), who covered the grouping and movements of the amphibious ships, troop-carrying vessels and escorts on the day before the landing, D–1, and on the night of D-day itself. He also detailed the launching and loading of landing craft just outside San Carlos, explaining that this would be timed so that the final approach to the northern entrance of Falkland Sound would take place in darkness in order to reduce the risk of attack from the air. Brigadier Thompson wanted the landing to begin as soon as possible after nightfall:

> I had wished to start landing as soon as possible after last light (the onset of darkness following sunset) to avoid the traditional dawn landing and have the maximum darkness in which to get the Brigade on to the high ground and clear any enemy off the sites from which the Rapier would defend the anchorage against air attack. However, a last light H hour would have meant a sea approach in daylight, which was clearly hazardous, given the adverse air situation. Clapp would have preferred a first light (the onset of daylight before sunrise) H hour with the maximum amount of darkness for the approach. However, with the usual spirit of cooperation a compromise solution was agreed within a few minutes of the problem being put to us both some days before the O Group. Even so, the SOO explained, at least half of the passage through the TEZ on D−1, and all within range of Argentinian

The assault ship HMS *Fearless* pictured off the Falklands. It was vital that both *Intrepid* and *Fearless* were deployed in Operation Corporate so that if one were hit, the landing craft of the second could still support an assault.

148 COMMANDO FORWARD OBSERVATION BATTERY

148 (Meiktila) Battery is the smallest unit in the British Army. Although it is part of 29 Commando Regiment RA, it mainly operates on its own. Its primary task is to provide fire direction for naval gunfire support (NGS) and in the Falklands the men of 148 were among the first to land with special forces. Teams from 148 took part in every battle across the Falklands and won great respect for their work. Based at Poole in Dorset the unit includes specialist Royal Navy radio operators who attend both the Royal Marines' commando course and The Parachute Regiment's P Company selection followed by the parachute course at RAF Brize Norton. Every man in 148 is trained to send and read morse code at eighteen words a minute. During Operation Corporate the forward observation (FO) teams carried everything they needed on their backs.

mainland-based air attack, would be in daylight. It would, the SOO promised, be the longest day.

Three days later came intelligence that resulted in alterations to Thompson's plan. On 16 May it was discovered that the Argentinians had positioned a small force on Fanning Head, which dominated the entrance to San Carlos Water from the north. It was thus decided to land a 25-strong force of SBS, accompanied by a forward observer party from 148 Commando Forward Observation Battery, after last light on D-day with the task of attacking Fanning Head from the east. Accompanying the force would be Captain Rod Bell RM, who spoke fluent Spanish and whose task it would be, using a loudhailer, to persuade the enemy company to surrender following a display of SBS firepower and a bombardment of naval gunfire.

More disturbing for Brigadier Thompson and his planning team was the news that the Argentinian air mobile reserve was being deployed north of Darwin, directly south of San Carlos, and not at Fitzroy as reported earlier. He said:

> The reports of the enemy strategic reserve being north of Darwin worried me more. If they got an inkling of the landing, even on the night of D-day, and moved fast they could get up on to Sussex Mountain, which overlooked the whole of the eastern arm of San Carlos Water, containing the major anchorage and three of the four beaches. Clearly Sussex Mountain must be seized as soon as possible, so I changed the order of landing. There were enough landing craft to land only two commandos or battalions simultaneously, so I brought 2 PARA forward from phase two to phase one to land alongside, but slightly before, 40 Commando. 45 Commando would land in phase two and not in phase one.

Royal Marines from 40 Commando's Recce Troop prepare to go ashore. The sniper on the left is armed with an L42 rifle.

Lieutenant Colonel H. Jones with A Company on Sussex Mountain.

Otherwise the plan remained unchanged. Commando and battalion objectives, beaches and landing craft allocation remained as before. The risk in this change of plan was that if there were enemy at Ajax Bay they would shoot into the backs of 40 Commando and 2 PARA landing opposite Ajax at San Carlos Settlement on Blue Beach One and Blue Beach Two respectively. For this reason I had wished to land at Ajax simultaneously with the landing at San Carlos Settlement. However, the possibility of the Argentinians seizing Sussex Mountain before the Commando Brigade arrived had to be considered and was a higher priority. If enemy did open up from Ajax they would have to be dealt with by gunfire from the frigate *Plymouth*, which was to accompany the first wave of landing craft right into San Carlos Water. Having made the necessary changes in the plan I visited

Special forces troops wait on the flight deck of the assault ship HMS *Intrepid* to be airlifted to *Hermes,* which is in the background. Both SAS and SBS troops worked ashore for several weeks before the Task Force came into the area. They were deployed by Sea King helicopters with pilots flying on night vision goggles.

Commanding Officers on 17 May in their ships to brief them. H. Jones, the CO of 2 PARA, in *Norland*; Whitehead, the CO of 45 Commando, in *Stromness*; Hunt (40 Commando), Vaux (42 Commando) and Pike (3 PARA) in *Canberra*.

By 17 May the Amphibious Task Group had rendezvoused with the RFA LSLs which, because of their slower speed, had left Ascension Island a week ahead. D-day was set for the night of the 20th/21st and final preparations were under way for it. It had been intended that units would disembark from the vessels in which they had sailed south and thus, during the period spent off Ascension Island, they had rehearsed the drills and procedures thoroughly. On 18 May, however, Northwood ordered Thompson to move two of the units aboard *Canberra* to other vessels because of the perceived risk of an enemy air attack on a major vessel during the day prior to the landing. 40 Commando and 3 PARA would have to be transferred to *Fearless* and *Intrepid* respectively, the latter also taking Z Company 45 Commando as her landing craft would be disembarking the rest of the commando from *Stromness* on D-day.

The transfer took place on the following day, the 19th. It was a major task, despite the reasonable sea state, with heavily burdened troops aboard *Canberra* having to leave

An Argentinian aircraft flies in low and fast over the Task Force ships. The Royal Navy was unable to win the air war before the amphibious assault and as a result the Task Force came under constant attack.

the vessel via a large door in her hull and then swing across on a rope to a narrow catwalk on the side of the LCU which was heaving up and down beside the liner. One member of 40 Commando slipped and fell between *Canberra* and the landing craft but was swiftly hauled out of the sea, soaked but unharmed. Meanwhile other units were being cross-decked by Sea King helicopter from the Carrier Battle Group to the vessels from which they would disembark for the landing on D-day. All went well until the last helicopter, transferring members of D and G Squadrons 22 SAS from *Hermes* to *Intrepid*, crashed after a large seabird flew into one of its engine air intakes. Twenty members of 22 SAS and its support element died along with the Royal Navy aircrew; it was the largest number of casualties suffered by the SAS in one day since the Second World War.

Dawn on 20 May found the Amphibious Task Group steaming towards the northern coasts of the Falkland Islands. All vessels were at action stations with weapons manned and radio silence imposed, communications between vessels being conducted by signal lamps. The weather was bad – a rough sea with drizzle, mist and a low cloud base – and remained so until the evening. It cleared as the task group headed for Foul Bay and the northern entrance to Falkland Sound which led to San Carlos Water. At midnight the troops of 40 Commando and 3 PARA aboard *Fearless* and *Intrepid* began to move down through the vessels to their docks, ready to embark on the landing craft. Aboard *Stromness* and *Norland* 45 Commando and 2 PARA prepared to do likewise.

Earlier that night 3 SBS had been landed by helicopter to the east of Fanning Head, dispatching a small party to check for any enemy on Green Beach One where 3 PARA would land in the second phase to secure Port San Carlos. Ajax Bay had been under SBS surveillance since the early part of May and an SBS patrol had been inserted successfully into the area of San Carlos Settlement five days earlier, but an attempt to do the same at Port San Carlos had been prevented by the presence of enemy in Foul Bay. Prior to the deployment of 3 SBS to Green Beach One, an aerial reconnaissance of the Fanning Head area was carried out by a Wessex helicopter fitted with a thermal imager. Aboard the aircraft were the commander of 3 SBS and Captain Hugh McManners of 148 Commando Forward Observation Battery, whose forward observation party would accompany the section. The Wessex flew from HMS *Antrim* to the north-west of East Falkland where it climbed to an altitude of 300 feet and the thermal imager was used to sweep Race Point and Middle Bay for signs of enemy forces. None was detected and the aircraft then turned its attention to the area north of Fanning Head where it observed enemy troops equipped with heavy weapons in positions both on the feature and to the north of it. They were elements of A Company 12th Infantry Regiment and C Company 25th Infantry Regiment which were based at Port San Carlos but had deployed a detachment, together with two 105mm recoilless rifles and a section of two 81mm mortars, to Fanning Head. The helicopter then returned to *Antrim* where the 3 SBS commander and Captain McManners briefed their men on the results of the reconnaissance.

Accompanied by the Spanish-speaking Captain Bell, 3 SBS and the forward observation party were flown to the east of Fanning Head in three lifts, the leading element clearing and securing the LZ while awaiting the arrival of the remainder. Thereafter, the 25-strong force, heavily armed with twelve GPMGs, headed west for Fanning Head. As Captain McManners later recalled in his book *Falklands Commando*:

> The going was very rough with large tussocks of grass and strange outcrops of what in the darkness looked like waist-high seaweed and huge lettuce plants. We were soon perspiring and opening our smocks to ventilate (wetness makes you terribly cold once you stop and cool down). We plodded up on to the ridge and sent scouts ahead with a thermal imager to 'vacuum' the ground, which appeared to be clear. On the top of the ridge it was rocky and although I was relieved because this meant it was unlikely to be mined, there was quite a bit of stumbling and falling which is very tiring.
>
> We could see Fanning Head looming in the darkness and again vacuumed ahead. We became a little nervous of the Head which, although beyond effective small arms range, was beginning to overlook us and it was possible that our slow progress was being observed.

At that point firing was heard to the north-west of Fanning Head and it was assumed that the enemy company was engaging ships out to sea with its heavy weapons. McManners immediately called for naval gunfire support from HMS *Antrim* which responded with a salvo from her twin 4.5-inch guns. This proved to be on target and McManners requested a further twenty salvoes of airburst shells which exploded 50 feet over the Argentinian positions. There was no further firing from the enemy and 3 SBS resumed its advance under covering fire from *Antrim* which launched sporadic salvoes to keep the enemy troops' heads down.

The SBS commander deployed his men in a line along a ridge from where they could observe the northern slopes of Fanning Head. Shortly afterwards they caught their first sight of the enemy. Captain McManners later said:

> Initially there was no sign, but then silhouetted against the spur of north Fanning Head we could see six or so figures of men digging in. I opened up (with the NGS) well beyond them (800m) and crept the fire backwards towards them. (Not only did I not want to hit them, but I did not want to hit *us*!) The

bright red images in the imager ran around, lay down or just stood still when the shells came down. Then a strange thing was seen – a line of two parallel files of men marched over the spur and lined up on our side, appearing to be deciding what to do next.

The figures then started to move towards us, moving away from their gun position and the NGS shells. We decided that this was the time to try and get the loudspeaker into action. It was very windy, blowing from the enemy towards us. A stream of tracer was aimed using an Armalite with a night-scope and then we opened up using one GPMG with a burst of tracer over their heads. The loudspeaker, which had been so carefully devised, packed, and carried, failed to work! Rod Bell tried shouting something about 'Royal Marine desperadoes', but even if they heard, it must have seemed like the voice of an angry god after the shelling and machine-gun fire.

The enemy split into two groups, one heading towards the SBS and the other in the opposite direction. Some of the Argentinians attempted to slip away back to their company's positions but were prevented from doing so by some well-aimed bursts in front of them from a weapon fitted with an image intensifier. Those who ignored the warning were subsequently shot and killed. At that point Bell, in an effort to prevent further bloodshed, went forward with some of the SBS to try to persuade the enemy to surrender but was unsuccessful.

Dawn was now approaching and the enemy company was still in possession of Fanning Head. The SBS commander decided that there was no alternative but to mount an attack. Once again, McManners called down fire from *Antrim*. As dawn approached, however, enemy troops were observed moving up the feature and into some bushes on its northern side. Suddenly, a machine-gun opened fire on the SBS, provoking a fierce response which resulted in the appearance of a white flag from the bushes. Six Argentinians surrendered and a search of the area revealed four more badly wounded. By then, the remainder of the enemy force had fled. It later transpired that the position had been occupied by a half-company, the other half being located in Port San Carlos. Questioning of the prisoners revealed they were a detachment of a composite 60-strong force of two platoons from A Company 12th Infantry Regiment and C Company 25th Infantry Regiment. Equipped with two 105mm recoilless rifles and two 81mm mortars, they had been in position for three days; poorly equipped and with no resupply, they had no rations and had resorted to killing sheep for food. Some were found to be wearing items of equipment looted from the Royal Marine barracks at Moody Brook.

Further south, D Squadron 22 SAS had been carrying out a diversionary attack on the Argentinian air-mobile reserve force near Darwin in what was named Operation

SBS SOLDIER ONE OF THE FIRST CASUALTIES

SBS Sergeant Ian 'Kiwi' Hunt was among the first special forces troops to set foot on the Falklands. His task was to collate information about enemy positions and relay it to the brigade commander. Both the SAS and SBS had allocated themselves 'areas of operation' but somehow two patrols clashed in the dead of night and opened fire on each other. 'Kiwi' was killed and the incident sparked a period of bad feeling between the two units, but they had to put their feelings aside and get on with the war. Sergeant Jan Rowe, an experienced climber who served with the Mountain & Arctic Warfare Cadre and fought in the Falklands himself, knew Sergeant Hunt well. He said: 'He was a very good operator – one of the fittest men I knew. He was in his element in the Falklands.'

Sergeant 'Kiwi' Hunt of the SBS who was killed in a tragic 'friendly fire' incident in the early days of the conflict. His patrol and an SAS patrol fired on each other by mistake.

Men of 3 PARA go ashore. The landing craft were an unfamiliar method of travel for the Paras and many could not wait to get their feet on dry land.

Tornado. Sea King helicopters from 846 Naval Air Squadron inserted the SAS and then launched a series of decoy landings to make the Argentinians think that Goose Green had been selected as the main site for coming ashore. During the night D Squadron had marched to its objective. It launched an attack with supporting gunfire from *Ardent*, pinning down the enemy force to prevent it moving north to counter the landings.

The Amphibious Task Group had anchored later than scheduled as a result of navigational problems caused by heavy mist at the northern entrance to Falkland Sound. Moreover, *Fearless* had suffered a problem with one of her ballast pumps which resulted in a delay in the flooding of her dock. Also, 2 PARA was taking longer than expected to disembark from *Norland*. Unlike the other units, the battalion had not been given the opportunity to carry out the night landing rehearsals at Ascension Island, having arrived only twelve hours before the departure of the Amphibious Task

Commander Rick Jolly, the commando doctor who managed the hospital at Ajax Bay. It was manned by commando and airborne medical teams and was dubbed the 'Red and Green Life Machine'. All who entered the hospital alive, no matter how bad their injuries, survived.

Casualties were flown to the hospital, which was erected in an old building in Ajax Bay.

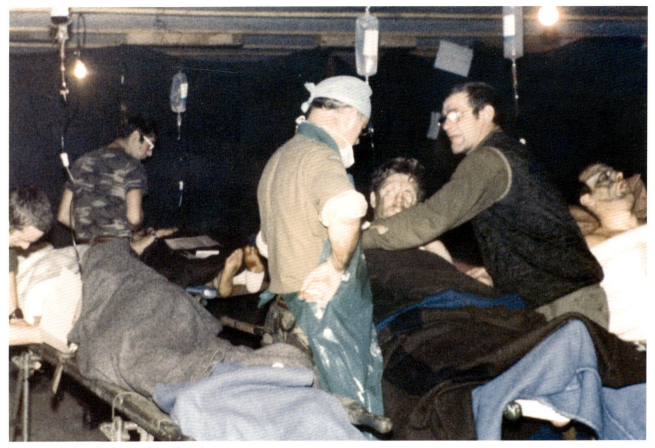

Medics in the 'Red and Green Life Machine'.

Group for the Falklands. The situation was exacerbated by a soldier falling between *Norland* and an LCU, suffering a crushed pelvis.

All these factors had resulted in H-hour being delayed from 2.30 to 3.30am. Eventually, the two groups of landing craft, comprising eight LCUs and four LCVPs, carrying 40 Commando and 2 PARA, under the overall command of Major Southby-Tailyour, set off, heading for the entrance to San Carlos Water. Two of *Fearless*'s LCUs carried two CVR-Ts, a Scorpion and a Scimitar, parked side-by-side at the bows ready to open fire over the lowered ramp at any enemy troops observed on the landing beach. Behind them were crammed elements of 40 Commando, the rest of which was carried by *Fearless*'s other two LCUs and four LCVPs which also contained the engineer detachment of 59 Independent Commando Squadron RE.

Off Ajax Bay the two groups of landing craft split. Those carrying 2 PARA headed for Blue Beach Two. As they did so, their crews were looking for torch signals from the 3 SBS reconnaissance patrol to confirm the beach was clear. No signals could be seen

The Type 42 destroyer HMS *Exeter* engages an Argentinian aircraft over San Carlos Water during the first days of the amphibious assault. Every day saw air attacks on the Task Force. In addition, reconnaissance aircraft flew over the area to film the British ships.

as the LCUs neared the shore some 50 yards apart and began lowering their ramps at approximately 4.30am, an hour later than scheduled. The LCU carrying C (Patrols) Company, commanded by Major Roger Jenner, was due to be the first ashore but had difficulty in beaching. B Company's LCU stopped 15 feet from the beach in some 3 feet of water: the men were forced to jump into the icy sea and wade ashore. As they did so, they were challenged by the 3 SBS patrol who had not been informed that the landings were taking place that night and had been expecting them on the 24th.

Having regrouped in the dark, the battalion set off for its objective, Sussex Mountain, with C (Patrols) Company moving on ahead to secure the start line. The 5-mile march proved difficult: most members of the battalion were carrying very heavy loads and the ground was covered with large tussocks of long grass which caused many to stumble and fall. Casualties and stragglers were collected by the battalion's medical section, aided by the padre, the Reverend David Cooper, who administered medicinal tots of

The men of 3 PARA go ashore from landing craft. Most carried spare mortar rounds, extra machine-gun ammunition and food. Many of the men in 2 PARA had a wet landing after their vessels grounded.

whisky once they had been grouped together and brought into the battalion rendezvous point (RV). Among the worst affected were the Blowpipe SAM operators of 32 Guided Weapons Regiment RA; lacking the physical fitness of the paratroops and weighed down by heavy and cumbersome containers holding missiles and launchers, they experienced considerable difficulty in keeping up with 2 PARA.

Dawn found the battalion climbing Sussex Mountain. Loads had been lightened, albeit slightly, because each man had deposited at the battalion RV the two 81mm mortar bombs with which he had been issued on *Norland*. Fortunately, the weather was good and morale rose as the sun appeared. Suddenly, however, a white parachute appeared in the sky and floated towards the ground with the pilot of a Pucara suspended below it. His aircraft had been shot down by a Stinger SAM fired by D Squadron 22 SAS which had been attacked by two Pucaras while withdrawing from the attack on the enemy air mobile reserve at Darwin. The second aircraft was shot down shortly afterwards by a missile from a warship. Major Jenner said: 'It was a wet landing and we had a long and difficult haul to the top of Sussex. Then in the daylight

Paratroopers dig in after being landed around San Carlos. They quickly prepared shelters against the weather and Argentinian air strikes.

from our lofty perch we could see the ships of the Task Force in the bay and witnessed the Argentinian air attacks. It was as though we were watching a huge TV screen.'

Other aircraft now appeared and shortly afterwards a Skyhawk attacked D Company, which was commanded by Major Phil Neame and was deployed in the centre of the battalion position with A Company on its right and B Company on the high ground to the south. C (Patrols) Company had set off on its march forward to the OP positions from which it would observe towards Goose Green.

The threat of air attack increased as more aircraft could be seen attacking ships of the Amphibious Task Group, some on the gunline in Falkland Sound and others which had weighed anchor at dawn and sailed into San Carlos Water to offload their cargoes. There was no air defence ashore because the Blowpipe detachments were not in position on the high ground and it would be some time before the Rapier SAM battery could be deployed and ready for action. As 2 PARA watched, an aircraft was shot down by a Sea Wolf fired by *Brilliant*. Shortly afterwards a Mirage flew over the battalion and the troops engaged it with some of their GPMGs. The Mirage was followed by a pair of Pucaras which made a single pass from the east to carry out a rocket attack before escaping unscathed.

Meanwhile 40 Commando had experienced no problems with its landing on Blue Beach One. The torch signals from the SBS reconnaissance patrol ashore had been seen clearly and the commando landed shortly afterwards, with A Company clearing White Rincon before advancing eastwards to establish defensive positions on the western slopes of Verde Ridge. Having cleared Little Rincon, B Company joined A Company while C Company cleared San Carlos Settlement. Then the three companies took up the positions allocated to each of them by the commanding officer.

Because of the hour's delay in the phase one landings, 3 PARA and 45 Commando had also been put ashore late, as Brigadier Thompson later recorded:

> After landing 2 PARA and 40 Commando, the landing craft returned to collect 3 PARA and 45 Commando. The planned loading time for the second wave was between 3.30am and 4.15am, with landing times of 6.05am for 3 PARA and 5.45am for 45 Commando. The first wave had not landed until about 4.30am and clearly the second wave would be correspondingly late. To add to the problem the radios from the Commando Brigade HQ in the amphibious operations room in *Fearless* to commandos and battalions were not working well.

3 PARA disembarked from *Intrepid* in her landing craft as dawn was breaking. While the LCUs and LCVPs were still some distance from the shore, radio contact was established with the SBS patrol which had reconnoitred the area of Green Beach One,

the latter confirming that it was clear of enemy. Shortly afterwards, the LCUs found themselves unable to reach the beach because the water was too shallow. B Company, commanded by Major Mike Argue, was aboard the four LCVPs which were able to come ashore, and the company disembarked dryshod before the landing craft returned to the stranded LCUs to ferry the rest of the battalion to the beach.

Having regrouped, 3 PARA set off for Port San Carlos with B Company in the lead. As it did so, however, a Sea King helicopter escorted by two Gazelles of 3 Commando Brigade Air Squadron, which was heading for a feature to the east called The Knob, came under fire from enemy troops of the composite force based at Port San Carlos who were withdrawing along the northern bank of the San Carlos River. The Sea King, which was carrying a reconnaissance party from the Rapier battery, swerved away unscathed but both Gazelles were hit. One succeeded in remaining airborne and

A Royal Marine stands guards over hooded Argentinian prisoners. They were part of a special forces team of forward air controllers and were captured by members of 40 Commando's Recce Troop near San Carlos.

Rapier anti-aircraft site established at San Carlos. The aim was to put these missile systems ashore to provide an air defence screen against the Argentinian air force.

returned to its parent vessel but the Royal Marine pilot in the other aircraft, Sergeant Andrew Evans, was hit and fatally wounded. Nevertheless, still conscious, he managed to land his aircraft on the water. Both he and his observer, Sergeant Edward Candlish, extricated themselves from the sinking aircraft but came under fire as they swam ashore. Twenty minutes after being pulled from the water by Sergeant Candlish and some islanders, Sergeant Evans died of his wounds.

As 3 PARA approached Port San Carlos, the Argentinians, comprising a group of forty and the other half of the company that had provided the force on Fanning Head attacked by 3 SBS, withdrew in haste and fled into the nearby hills. As they did so, they shot down another Gazelle as it flew over Cameron's Point towards The Knob. 3 PARA dispatched a patrol from A Company to rescue the two-man crew but both were dead.

The battalion managed to secure all its objectives. C Company, commanded by Major Martin Osborne, moved up the valley and occupied the high ground above Port San Carlos known as Settlement Rocks, while the rest of the battalion took up positions around the settlement itself. Lieutenant Colonel Hew Pike and his battalion headquarters established themselves in the house belonging to the manager of the settlement, which was inhabited by some forty islanders.

At Ajax Bay 45 Commando's disembarkation from *Stromness* had been hampered by a breakdown in radio communications and the absence of *Fearless*'s fourth LCU which had broken down. The commando had to cram itself into the remaining three landing craft and dawn was beginning to break by the time it was en route to its landing beach. Thereafter, in spite of being behind schedule, the landing proceeded without further problems and the commando secured Ajax Bay without encountering any opposition and then deployed to the high ground above it.

In San Carlos Water and out in Falkland Sound Argentinian aircraft had scored their first success with an attack on the frigate *Argonaut* two hours after dawn. An Aermacchi M339 carried out a low-level approach and fired a salvo of four rockets, which missed the vessel, and then strafed it with cannon, damaging the ship's surveillance radar and wounding three of her crew. Earlier, another Aermacchi had carried out a bomb attack on the RFA *Fort Austin*, which fortunately escaped unharmed.

Shortly after the attack on *Argonaut*, enemy aircraft appeared in force and attacked 3 Commando Brigade and the Task Force vessels in waves. From the troops ashore rose a hail of small arms fire and Rapier and Blowpipe SAMs. Meanwhile the warships launched Sea Slug, Sea Cat and Sea Wolf SAMs, while also bringing their guns to bear on the enemy aircraft which raced in at low level to press home their attacks with what at times appeared to be suicidal determination. The RFA vessels also opened fire with their air defence weapons, while troops aboard the merchant vessels, including

By the end of 21 May, the day of the landings, HMS *Ardent* had been hit and was sinking and *Argonaut*, *Brilliant*, *Antrim* and *Broadsword* were damaged. Later *Coventry* was hit, *Antelope* bombed and the *Atlantic Conveyor* sunk.

Canberra, added to the heavy volume of fire with Blowpipes, GPMGs, LMGs, 66mm LAWs and rifles.

Despite this determined defence, hits were scored on other vessels. The two Type 22 frigates *Brilliant* and *Broadsword* were strafed with cannon fire by two Mirages, while *Antrim* was hit by bombs and rockets on her port side; fortunately, the bombs failed to explode but one passed through her magazine, disabling her SAM systems. *Argonaut* was again the target of an attack when six Skyhawks dropped a number of 1,000lb bombs, scoring two hits. One bomb entered the boiler room; although it failed to explode, it did cause considerable damage and stopped both the frigate's engines. The other bomb pierced the ship's hull below the waterline, passing through a fuel tank; although it also failed to explode, it destroyed the forward magazine and set off much of the vessel's ammunition. Two of the crew died in this attack. Subsequently, *Plymouth* came to *Argonaut*'s aid and towed her into San Carlos Water.

By the end of the afternoon all the frigates had been hit – *Ardent* had been subjected to no fewer than seventeen attacks in Grantham Sound while she was bombarding enemy forces at Goose Green and Darwin. She was initially attacked by Pucaras, then by Mirages and Skyhawks which straddled her with 500lb bombs. Eventually, a pair of Skyhawks attacked simultaneously, hitting her with two bombs, causing considerable damage, knocking out the frigate's aft SAM system and setting her on fire. As she withdrew from Grantham Sound and headed for San Carlos Water, she was hit by further bombs and shortly afterwards another six aircraft also launched attacks on her. Throughout this period *Ardent* put up a fierce defence but by dusk she had lost all power and was ablaze aft of her funnel with the fire spreading to her magazines. At that point her captain, Commander Alan West, gave orders for her anchor to be dropped

The Type 21 frigate HMS *Ardent* sank the morning after she was bombed during an Argentinian air raid.

An Argentinian air force A4 Skyhawk armed with a 1000lb bomb refuels from a KC-130 before heading to the Falklands. The aircraft made regular daily attacks on the ships of the Task Force, the heaviest being on 21 May, the day of the landings.

Argentinian fighter pilots who attacked the British naval Task Force pose at their mainland base. Left to right: Lieutenant Rodriguez Mariani, Lieutenant Julio Barrasa, Lieutenant Commander Agotegaray, Commander Jorge Colombo, Lieutenant Commander Augusto Bedacarratz, Lieutenant Commander Roberto Curilovic, Lieutenant Commander Alejandro Francisco, Lieutenant Collarinco, Lieutenant Armando Mayora.

and for his crew to abandon the ship. By the time the action ended *Ardent* had received hits from seven 1,000lb and 500lb bombs which had killed twenty-two of her crew and wounded thirty. Shortly afterwards, West and his men were taken off by *Yarmouth*.

Meanwhile aboard *Fearless* Brigadier Thompson watched as his units and the rest of the task fought back against the air attacks, which eventually ceased during the afternoon. It was not until evening that he boarded a Scout helicopter and made his way to 3 PARA, 40 Commando and 42 Commando. The latter had been disembarked during the afternoon when it became obvious that the unit was increasingly at risk while it remained aboard *Canberra*. Moreover, as a result of 3 PARA's reports of enemy in the vicinity of Port San Carlos, Thompson had decided to reinforce that area of the beachhead.

With the brigade ashore and its Rapier air defence and artillery batteries in place and ready for action, Thompson now concentrated on offloading all his supplies and logistical support from the Amphibious Task Group vessels and establishing his Brigade Maintenance Area (BMA) at Ajax Bay.

The Argentinians lost sixteen aircraft during their attacks on the Task Force on 21 May. From the east, out of enemy aircraft range, *Hermes* and *Invincible* had deployed their Sea Harriers to provide cover for the Amphibious Task Force. These aircraft had established three CAP positions, each comprising two planes: the first to the north of the islands, the second over West Falkland, and the third over the southern entrance to Falkland Sound. Early on 21 May the Harrier force had succeeded in drawing first blood by shooting down two helicopters, a Chinook and a Puma. During the following days, it scored further successes, mainly against enemy aircraft withdrawing after attacking the Task Force in San Carlos Water. On one occasion two Harriers of 899 Naval Air Squadron spotted a wave of enemy aircraft and attacked, shooting four down with their AIM9L Sidewinder air-to-air missiles (AAM). Two hours later Lieutenant Clive Morell and Flight Lieutenant John Leery downed two more.

The principal problem facing the Task Force at this point was how to locate attacking aircraft sufficiently early for air defence systems to be made ready. The submarine force, which had been reinforced by HMS *Valiant* on 16 May, was deployed off the Argentinian mainland, reporting the take-offs of enemy aircraft which were tracked as they flew at altitudes of around 19,000 feet to conserve fuel. However, once they dived to sea level, at a range of some 50 miles from the Falklands, they vanished from Task Force radars and were picked up again only as they appeared weaving between the hills of the islands or hugging the inlets as they made their final approaches along Falkland Sound. An added difficulty was that Sea Harriers could only remain on station for twenty minutes before returning to the carriers to refuel and rearm. Moreover, comprising a force of only twenty, they were far outnumbered by the enemy's seventy-two aircraft. It was thus inevitable that a large number of attacks would succeed in getting through.

The ferry *Norland*, which was requisitioned to ferry 2 PARA to the South Atlantic, under heavy attack in San Carlos Water. The STUFT ships came under regular bomb attack but none was sunk at San Carlos.

The following day, Saturday 22nd, saw no air attacks because of low cloud. During the previous night *Coventry* and *Broadsword* had been deployed to the north-west of the islands ready to intercept enemy aircraft while they were still flying at high altitude. At the same time the damaged *Antrim* was replaced in Falkland Sound while *Canberra*, having disembarked her troops, withdrew with other STUFT Task Force vessels from San Carlos Water and, escorted by HMS *Brilliant*, sailed out to sea beyond the range of enemy aircraft. The STUFT vessels would only return under cover of night to offload their cargoes for ferrying ashore to the BMA at Ajax Bay.

Enemy aircraft attacked in force again on Sunday 23 May. Just after midday a pair of Skyhawks appeared, flying in at low level from the east, and attacked HMS *Antelope*, which shot down one aircraft with a Sea Cat SAM. Seconds later, another pair appeared from the north, one of these being downed by *Antelope*'s 20mm Oerlikon anti-aircraft guns. Seconds later, however, the frigate was hit by a 1,000lb bomb which pierced her aft starboard side but failed to explode. Shortly afterwards, another hit her port side below the bridge. The second bomb also failed to explode but careered into the petty officers' mess where it killed a steward and two sickberth attendants. Evading further attacks, *Antelope* succeeded in entering San Carlos Water under her own power during the early afternoon and anchored close to *Argonaut* as efforts were made to deal with the two unexploded bombs inside her by a Royal Engineers Explosive Ordnance Disposal team comprising Warrant Officer 2 Phillips and Staff Sergeant Jim Prescott. As the two men set to work, the majority of the ship's company moved to the forward area of the ship while skeleton crews manned her weapons. That evening, Phillips and Prescott carried out a controlled explosion to defuse the bomb; as they approached it to

Royal Marine Commandos with a hooded Argentinian special forces soldier who surrendered during a firefight in the early hours of the landings.

A Royal Marine armed with a Blowpipe missile system mans an air defence position above San Carlos Water.

inspect the results, it exploded, killing Prescott and wounding Phillips badly. A huge blaze started and soon engulfed *Antelope*. Her commander, Captain Nick Tobin, gave the order to abandon ship, his crew being evacuated by landing craft which had sped to the vessel's aid immediately after the explosion. On the following morning, her back broken, *Antelope* sank in San Carlos Water.

The 24th saw enemy aircraft attacking in waves once again. Such were their numbers that *Coventry* and *Broadsword*, deployed to the north of West Falkland, were unable to intercept and engage them. At 9.15am the RFA LSLs *Sir Galahad* and *Sir Lancelot* were both hit by bombs from Skyhawks, all of which failed to explode. Both vessels were deliberately run ashore to be salvaged and withdrawn once the bombs had been defused and removed.

Meanwhile the Task Force hit back with increasing success. The Rapier crews, their launchers sited on the high ground around the anchorage and 3 Commando Brigade positions, shot down three aircraft while a further two were shot down by *Fearless*'s

A Leander class frigate narrowly escapes a direct hit as a bomb drops short of her stern.

Sea Cat SAMs. Three more fell victim to the Sea Harriers of Lieutenant Commander Andy Auld and Lieutenant David Smith who attacked a formation of four Mirages.

The following day, 25 May, was Argentina's National Day and all members of the Task Force were well aware that it was more than likely the enemy would mark the occasion with further heavy attacks. Enemy aircraft appeared in strength but were met with a formidable response from the Task Force. *Coventry* claimed three with her Sea Dart SAMs while two more were shot down by *Yarmouth* and a Rapier. During the afternoon, however, the Argentinians succeeded in striking a devastating blow. At 2pm a pair of Skyhawks approached *Coventry* and *Broadsword* at low level from Pebble Island. Both vessels' guns opened fire as one aircraft, heading for *Coventry*, swung away towards *Broadsword*, which was steaming at full speed half a mile astern. The latter's Sea Wolf SAM system chose this moment to switch itself off and one of the Skyhawks succeeded in dropping a bomb which pierced the starboard side of the frigate. Failing to explode, it made its exit via the flight deck, destroying *Broadsword*'s Lynx helicopter. At that point, the frigate's reactivated Sea Wolf locked on to a second pair of Skyhawks but was unable to launch because *Coventry*, swinging sharply to starboard to minimise her profile as a target, cut across *Broadsword*'s bows.

Coventry launched a Sea Dart SAM which missed, her 4.5-inch main armament and anti-aircraft guns continuing to fire at the two incoming aircraft. Seconds later, four 1,000lb bombs were dropped on the destroyer: one missed, falling astern, but the other three hit the vessel along her port side, all exploding inside her and damaging her fatally. With all power gone, she began to list heavily to port. There was nothing that could be done for her and the crew, led by their commanding officer Captain David Hart-Dyke, abandoned ship soon afterwards They were rescued by Sea King and Wessex helicopters dispatched with all haste from San Carlos Water. Shortly afterwards *Coventry* rolled over and sank.

The 25th also saw the second use of Exocet missiles by the Argentinians. Following the attack on the Carrier Battle Group on 4 May, in which two missiles were expended, there were now only three Exocets in the Argentinian Navy's arsenal. Two were now deployed on a pair of Super Etendards of the 2nd Attack Squadron based at Rio Gallegos. Having taken off, the aircraft flew north, refuelled in mid-air and then headed to a point 110 nautical miles north-north-east of the Falkland Islands where they turned south. Shortly afterwards, they picked up the Carrier Battle Group on their radar.

The two Super Etendards were at a range of 30 miles when they were detected by *Ambuscade*, which opened fire with every weapon on board while also launching her

Opposite: Sailors man anti-aircraft guns. Anyone who was free manned anti-aircraft guns on the upper decks of the ships at anchor in San Carlos. In many cases GPMGs were used on dedicated mountings but some were simply lashed to guard rails.

chaff decoys. According to those who witnessed the attack, both aircraft launched their Exocets. One missile was reportedly aimed at *Invincible*, which, like every other warship in the battle group, was firing her chaff. Half-way to its target, the Exocet suddenly veered away and headed for the *Atlantic Conveyor*, a large container ship carrying four Chinook and six Wessex helicopters earmarked by Brigadier Thompson for 3 Commando Brigade's break-out from the beachhead. A week earlier the vessel had also been carrying a number of Sea Harriers but those had been transferred to the carriers. One of the Chinooks had already been deployed from the vessel, which was due to enter San Carlos Water that night so that the remaining aircraft could be flown off her.

Without any chaff or air defence weapons to protect her, *Atlantic Conveyor* was a sitting target for the Exocet. It hit the vessel below her superstructure on the port side. The ship caught fire and within an hour her cargo of helicopters had been completely destroyed. Her crew, along with the RAF and naval personnel aboard, leapt into the sea with the ship's liferafts. Twelve men died, including the *Atlantic Conveyor*'s master, Captain Ian North, a very popular figure known to all as 'Captain Birdseye'. He was last seen swimming towards a liferaft.

Fortunately, 25 May marked the end of the heavy air attacks on the beachhead and the Amphibious Task Group. By that time the Argentinians had suffered unsustainable losses in pilots and aircraft, totalling one-third of their strength. While the Task Force still had not wrested control of the air from the enemy, it had succeeded in reducing the threat.

Meanwhile at his headquarters ashore Brigadier Thompson was under increasing pressure from the joint headquarters at Northwood and politicians in the War Cabinet to break out from the beachhead. As he later explained, it would have been premature to do so at that stage:

> Other than pushing out patrols, there was no point in the Brigade moving out of the beachhead until a substantial part of its bullets, beans and fuel was ashore and achieving this would use up most of the medium helicopters and all the landing craft for several days to come.
>
> If the Brigade did advance out of the beachhead, the distances over which it would need to be kept supplied would increase with every kilometre it moved away from the anchorage. Contact with the enemy would result in ammunition being used and having to be replaced immediately.
>
> As the Brigade moved away from the protection of its own artillery, the guns and ammunition would have to be shifted forwards to catch up. To lift one light gun battery and 500 rounds per gun, enough for one battle, takes eighty-five Sea King helicopters, or eight Sea King helicopters flying almost eleven times each, or any permutation thereof – and there were four light gun

batteries. It is a fact of military life that the deeper you advance into enemy territory, your needs expand accordingly; more and more has to be transported further and further.

As the Brigade moved further from the air defence umbrella round San Carlos Water it stretched its resources. But more critically its line of supply would be exposed to air attack. Infantry on the ground, well dispersed, dug-in, or taking cover and aggressively firing back, would not be too vulnerable to attack from the air unless the enemy used cluster bombs, which the Argentinians did not have, or napalm which they did possess but fortunately only used once.

On the other hand, the Brigade's arteries, along which the bullets, beans and fuel had to flow, were totally reliant on helicopter lift and the enemy possessed air superiority. Resupply in daylight would lead to helicopters being shot down and, with only eleven Sea Kings and five Wessex helicopters available for medium-lift tasks at this stage, even small losses would be a major setback. Night helicopter resupply with only four passive night vision goggle-equipped helicopters would be totally inadequate.

While 3 Commando Brigade built up its logistical stockpiles, it was already probing forward for details of the enemy's strengths and dispositions. The Mountain & Arctic Warfare Cadre, deployed in its role as the brigade reconnaissance troop, had inserted two OPs at last light on 21 May at Bull Hill and Evelyn Hill. Meanwhile each commando was using its reconnaissance troop to deploy OPs and patrol its front and flanks, while 2 and 3 PARA did likewise with their patrol companies.

Meanwhile in Britain there was increasing government anxiety that the United Nations would demand a ceasefire which would leave the Task Force in control of the beachhead and the Argentinians still in possession of the Falkland Islands. Moreover, the continuing losses sustained by the Task Force were prompting increasing public demand for positive action. This resulted in further pressure on Brigadier Thompson who was summoned to the Brigade's satellite communication terminal at Ajax Bay. There he received a call from Northwood advising him to crack on and take Goose Green. Thompson responded by stating that Goose Green was irrelevant and that once Port Stanley had been captured, Goose Green would automatically fall. He continued by saying that he planned to leave a small force to mask any advance by the enemy from Goose Green while concentrating on moving east to Mount Kent which would be secured prior to the advance on Stanley. The response from Northwood and Admiral Fieldhouse was clear: Thompson could by all means advance east but a force *had* to be dispatched to Goose Green.

SEVEN

DARWIN & GOOSE GREEN

FIGHTING LIKE LIONS

The battle at Goose Green has been the subject of much analysis by armchair experts who have suggested, with the benefit of hindsight, that Brigadier Julian Thompson should not have sent 2 PARA to fight. The facts are that Goose Green was initially planned as a raid. It was a secondary priority to securing the high ground overlooking Stanley and when it became clear there would be insufficient helicopters to support 2 PARA following the loss of *Atlantic Conveyor*, the operation was cancelled. However, as in so many actions throughout history, commanders back in the 'puzzle palace' at Northwood wanted their plan to be implemented and ignored the advice of the man on the ground. The higher command forced the Brigadier to go to Goose Green.

On 12 May Thompson had received a directive by signal from Major General Sir Jeremy Moore who was due to embark on 20 May aboard the liner *QE2* with his headquarters and 5 Infantry Brigade. It read:

> You are to secure a bridgehead on East Falkland, into which reinforcements can be landed, in which an airstrip can be established and from which operations to repossess the Falkland Islands can be achieved. You are to push forward from the bridgehead area so far as the maintenance of its security allows, to gain information, to establish moral and physical domination over the enemy, and to forward the ultimate objective of repossession.
>
> You will retain operational control of all forces landed in the Falklands until I establish my headquarters in the area. It is my intention to do this aboard *Fearless*, as early as practicable after the landing. I expect this to be approximately on D+7. It is then my intention to land 5 Infantry Brigade into the beachhead and to develop operations for the complete repossession of the Falkland Islands.

On 23 May Northwood told Thompson that his objective was now 'to invest Stanley'. In Britain pressure had been increasing from the War Cabinet for a rapid breakout from the beachhead; a day earlier the Chief of Defence Staff, Admiral Sir Terence Lewin, had stated: 'We're going to move and move fast.' The result was further pressure on Thompson to get moving.

A Royal Marine of the Air Defence Troop marching to Goose Green. The small specialist unit was armed with Blowpipe missiles and was assigned to the Paras as a protection force against air attack. It played a key role in shooting down a Pucara which was attacking the battalion.

However, after Thompson had received Moore's directive, and was told by Northwood that investing Stanley was his priority, *Atlantic Conveyor* had been sunk, taking with her most of the Task Force's helicopters. This left 3 Commando Brigade desperately short of lift capacity. Thompson said:

The sinking of *Atlantic Conveyor* left 3 Commando Brigade and Commodore Clapp's Amphibious Task Group with the eleven Sea King Mark IV and five Wessex helicopters with which they had carried out the amphibious landing on D-day. Although one Chinook had survived from *Atlantic Conveyor*, it was not made immediately available. Out of the eleven Sea Kings, one was permanently allocated to the Rapier Battery every day during daylight hours, to carry fuel to the firing post generators and REME fitters to maintain the equipment.

The firing posts could not be allowed to go out of action for lack of fuel or maintenance. Of the remaining ten Sea Kings, the four night vision goggle-equipped aircraft were not available for daylight tasks except in an emergency and then only for short periods, because the aircraft must be maintained and their crews rested after the exhausting and dangerous business of nightly sorties.

The remaining six Sea Kings and five Wessex were all that were available for all troop, equipment and logistic movement ashore by the Brigade and the continuing offload being carried out by the Logistic Regiment and by Clapp's amphibious ships and STUFT. Clapp retained operational control of all the helicopters because, rightly, he judged that the offload must have priority.

Prior to the loss of *Atlantic Conveyor*, Thompson had planned to lift 3 Commando Brigade eastwards from San Carlos to Mount Kent, some 5 miles west of Port Stanley. It overlooked the capital and had been under observation by a patrol from G Squadron 22 SAS. The initial stage of the move eastwards had already been made on the night of 24 May with an advance party of D Squadron inserted by helicopter on to Mount Kent. The men found Kent to be only lightly held by the Argentinians. The rest of the squadron was aboard the RFA LSL *Sir Lancelot*, from which it was to have been flown in to the LZ below Mount Kent on the night of 25 May. Thompson had intended to follow up this move by flying in 42 Commando and a battery of guns on to the same LZ at night, the rest of the brigade being lifted in thereafter. With the greatly reduced number of helicopters available, however, such a plan was now unworkable because only one rifle company, a section of mortars, half a battery of light guns and a limited amount of ammunition could be lifted forward each night. There was no alternative to the brigade making its way eastwards on foot.

The planned operation at Goose Green was also in accordance with the part of Moore's directive that ordered Thompson to push forward. Thompson said: 'We had planned to raid Goose Green before 5 Brigade arrived – a battalion raid by 2 PARA, with gunfire support, wellie-in, duff-up the garrison and bugger off. That's all.'

Thompson had first briefed the commanding officer of 2 PARA, Lieutenant Colonel H. Jones, about the operation when he visited the battalion on 22 May after coming ashore from *Fearless*. Jones had submitted his plan to the Brigadier on 24 May, basing it on the use of helicopters to lift his battalion the 15 miles from San Carlos to Goose Green. Informed that the only aircraft available were the four night vision goggle-equipped Sea Kings, which were only to be used to lift in three light guns and ammunition to provide artillery support, Jones then suggested the use of landing craft to move 2 PARA at night from Port Sussex via Brenton Loch to a beach at Salinas opposite Goose Green. Once again, his plan was turned down on the grounds that navigation along Brenton Loch at night would require the use of radar which could be detected by the Argentinians. Moreover, without air superiority, a heliborne or seaborne approach would be too risky. There was no alternative: 2 PARA would have to make the long approach march on foot. On the 24th, Jones submitted his revised plan which was approved by Thompson. While Jones was at the Brigade headquarters with his operations officer, 2 PARA's Intelligence Officer, Captain Alan Coulson, visited *Intrepid* where he obtained information on the enemy forces at Darwin and Goose Green from members of D Squadron 22 SAS who had carried out the diversionary raid there on the night of 21 May. They had attacked Burntside House at the northern end of the Darwin

Paratroopers waiting for the order to move. Helicopters were in short supply in the Falklands. Brigadier Thompson wanted to cancel the plan to attack Goose Green because he could not get helicopters to ferry in guns in support of the operation, but he was ordered to go ahead regardless.

isthmus and estimated the enemy's strength as being a company; this differed greatly from the assessment already given to the battalion prior to the landing.

Like 3 PARA and the three commandos, 2 PARA had been active in patrolling the areas to its front and on its flanks. C (Patrols) Company's OPs had reported enemy activity in the area of Canterra House, approximately 5 miles south of Sussex Mountain. On the night of 23 May 12 Platoon of D Company, commanded by Lieutenant Jim Barry, had been dispatched by helicopter to search and clear the area surrounding the house. After being inserted just over a mile from its objective, the platoon had located the building with the help of artillery fire and cleared it, finding no trace of any enemy. It remained at Canterra House for the rest of the night and throughout 24 May because its presence there tied in with Lieutenant Colonel Jones's plan for the attack on Goose Green.

On his return from Brigade headquarters, Jones briefed his company commanders on the forthcoming operation. The battalion would move that night with the aim of reaching Camilla Creek House, which lay approximately 3½ miles south-east of Canterra House and some 8 miles south of Sussex Mountain, by dawn on 25 May. D Company, commanded by Major Philip Neame, and 12 Platoon from Canterra House, would clear and secure a gunline for three light guns of 8 Commando Battery RA which would be lifted in after last light by the night vision goggle-equipped Sea Kings. The company would also clear the area of Ceritos House, some 4 miles to the east. In the meantime, A and B Companies would push on to attack Darwin.

D Company set off at last light on the 24th but, having covered half the distance to Camilla Creek House, received a radio message ordering it to return to Sussex Mountain; the operation had been aborted because of a problem with the helicopters. The four Sea Kings had earlier deployed D Squadron 22 SAS's advance party to Mount Kent and were preparing to lift the three light guns to Camilla Creek House when the weather deteriorated and they could not fly. As the operation could not be carried out without artillery support, Thompson aborted it.

On the morning of 25 May Lieutenant Colonel Jones decided to deploy D Company forward by helicopter to Canterra House, from where it would move on foot to Camilla Creek House. Once again, however, the weather conditions prevented flying and the operation was cancelled. Then, on 26 May, Thompson was ordered by

Camilla Creek House from the air.

29 COMMANDO REGIMENT ROYAL ARTILLERY

The gunners of 29 Commando Regiment RA are a vital asset among the Brigade's combat support units and have been with 3 Commando since the 1960s. In 1961 the Army agreed to a request from the Royal Marines to provide artillery support for the Commando Brigade. It was decided that 29 Field Regiment should fill this role and as such should also be commando trained. During January and February 1962 the first commando course for gunners was held at Lympstone and on 15 May 1962 the first commando gunners were formally presented with their green berets. During Operation Corporate the gunners of '29' were equipped with the 105mm light gun. Weighing 1,806kg, it could be underslung by Sea Kings and had a range of 17,200 metres. The Regiment took three six-gun batteries to the Falklands and the guns were constantly in demand by commanders. The batteries were 79 (Kirkee), 7 (Sphinx) and 8 (Alma).

Northwood to dispatch 2 PARA to Goose Green with all haste and to move east without further delay.

Jones, who had become increasingly frustrated and annoyed by the cancellations, was delighted to be summoned to Brigade headquarters to hear the operation was on again. On his return, he quickly briefed Major Neame so that D Company could move off without delay to carry out its task of clearing Camilla Creek House, securing the gunline for the three light guns and clearing the area around Ceritos House. 2 PARA would move in light order, carrying the minimum amount of equipment in addition to its weapons and ammunition. Jones initially decided not to take the battalion's eight 81mm medium mortars because the lack of vehicles meant only a limited number of bombs could be carried for them. However, he heeded the advice of the commander of 8 Commando Battery, Major Tony Rice, who suggested that a section of two mortars should accompany the battalion. He also decided that the Machine-Gun Platoon should carry six GPMGs in the light role, and that the Anti-Tank Platoon should take three Milan firing posts and seventeen missiles.

2 PARA left Sussex Mountain before last light on 26 May and set off for Camilla Creek House with A Company, commanded by Major Dair Farrar-Hockley, in the lead. It was accompanied by: Major Hector Gullan, an officer in The Parachute Regiment serving on the staff of 3 Commando Brigade, who would be Thompson's liaison officer during the operation; Squadron Leader Jock Penman, an RAF forward air controller (FAC); and the sixteen-strong reconnaissance troop of 59 Independent Commando Squadron Royal Engineers, led by Lieutenant Clive Livingston. That afternoon C (Patrols) Company had withdrawn its OPs and and set off for Camilla Creek House where it would rendezvous with D Company.

As darkness fell the battalion found the going difficult. The men had to negotiate ankle-turning grass tussocks, large peat pools and stretches of soft mud interspersed with steep-sided gullies. Eventually, they resorted to using the track which D Company had cleared earlier. 2 PARA then moved at a cracking pace but the strain began to tell as the battalion headed south through the darkness. Fatigue set in, particularly among radio operators and members of the medical team who were carrying heavy loads and struggled to keep up. Squadron Leader Penman became separated from the column in the darkness and fell, spraining his ankle; fortunately, he was spotted by Captain Peter Ketley, the Anti-Tank Platoon commander. Two members of A Company also fell, one twisting his ankle and the other falling unconscious. The battalion's medical officer, Captain Steve Hughes, who was already exhausted after going without sleep for two nights while tending injured men on Sussex Mountain, also injured an ankle. However, he pressed on; it later transpired that he had a hairline fracture.

In the difficult conditions companies became separated. In the rear, Support Company had fallen behind after halting to look after Squadron Leader Penman, who was left with a medic to look after him. Lieutenant Colonel Jones left members of his 'R' Group to wait for Support Company while he went on with A and B Companies. As the battalion headed for Camilla Creek House, artillery air bursts could be seen to the left in the distance. They came from Argentinian 105mm guns at Goose Green engaging a C (Patrols) Company group, commanded by Sergeant Higginson, which had been spotted by an enemy helicopter while making its way to rendezvous with the battalion.

By this stage D Company was approaching the area of Camilla Creek House. Halting at a distance of just over a mile from the buildings, the leading platoon commander, Lieutenant Chris Waddington, observed the target through a night vision device before reporting that the area seemed clear of enemy. Taking no chances, Major Philip Neame called down artillery fire which was followed by an assault by 10 Platoon, commanded by Lieutenant Shaun Webster. The buildings were found to be deserted although there were signs of very recent occupation, including a leg of lamb roasting in the oven. Having cleared Camilla Creek House, 10 Platoon moved away quickly, knowing it was likely that they had already been registered as a defensive task by Argentinian artillery. Major Neame then deployed two of his platoons to cover the most likely enemy approaches as he awaited the arrival of the rest of the battalion.

A and B Companies arrived, with Support Company following close behind. Although it was risky course of action, Lieutenant Colonel Jones decided to use Camilla Creek House and its surrounding farm buildings and outhouses for shelter. His exhausted soldiers found themselves under a roof for the first time since the landing at San Carlos five days earlier. Men slept wherever they were able to find a space, the headquarters element of 11 Platoon commandeering a lavatory while one of the rifle sections squeezed into a cupboard. Outside, a screen was deployed to warn of any enemy approach.

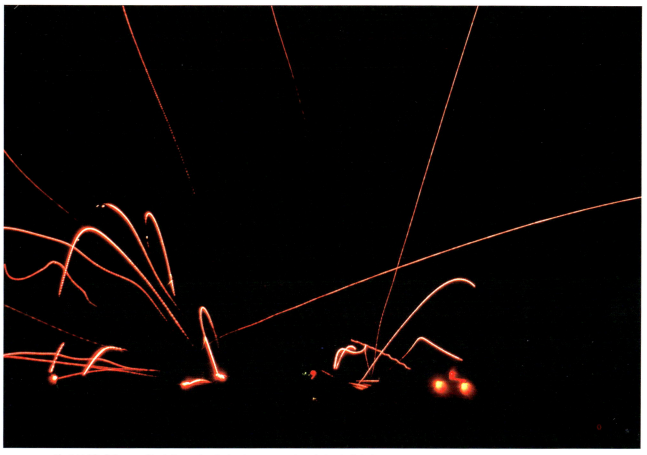

The initial firefight started in darkness, but the battle was to continue during daylight hours.

Meanwhile a patrol from C (Patrols) Company, commanded by Corporal 'Taff' Evans, together with a four-man party of forward air controllers (FACs) under Captain Peter Ketley, who had commanded the Milan platoon and had taken over from Squadron Leader Penman, pressed on to positions 450 yards apart, from where they could observe enemy troops on the Goose Green isthmus. Another patrol under Lieutenant Colin Connor, the Reconnaissance Platoon commander, was doing the same 700 yards away to the south-west. Both patrols had been tasked with locating the 105mm guns that had fired on Sergeant Higginson's patrol earlier, so that they could be registered as targets for the three light guns supporting 2 PARA.

At first light on 27 May the two patrols and the FAC party found themselves about 500 yards away from an enemy company position dug in on a forward slope and the crest of a small hill on the other side of Camilla Creek. Previous intelligence had indicated that the enemy guns were located by the bridge over the Ceritos Arroyo at the north-eastern tip of the creek, but it soon became apparent that they had been moved. Observing from his OP, Corporal Taff Evans could see a recoilless rifle being dug in to the east of the track on the northern side of Coronation Point. Further to the south-east he observed sixteen trenches and a number of men digging in. To the south, in the area of Boca House, there was another defensive position comprising five bunkers, while between Boca House and the company to the front of his OP was a platoon in a position overlooking Camilla Creek.

Back at Camilla Creek House consternation reigned. At dawn Lieutenant Colonel Jones and some of his officers had listened with incredulity and anger to a BBC World Service radio broadcast announcing that a parachute battalion was within 5 miles of Darwin and Goose Green which it was preparing to attack. 2 PARA had succeeded in moving undetected during the night and then concealing itself under cover, but the entire operation had now been jeopardised by a breach of security that would inevitably alert the Argentinians. The bulk of the battalion immediately evacuated the buildings and took up positions in the valleys nearby, although battalion headquarters remained inside Camilla Creek House itself.

The enemy positions were ideal targets for artillery or an air strike. Jones was concerned about betraying the position of his three light guns and decided to call instead for a strike by Harriers. He summoned Captain Ketley. Lieutenant Colin Connor and Corporal Taff Evans had already provided details by radio of six targets for strikes and, unaware that Ketley was already deployed forward with them, Jones called him on the radio, instructing him to report to the battalion headquarters to collect the necessary information.

Ketley thus withdrew with his party and set off back towards Camilla Creek House. On reaching HQ and reporting to Jones he learned that the air strike was already on its way and set off immediately to resume his position near the OPs. As they headed back along the track, he and his party observed a civilian Land Rover approaching. The vehicle stopped. At that point Ketley realised that it contained enemy troops and opened fire. The occupants surrendered immediately and were taken to battalion headquarters where they were interrogated by the Intelligence Officer, Captain Alan Coulson, assisted by the Spanish-speaking Royal Marine officer, Captain Rod Bell, who was attached to 2 PARA for the operation. One of the prisoners was an officer. He revealed that he and his men had been using Camilla Creek as an OP and had been patrolling the area for the past four days.

Meanwhile the Harrier air strike had arrived over the enemy positions at Camilla Creek. The leading aircraft, flown by Squadron Leader Bob Iveson, made its approach from the north and then banked away after identifying the positions opposite Corporal Evans's OP. The second aircraft made its attack but succeeded only in hitting the reverse slope behind the enemy company. Iveson then made his second run in but was

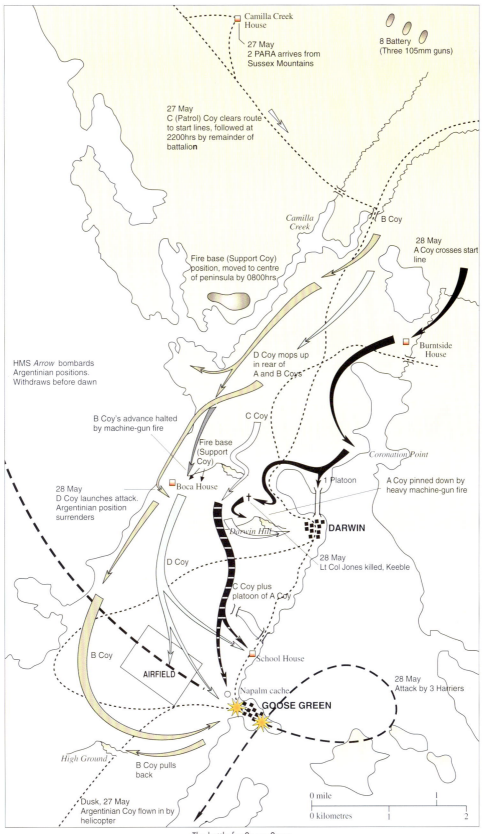

Camilla Creek
House

27 May
2 PARA arrives from
Sussex Mountains

8 Battery
(Three 105mm guns)

27 May
C (Patrol) Coy clears route
to start lines, followed at
2200hrs by remainder of
battalion

*Camilla
Creek*

B Coy

28 May
A Coy crosses start
line

Fire base (Support Coy)
position, moved to centre
of peninsula by 0800hrs

Burntside
House

D Coy mops up
in rear of
A and B Coys

HMS *Arrow* bombards
Argentinian positions.
Withdraws before dawn

B Coy's advance halted
by machine-gun fire

C Coy

Fire base
(Support
Coy)

Coronation Point

1 Platoon

A Coy pinned down by
heavy machine-gun fire

28 May
D Coy launches attack.
Argentinian position
surrenders

Boca House

Darwin Hill

DARWIN

D Coy

28 May
Lt Col Jones killed, Keeble

C Coy plus
platoon of A Coy

B Coy

School House

AIRFIELD

28 May
Attack by 3 Harriers

Napalm cache

GOOSE GREEN

High Ground

B Coy pulls
back

Dusk, 27 May
Argentinian Coy flown in by
helicopter

0 mile   1

0 kilometres   1   2

The battle for Goose Green.

hit by anti-aircraft fire. Ejecting from his aircraft to the south of Goose Green, he landed safely and avoided capture until the battle ended two days later.

At 3.30pm the two OPs came under fire from the enemy company opposite Corporal Taff Evans's position. Lieutenant Colin Connor called for artillery support but this was not available – nor were the battalion's two mortars bedded in. Connor and his patrol crawled into dead ground as the enemy brought fire to bear with .50 calibre heavy machine-guns. Meanwhile Corporal Evans called for air support which arrived shortly afterwards. As the Harriers attacked, Evans and his men withdrew in pairs and, having reached the safety of dead ground, they pulled back to Camilla Creek House.

Jones had planned to issue his orders for the forthcoming attack at 3pm but a delay in his company commanders' arrival from their dispersed locations, and the news of Ketley's capture of the Argentinian patrol in the Land Rover, forced him to postpone his 'O' group until 7pm. It began, as is normal practice, with a detailed description of the ground over which 2 PARA would be fighting. This was given by a Royal Marine officer, Lieutenant John Thurman, who had served previously in the Falkland Islands. He described the terrain in detail, indicating features and the settlements of Darwin and Goose Green. He was followed by the Intelligence Officer, Captain Coulson, who provided all the available details about enemy units, their strengths and dispositions, including the locations of known minefields which had been discovered from a map found on a captured Argentinian engineer officer. Jones then proceeded to reveal his plan and to give his orders for the capture of Darwin and Goose Green. The operation was to be a six-phase attack starting before dawn on 28 May and continuing throughout the day until all objectives had been taken.

Phase One would see Major Jenner's C (Patrols) Company reconnoitring and clearing the route from Camilla Creek House, and then securing the battalion's start line which would stretch from Camilla Creek to Burntside House, spanning the track between the two points. The company would also be responsible for clearing the area of the bridge over the Ceritos Arroyo. Phase Two would comprise an attack on the nearest two enemy positions by A and B Companies, with A Company attacking a tented area at Burntside House and B Company the enemy company position dominating Camilla Creek. In Phase Three A Company would attack enemy positions at Coronation Point while D Company assaulted another position on the west coast of the isthmus, to the south of the first one. In Phase Four B Company would pass through D Company and attack the enemy at Boca House. In Phase Five A Company would move forward to Darwin while B and D Companies would move on to Goose Green. Meanwhile C (Patrols) Company would clear the airfield. Phase Six would see Darwin and Goose Green captured while C (Patrols) Company advanced further south.

Naval gunfire support for the operation would be provided by the frigate HMS *Arrow* which would remain in support until 8.30am. From first light Harriers and armed helicopters would be on call, as would helicopters for resupply and casualty evacuation. The three light guns of 8 Commando Battery RA would be in direct support, while two Blowpipe detachments would provide air defence, one located at Camilla Creek to protect the gunline while the other advanced with 2 PARA. Forward observation officers (FOOs) from 8 Commando Battery would go with A, B and D Companies, and each company would have a mortar fire controller (MFC). Sections of the 59 Independent Commando Squadron RE reconnaissance troop would also be attached to each company. Support Company would establish a fire support base on the western side of Camilla Creek. In addition to the Anti-Tank Platoon's three Milan firing posts, the six GPMGs of the Machine-Gun Platoon and the section of two 81mm mortars, it would include 2 PARA's snipers and a party from 148 Commando Forward Observation Battery RA. It would be commanded by Captain Kevin Arnold, who would direct supporting fire from *Arrow* and act as an FAC for any air support tasks. During phase four the fire support base, having provided support for the B and C Company attacks, would rejoin the battalion and remain in reserve for phases five and six.

A Royal Marine of the Air Defence Troop at Goose Green. Like other troops, the marines carried all their own equipment but also bore the weight of Blowpipe missiles.

At 11pm on 27 May Support Company and the other elements of the fire support base moved off from Camilla Creek House and by 2am they were in their allotted positions on the western side of Camilla Creek. Thirty minutes later *Arrow*, directed by Captain Kevin Arnold, began bombarding enemy positions, in particular an artillery piece firing further to the south. In the meantime, C (Patrols) Company was reconnoitring and clearing the battalion's initial approach route and start line, with A and B Companies being led to their start lines by guides from the Reconnaissance and Patrols Platoons. At 6.35am A Company crossed its start line with 3 Platoon, commanded by 2nd Lieutenant Guy Wallace, on the left and 2nd Lieutenant Mark Coe's 2 Platoon on the right. Moving behind them came Major Farrar-Hockley's company headquarters, with 1 Platoon, commanded by Sergeant Ted Barrett (in the absence of Lieutenant Johnathan Shaw, who had been injured during the march from Sussex Mountain to Camilla Creek House), following in reserve.

The company's advance on Burntside House was initially hindered by *Arrow* registering her 4.5-inch gun on the objective. Nevertheless, the flashes from the exploding shells enabled the leading platoons to pinpoint the building in the darkness. As 3 Platoon moved up to attack it, 2nd Lieutenant Wallace ordered his Carl Gustav MAW team to open fire on the building; unfortunately they missed with the first round and then suffered two misfires. The men, by then joined by 2 Platoon, resorted to rifles, GPMGs and 66mm LAWs, bringing a heavy volume of fire to bear on the building. As 3 Platoon moved in for its final assault, voices could be heard inside the house, shouting in Spanish. They belonged to four islanders who had called out, thinking the attacking troops were Argentinian. Shaken but unharmed after their ordeal, they emerged from under a heap of mattresses where they had taken cover. A search of the area shortly afterwards revealed signs of an Argentinian platoon's hasty departure; two dead Argentinians were found after the operation ended. Once the entire area of Burntside House had been cleared, 1 Platoon moved forward to check an area nearby where the C (Patrols) Company OPs had earlier spotted some camouflage nets. Nothing was found.

In the meantime B Company had crossed its start line at 7am. 6 Platoon, under Lieutenant Clyde Chapman, advanced on the left with Lieutenant Ernie Hocking's 4 Platoon on their right, and Major John Crosland and his company headquarters following behind. In reserve moved 5 Platoon, commanded by Lieutenant Geoff Weighell. The first sighting of the enemy came when Private McKee of 6 Platoon spotted a figure sitting on the ground. As he shouted a warning, the man stood up and began walking through McKee's section. The commander, Corporal Margerison, challenged the figure and, after receiving no reply, opened fire.

At that point Margerison spotted some trenches. Warning his platoon commander, he led his section in an immediate attack and stormed the position. The majority of the enemy troops made no effort to defend themselves but the remainder resisted and nine

Major John Crosland, commander of B Company 2 PARA, cleaning his weapon.

were killed. Thereafter B Company pressed on with 4 Platoon, encountering no resistance on the right where it had expected to find the enemy company position overlooking Camilla Creek.

It seemed that the Argentinians had withdrawn because six abandoned trenches were found by 5 Platoon. Shortly afterwards 5 Platoon was ordered by Major John Crosland to move through and advance on the next known enemy position, which was to have been D Company's objective in phase three. Once again it appeared that the enemy had fled; more empty trenches were found, with mortars and rocket launchers lying abandoned around them. On the left Corporal Mick Connor's section discovered yet more trenches, while a contact took place on the right during which Lance Corporal Dance's No. 2 Section took three prisoners. At that point 5 Platoon came under fire from enemy positions to the front. Parachute illuminating flares were fired and it was clear the firing was coming from two trenches. Sergeant Aird engaged both with his M-79 40mm grenade launcher but the enemy fire continued. However, under covering fire from a member of No. 2 Section, Lieutenant Geoff Weighell and Sergeant Ian Aird succeeded in moving forward and clearing both trenches with grenades. During this action Major John Crosland and his company headquarters came under fire from enemy mortars and artillery; at one point two shells landed between Crosland and his second-in-command, Captain John Young, but fortunately they failed to explode.

In the meantime D Company had followed Lieutenant Colonel Jones and his Tac HQ along the track which marked the battalion's axis of advance. Although the company was in reserve and thus following behind the other units, navigation was difficult in the dark and the men took a wrong turning; they had already failed to rendezvous with their guide from C (Patrols) Company. By the time D Company reached the battalion RV, Jones was becoming extremely anxious about the slow rate of progress. He ordered Major Neame to push forward and sweep both sides of the track to clear an enemy machine-gun position which he thought was on the left and which had been missed by B Company.

D Company advanced with 12 Platoon, commanded by Lieutenant Jim Barry, in the lead. 10 Platoon, under Lieutenant Shaun Webster, followed behind and to the left, while 2nd Lieutenant Chris Waddington's 11 Platoon moved behind and to the right. As the company pushed forward, it came under fire from the right. Webster spotted six trenches to his front and, crawling to within throwing range, knocked out the nearest with a white phosphorous grenade. As he did so, he and the other members of his platoon with him came under fire at close range and two men were wounded. Meanwhile 11 Platoon carried out a right flanking assault, during which one man was killed, and 12 Platoon attacked the enemy to its front.

At 8.50am Support Company moved forward from its fire support base position. C (Patrols) Company also moved up in reserve, being joined by the Assault Pioneer Platoon which had already brought forward an ammunition resupply and would now evacuate D Company's casualties. By now enemy artillery was bringing down heavy fire on the area. Jones and his Tac HQ, located behind D Company, suffered a number of near misses, one of which landed between Jones and his adjutant, Captain David Wood.

A Company now advanced on Coronation Point, its phase three objective; it reached the target at 9.20am and found it to be unoccupied. With the agreement of the commanding officer, who joined the company at that point, Major Farrar-Hockley pushed on to the next objective, Darwin Hill, which dominated the settlement. First light was approaching as the company advanced, having left 3 Platoon to provide fire support from a position overlooking Darwin from the northern side of the inlet. 2 Platoon was in the lead and as it moved up a gully its leading section spotted three men on the high ground to the right. They were engaged once it became apparent that they were enemy troops and shortly afterwards the platoon came under fire from positions to its right. Corporal Steve Adams led his section, which had been caught in

RADIO OPERATOR STEVE TAYLOR

Paratrooper Private Stephen Taylor had a narrow escape at Goose Green when a bullet passed through the side of his helmet but didn't leave a scratch on him. Private Taylor, who had joined The Parachute Regiment aged sixteen, was also the man who picked up the BBC World Service report announcing that the Paras were heading for Goose Green.

In 1982 he was one of the youngest men in the battalion. At just twenty and with several tours of Northern Ireland already under his belt he deployed south as a company radio operator. He takes up the story:

> We all heard about the invasion on the news and the next thing we were being recalled. Five of us lived in Portsmouth and we all called each other and made our way to Aldershot. When we landed we got wet feet and we convinced ourselves that the marines had done it on purpose, leaving us soaking as we made our way up Sussex Mountain. The sight from the top was amazing, but we felt very helpless as we watched the Task Force come under air attack.
>
> On the way to Goose Green we stopped for a brew and as the radio operator I quickly tuned the set into the BBC World Service. I couldn't believe it when I heard the BBC report that we were heading for Goose Green. I told the commander and he passed it to Colonel H. who was furious. Later we saw helicopters flying in to resupply the enemy, which we later learned had in fact dropped more troops to reinforce their positions.
>
> Later, as the battle was in full progress, I stood up to put a bigger aerial on the set. On reflection it was a mistake. I was suddenly blasted off my feet. It felt as though someone had smacked me in the head with a brick. I was thrown to the floor and then realised I had caught a round in the side of my helmet. Another centimetre and it would have killed me. I was very lucky and I have still have the helmet at home to remind me.

Clearly the job of radio operator was a dangerous one in Operation Corporate because a similar incident happened to a signaller in the commanding officer's 'R' Group of 3 PARA on Mount Longdon. Private McLoughlin was struck by a bullet which penetrated his helmet but it too caused no injury.

the open, forward in a charge to the other side of the spur towards a gully offering cover. He was wounded in the shoulder, and the section's GPMG gunner was also hit. At that point Adams, realising the strength of the enemy position that he was attacking, withdrew his section to rejoin the rest of 2 Platoon.

By this time Company Headquarters and 1 Platoon had been caught in the open and were under heavy fire. Sergeant Barrett led the platoon up the gully but it suffered several casualties. In the meantime Captain James Watson, the artillery FOO attached to the company, and two members of 2 Platoon – Corporal John Camp and Private

Dennis Dey – succeeded in attacking and knocking out some of the nearer enemy positions with grenades and 66mm LAW rockets. As his platoons fought their way up the gully, Major Farrar-Hockley ordered 2 Platoon to carry out a left flanking attack but this was thwarted by heavy fire from the right, during which one man was hit.

A Company was now scattered in sections through the gully, with men seeking what little cover was available as they tried to engage enemy troops who outnumbered them and were in well-sited bunkers. As the nearest positions were cleared, Major Farrar-Hockley, who had earlier ordered Sergeant Barrett to concentrate as many of the company's GPMGs as possible into a fire base, decided to group the guns on a mound at the head of the gully. Six GPMGs were brought forward but it was then found that the main enemy positions were further to the right and out of range. Moreover, no back-up was available from the battalion's two 81mm mortars as Support Company was also out of range. 3 Platoon, which was providing fire support from the northern end of the causeway on the other side of the inlet, had come under fire from enemy mortars and had suffered a number of casualties. Nevertheless, it continued to provide covering fire.

Dawn had arrived by now and with it came an increase in the volume of fire being laid down by enemy artillery and mortars. A Company was calling for supporting fire from the three light guns of 8 Commando Battery but this was refused because of the confused situation. Moreover, the guns, which had been in action almost constantly since the beginning of the battle, were running low on ammunition and at the same time they were under counter-battery fire from enemy artillery. Shortly after first light they were attacked by two Pucaras which were engaged by the Blowpipe detachment defending the gunline. The situation was made all the worse by bad weather at sea which prevented Harriers carrying out strikes.

Meanwhile B Company mounted its attack on the enemy at the derelict Boca House. The final approach was down a slope covered by a line of gorse and as the company descended towards the group of buildings the enemy opened fire. 4 Platoon – the right assault platoon – came under fire from a machine-gun on the enemy's left flank. Taking cover, Lieutenant Ernie Hocking and his men engaged a number of bunkers and a machine-gun position to the south of the objective. Soon, however, the platoon found itself very exposed and withdrew into some dead ground as the weight of fire from enemy machine-guns and snipers increased.

5 Platoon, which was in reserve, had taken cover in a re-entrant. Lieutenant John Weighell decided to withdraw under cover of smoke but his 2-inch mortarman, Private Street, was wounded in the leg as he began firing the first bombs. Corporal Stan Standish and Private Andy Brooke came forward. Despite heavy machine-gun fire then raking the slope, they succeeded in reaching Street and carrying him back into dead ground. Moments later the platoon suffered another casualty when Private Steve Hall was also hit. He was rescued by two other members of his section, Private Stephen

Illingsworth and Private Poole, who gave him first aid before dragging him into dead ground. Illingsworth then went back to fetch Hall's weapon and webbing but was killed doing so. His body was retrieved by Sergeant Aird and 5 Platoon's signaller Private Andrew Williamson. Shortly afterwards Captain John Young, the company second-in-command, was seriously wounded.

6 Platoon was the left assault platoon and had come under fire from two machine-guns in a position on a hill line. Skirmishing forward, Lieutenant Clyde Chapman and two sections advanced on a bunker which proved to be unoccupied. As they pushed on, however, they came under fire from a machine-gunner who narrowly missed hitting Chapman and then fled. At that point the platoon came under fire from Boca House and took cover in the gorse.

Meanwhile C (Patrols) Company was moving forward on the left of the battalion's axis, with D Company on the right. Both came under artillery and mortar fire which was adjusted as they advanced. Fortunately the soft ground reduced the effect of the shell bursts, although there were a number of near misses – one bomb landed very close to the Patrols Platoon commander, Captain Paul Farrar.

When they reached the gorse line, Major Jenner and his men could see A Company below them. The enemy positions above the gorse had A Company pinned down. Over the radio Major Jenner offered to provide fire support for an A Company attack with the twelve light machine-guns carried by his men. This was refused by Lieutenant Colonel Jones, as was an offer of help from D Company which was ordered to maintain its position. As both C and D Companies observed the A Company action, the battalion's two mortars attempted to provide some much-needed support, but this proved to be in vain.

D Company was now suffering from constant enemy artillery fire and Major Neame decided to move his men forward into cover. At that point a body of enemy troops was observed on the western side of the isthmus, heading in the direction of Boca House. They were engaged by the Reconnaissance Platoon and 12 Platoon but with little effect because the range was too great.

Still exposed to enemy shelling, C (Patrols) and D Companies pulled back into the lee of a hill. D Company, in the time-honoured fashion of the British Army, brewed up and while it was doing so Major Neame took stock of the shoreline. Realising that it offered possibilities for a flanking move, he contacted Lieutenant Colonel Jones over the radio but the latter rejected his suggestion. Shortly afterwards Support Company arrived on the scene and Major Hugh Jenner offered to provide supporting fire but this idea was also rejected by Jones who was unwilling to commit any more of the battalion's resources because of the heavy artillery and mortar fire falling on the spur opposite the enemy positions confronting A Company. Although it offered a good vantage point from which to observe the enemy, casualties would have been high among any troops using it.

The enemy positions were well sited and the troops of Lieutenant Colonel Italo Piaggi's 12th Infantry Regiment in them were putting up a stout resistance, causing 2 PARA severe problems as a result. Piaggi's orders from his brigade commander, Brigadier General Omar Parada, stated that he was to defend Goose Green, Darwin and the airstrip against assault from both land and sea. During the weeks prior to the Task Force landing, Piaggi's men had dug bunkers and trenches. They had also laid minefields in the centre of the isthmus to the north of Darwin, behind the beaches on its western side, and to the north of the airstrip and Goose Green settlement. Other mines were laid on the very end of the Goose Green peninsula and further to the south. Despite the evident interest of the British in Goose Green – manifested by a series of air strikes by Sea Harriers – no Argentinian reinforcements were sent there. Indeed, Piaggi had been ordered to dispatch a composite force comprising sixty men of A Company and C Company 25th Infantry Regiment under the command of Lieutenant Carlos Esteban to Port San Carlos with the mission of keeping a watch on Falkland Sound and giving early warning of any landings.

Following news of the landing at San Carlos, Piaggi had been well aware that his unit was closest to the enemy. His principal concern had been the lack of supporting artillery but it was not until 21 May that his requests were answered and two 105mm pack howitzers were dispatched to Goose Green aboard the supply vessel *Rio Iguazu*, which sailed from Port Stanley two hours before last light on the 21st. However, halfway up the Choiseul Sound she was attacked by two Sea Harriers, one of which strafed her with its cannon, setting her ablaze as she ran aground on the beach. On hearing of the attack, Piaggi dispatched a salvage party by helicopter. It succeeded in retrieving both guns and a quantity of stores from the beached vessel. The guns had been damaged but Piaggi's men were able to make one of them serviceable. A few days later two more pack howitzers were flown in by helicopter. As a result, when battle was joined on 28 May, both sides possessed precisely the same amount of supporting artillery.

At 11.25am, with A Company still pinned down, air support was requested by 2 PARA but was refused because of bad weather out to sea which prevented the Harriers taking off from HMS *Hermes*. To add insult to injury, three Pucaras flew over the battalion shortly afterwards en route for 2 PARA's A Echelon and 8 Commando Battery's gunline at Camilla Creek House. Ten minutes later they attacked and one was shot down by a Blowpipe. The two remaining aircraft carried out a further attack five minutes later, both escaping unscathed.

At this point Lieutenant Colonel Jones went forward to A Company to see the situation for himself. On arrival, he encountered Major Farrar-Hockley who was with the company fire support team of massed GPMGs on the mound at the head of the gully. Jones ordered 2nd Lieutenant Mark Coe to take the Mortar Platoon commander, Captain Mal Worsley-Tonks, up to the gorse line to a position from which support from the battalion's two 81mm mortars could be directed on to the enemy positions.

A Scout helicopter flies over soldiers of 2 PARA at Goose Green. The lack of natural protection from enemy fire is clear from this picture.

The two officers set off but were recalled after Major Farrar-Hockley convinced Jones that such a move was extremely dangerous.

Farrar-Hockley then ordered Coe to try to take his platoon around to the right of the mound. As Coe and his men started to move out of the gully, they came under heavy fire and were forced to withdraw.

Meanwhile the enemy artillery and mortars kept up an incessant bombardment on the open ground in front of the gorse which was now in flames. The seven trenches on the mound had been cleared and the main volume of enemy fire was coming from positions on the flank of the A Company GPMG fire support team. The three guns of 8 Commando Battery responded to a call for artillery support but the high winds affected the fall of the shells, some of which landed in the area of B Company's action.

Jones then ordered Farrar-Hockley to attack a well-defended position some 55 yards away, above and to the right of A Company. An attempt to take it had been made an hour earlier but had failed, several casualties being sustained in the process. Farrar-Hockley assembled a 16-strong group and led it towards the enemy position which was located on a ledge. Among those in the group were his second-in-command, Captain Chris Dent, and, unbeknown to him, the Adjutant, Captain David Wood. The group did not get far before coming under fire; Dent was killed almost immediately and two other men were hit. Shortly afterwards Captain Wood and Corporal David Hardman were also killed. Farrar-Hockley now had no alternative but to withdraw into the safety of dead ground.

Only then did he realise that Lieutenant Colonel Jones had moved off on his own around the spur and into the gully where Corporal Adams and his section of 2 Platoon had taken cover earlier in the battle. Shortly beforehand Jones had been urging A Company on to its feet. Captain Worsley-Tonks was calling down white phosphorous smoke from his two mortars and this appeared to be having some effect because the enemy fire now became more sporadic. It seems Jones may have been under the mistaken impression that only one bunker was still holding out – small groups of enemy troops were attempting to flee from the furthermost positions by that time. He ran down to the side of the mound, followed at a short distance by his escort, Sergeant Barry Norman and Lance Corporal Colin Beresford, and his signaller, Sergeant Blackburn.

As Jones entered the gully he paused to check his Sterling submachine-gun before pressing on alone towards an isolated enemy position which he had spotted on the left of the gully and which had previously remained unnoticed. At that point Sergeant Norman shouted a warning to Jones who was not only nearing the lone position but was also climbing into view of the other trenches which he had originally intended to attack. Almost immediately an enemy machine-gun opened fire and seconds later Jones fell. He had been shot; the round entered his shoulder and exited his lower back by his spine. Rick Jolly, naval surgeon, carried out a post-mortem on the body.

Lieutenant Colonel H. Jones, the commanding officer of 2 PARA, who was killed at Goose Green. He was awarded the Victoria Cross for his gallant action.

The cairn laid to remember Lieutenant Colonel H. Jones stands on the spot where he died and is regularly maintained by military staff based in the Falklands.

The message 'Sunray is down' was transmitted by Sergeant Blackburn over the battalion radio net, the information being flashed to headquarters 3 Commando Brigade. Unfortunately San Carlos was being subjected to an air attack and it was some time before there could be a response to the request for a helicopter to evacuate the commanding officer. There was, however, no hope of even reaching Jones, who was unconscious. The battle continued.

Slowly but surely A Company began to win the upper hand as sections worked their way forward, each covering the other. No sooner had Corporal David Abols knocked out a trench with a 66mm LAW than a white flag appeared. Major Farrar-Hockley ordered his men not to move forward until the enemy showed themselves. Orders to cease fire could be heard echoing throughout the Argentinian positions and calls went out to the enemy troops to surrender. But they were too frightened to move and firing from the trenches suddenly resumed. A Company responded by firing back and the white flag appeared once again. As the shooting died away for a second time, the enemy troops clambered out of their positions and surrendered.

Company Sergeant Major Colin Price and Sergeant Blackburn tried to resuscitate Jones. They were joined by Major Farrar-Hockley who gave orders for Jones to be moved to the mound at the head of the gully to await evacuation. The commanding officer died fifteen minutes later, with Farrar-Hockley waiting beside him for the helicopter. Shortly afterwards two Scouts arrived at battalion headquarters at Camilla Creek House. Having been briefed on Jones's location by the Signals Officer, Captain David Benest, the pilot, Captain Richard Nunn, took off at 2.45pm and headed for A Company's position. A few minutes later, however, he was intercepted by two Pucaras who shot the aircraft down, killing Nunn in the process. The other Scout, flown by Geoff Niblett, escaped the Pucara attack.

Despite continuing artillery and mortar fire, A Company rounded up its prisoners and tended to the wounded. It was only then that the strength of the force attacked by A Company became apparent: ninety-two enemy had been accounted for, of whom eighteen had been killed and thirty-nine wounded, while many more had escaped. Enemy wounded were treated with the same care and consideration as the men of 2 PARA. Two medics, Lance Corporal Fraz Framingham and Private Paul O'Rourke, dressed their wounds. The prisoners were given tea and the wounded received extra clothing in accordance with Jones's orders that any captured Argentinians were to be treated correctly.

A number of helicopters appeared, bringing forward, among others, the battalion's two medical officers, Captains Steve Hughes and Rory Wagan; the latter had previously been 2 PARA's medical officer and had been returned to his old battalion for the operation. They supervised the evacuation of A Company's casualties, which numbered three killed and twelve wounded, in addition to the commanding officer, the adjutant and Corporal Mick Melia from 59 Independent Commando Squadron RE.

During A Company's action at Darwin Hill, B Company had remained in its position on the reverse slope of the ridge forward of Boca House. An attack over the open ground to the front could not be considered, so the company had to remain where it was, engaging the enemy at every opportunity. There was little that could be done to help A Company other than trying to knock out the enemy positions thought to be causing trouble. Corporal Kev Dunbar, a section commander in 4 Platoon, had already attacked these positions at first light but to make sure they were out of action Lieutenant Ernie Hocking and Lance Corporal Barrie, covered by Privates Maitland and Steven Walton, began to move forward to throw grenades into them. As Hocking moved up on to the hill, however, he was ordered back because an air strike had been called in on Boca House. As he withdrew, he spotted between fifty and a hundred enemy troops standing in the open beside their trenches but had no chance to engage them because of the imminent air strike.

Meanwhile 6 Platoon was still pinned down by enemy mortar fire in the gorse line. From his position Lieutenant Clyde Chapman could observe two bunker positions approximately 370 yards apart with a number of tents nearby. Corporal Margerison moved his section forward so that it could obtain a better view of the enemy. At that

Darwin Hill, reverse slope, after the battle. Smoke can be seen drifting across the battlefield.

point, a rocket was fired from one of the bunkers and landed among the platoon, fortunately without exploding. Chapman responded by calling for artillery support but the firing was inaccurate and the shells fell wide of the mark. 6 Platoon remained in this situation for the next hour and a half before Major Crosland decided to withdraw it. Under cover of smoke laid down by the battalion's two mortars and its own smoke grenades, the platoon pulled back. Corporal Margerison was wounded as he waited for his GPMG group to catch up; as he fell, another bullet hit the stock of his rifle and shattered it. Two members of his section, Lance Corporals Bardsley and Barry, immediately dragged him to safety.

By this time the battle at Darwin Hill was over and 2 PARA's second-in-command, Major Chris Keeble, was already coming forward to assume command of the battalion. Over the radio he ordered Major Crosland to take control of the battle while he was en route. At the same time he told C (Patrols) and Support Companies to move up to the three rifle companies with all haste.

Meanwhile Major Neame was still contemplating the western shoreline along which D Company could carry out a flanking attack on Boca House. Although the tide was coming in, the small cliff and a narrow strip of rock offered a covered approach which was unlikely to be mined because of the hardness of the beach. Accompanied by Lieutenant John Page, Sergeant Bullock and a section, he set off to reconnoitre the route. Making their way carefully along the shore, and using the cliff as cover, Neame and his group moved in the direction of the enemy. When he found a suitable position, Neame used the radio to call forward 11 and 12 Platoons. He massed their nine GPMGs and positioned them so that they could provide covering fire for an assault.

The nine GPMGs opened fire and the enemy was left in little doubt that a withdrawal was now impossible. Via his second-in-command, Lieutenant Peter Adams, Major Neame informed Major Keeble that he and his platoons could not remain on the beach indefinitely because of the incoming tide. Back on the ridgeline, meanwhile, Major Crosland had asked for the Anti-Tank Platoon and its three Milan firing posts to be sent forward. Major Keeble had agreed to this but ordered D Company not to begin a flanking attack until B Company had been resupplied with ammunition which he had brought forward with him.

Captain Ketley and his three firing posts soon arrived and minutes later two missiles were launched at the enemy bunkers. By this time D Company was beginning its flanking attack and the Machine-Gun Platoon, which had arrived and deployed its six GPMGs only shortly beforehand, opened fire. Almost immediately came a radio message from the commander of 10 Platoon, Lieutenant Shaun Webster, telling the guns to cease fire as the enemy troops were indicating they wished to surrender.

As D Company advanced, a member of 12 Platoon shouted to Lieutenant Jim Barry that they were in a minefield. The latter, who was already well aware of the fact, told him to keep moving because it was too late to stop. At that moment a mine was detonated by Private Steve 'Spence' Spencer, who walked into a tripwire. The blast knocked him and three others over but fortunately did not injure them. Under the impression that the platoon was under attack, a GPMG gunner on the ridgeline opened fire, as did one of the Milan firing posts, endangering 12 Platoon which was now out in the open. Had the enemy retaliated, D Company would have suffered heavy casualties. Over the radio Major Neame ordered all firing to cease.

On the ridgeline, meanwhile, enemy mortar fire was still causing problems and three members of the Anti-Tank Platoon were wounded. Behind the ridge men took cover as best they could while medics gave emergency treatment to the injured, moving them to a makeshift first aid post behind a small wall of peat constructed to provide shelter from the wind and rain.

D Company had now cleared the enemy positions around Boca House, taking fifteen prisoners, some of them badly wounded, and finding twelve dead. Six other Argentinians had been observed fleeing. Not bothering to regroup, Major Neame pushed on, leaving his company sergeant major and a section to cope with the

Men of D Company 2 PARA organise Argentinian prisoners after an enemy position is taken during the battle for Goose Green.

prisoners. The plan was now for D Company to exploit forward to the high ground around the airfield overlooking Goose Green and attack an enemy position in the area of the schoolhouse. A Company would remain in its positions on Darwin Hill, less 3 Platoon which, attached to C (Patrols) Company, would clear all the enemy positions near the gorse line – above the scene of A Company's action – before clearing Darwin itself. B Company, meanwhile, would make a flanking move down the western side of the isthmus, looping south to cut off Goose Green from that direction.

The Anti-Tank and Machine-Gun Platoons took up positions ready to support the other companies. They were joined by the section of mortars, which had done its utmost to provide support throughout the battle but for much of the time had been out of range. The absence of the battalion's other six mortars had prevented the leap-frogging of baseplates to ensure continual support. The lack of ammunition was also causing problems. The section had run out of bombs at 1pm, during A Company's action, and it had become necessary for further supplies to be manpacked forward from the old baseplate position at the battalion RV to the new one at Burntside House; this was a gruelling task. Nevertheless, the section's two mortar crews had fired over 1,000 bombs in the two hours of the A Company action, the mortars themselves sinking further and further into the soft peat until eventually only their muzzles were visible. Moreover, the barrels became so hot that it was necessary for the number two in each crew to pour cold water over them continually.

The three light guns of 8 Commando Battery RA were also prevented from providing support. The close proximity of the 2 PARA companies meant that for much of the time the risks of bringing down artillery fire were too great. It was only during the action at Boca House, when B Company was at a sufficient distance from its objective, that they could fire, and even then only with dubious accuracy.

While A Company regrouped and reorganised, C (Patrols) Company began clearing Darwin. At this point, however, the plan for the next phase of the operation was changed and Major Roger Jenner was ordered to advance on the airfield at Goose Green. B Company had already begun its flanking move and D Company was advancing towards the airfield from Boca House. Jenner and his men, followed by the Anti-Tank and Machine-Gun Platoons, headed over the crest of the ridge above Goose Green and began descending the slope towards the schoolhouse. In front of them lay the airfield where enemy troops stood transfixed at the sight of the advancing company. They did not take long to react, however, the anti-aircraft gunners among them running for the three 35mm guns which opened fire. As they did so Major Jenner called for artillery support but none was available. At that moment a member of the Machine-Gun Platoon, Private Steve Russell, was badly wounded in the neck by a burst from an Oerlikon and Major Jenner and one of his signallers, Private Holman-Smith, ran across to give him first aid. As they reached Russell another burst from the Oerlikon killed Holman-Smith and slightly wounded Jenner and his other signaller, Private Charlie Holbrook. Jenner then attempted to make radio contact with his two platoons, whom he could see advancing below, but was unable to do so. Under heavy fire, he withdrew to the gorse line from where Major Keeble was observing the battle. The latter ordered him to withdraw his company but all radio contact had been lost.

By this time enemy troops in the schoolhouse had opened fire and the two C (Patrols) Company platoons and B Company, which was approaching from the west, were both very exposed. 3 Platoon, which was still in reserve, pulled back and took cover in the gorse line after suffering three casualties, including Sergeant Jim Beattie. Meanwhile the Reconnaissance and Patrols Platoons moved forward and took cover in dead ground, where they were joined shortly afterwards by the company second-in-command, Lieutenant Peter Kennedy. The Anti-Tank and

Machine-Gun Platoons deployed to the left, the machine-gunners advancing to positions from which the schoolhouse would be in range of their six GPMGs. 2 PARA's snipers also took up positions in the gorse from which they could bring down harassing fire on the airfield.

D Company was now advancing rapidly towards the airfield. 12 Platoon was in the lead as it moved under cover of a re-entrant towards its objective. As the platoon commander, Lieutenant Jim Barry, and his men caught sight of the airfield, they observed enemy troops withdrawing on a tractor. Corporal Sullivan's section opened fire, causing casualties. At that moment more enemy were spotted withdrawing into dead ground towards the schoolhouse. Meanwhile the company continued to push on to the south-east, leaving the airfield on its right and avoiding the fire of the Oerlikons by using the river valley leading to the schoolhouse. Having advanced a further 900 yards or so, D Company spotted troops crossing a footbridge over the estuary ahead and running towards the schoolhouse. At the same time Major Neame caught sight of what he suspected to be an enemy command post in a hollow on the high ground at the western end of the airfield. He immediately dispatched 10 Platoon to attack it.

Lieutenant Shaun Webster and his two sections advanced on the suspected command post position but found it abandoned. As they moved further forward they came under fire from two snipers to the south-west. With Corporal Taff Stodder and his section providing covering fire, Webster led his remaining section and platoon headquarters in a left flanking attack. But as he and his assault group advanced on a second abandoned position, they were subjected to very heavy fire from an enemy platoon on the southern side of the airfield. They took cover behind the empty trenches. No sooner had Neame ordered Webster to advance no further than the lieutenant and his men found themselves under very heavy and accurate machine-gun fire which forced them to take cover in the abandoned trenches. It rapidly became apparent that this was not enemy fire but that of the Machine-Gun Platoon which had mistaken them for enemy troops. Once the volume of fire had decreased, Webster and his men hoisted their maroon berets on sticks and waved them above the trenches, while Webster himself attempted to establish radio contact with D Company headquarters. Fortunately, the Machine-Gun Platoon spotted the berets and ceased fire, enabling Webster to regroup his men.

The remainder of D Company had continued advancing along the river valley until it neared the estuary. A minefield on the right forced Neame and his men to head for the schoolhouse and the track which led to it. As they observed the building, a large group of enemy troops was seen regrouping in it and Neame thus decided that he would attack it first. At that moment, however, the enemy spotted the company and opened fire. Having dropped off 12 Platoon to provide covering fire from a position on the track, Neame led 11 Platoon in an assault from the creek. Lieutenant Jim Barry of 12 Platoon then observed white flags flying from the windows of the schoolhouse and ordered his signaller, Private Steven 'Geordie' Knight, to pass this information to company headquarters. Unfortunately, in the ensuing confusion of the attack, the message did not get through. Moreover, some of the enemy, despite the white flags, were still continuing to fire from other positions in the area of the schoolhouse.

As Neame and 11 Platoon advanced on the objective, the Reconnaissance and Patrols Platoons also came under fire from the same area. From a point higher up the slope, Captain Paul Farrar watched as enemy troops abandoned three bunkers facing the sea to the east of the schoolhouse and moved into a small building to the south-east, obviously aware that the threat was coming from behind them. Meanwhile the Patrols Platoon had split into two groups, with Company Sergeant Major Barry

Members of 2 PARA after the battle for Goose Green. The soldier wearing a beret is a Royal Marine, possibly from the Air Defence Troop which was attached to the battalion for the attack.

Greenhalgh taking one forward into dead ground while the other, under Captain Farrar, also advanced as enemy artillery and mortars began bringing down a bombardment.

Shortly afterwards Farrar and his group engaged one of the Oerlikon 35mm anti-aircraft guns at a range of some 135 yards with a 40mm grenade launcher, before rejoining Company Sergeant Major Greenhalgh and his men. Thereafter, Farrar divided his platoon into three groups for an assault on the schoolhouse; the third of these, commanded by Corporal Russell Bishop, comprised all the platoon's LMGs which would provide covering fire.

11 Platoon had already attacked the outbuildings to the west of the schoolhouse, firing four 66mm LAWs into one of them. Under covering fire from the remainder of the platoon, Corporals Wally McAuley and Tom Harley then charged the building, throwing in grenades and setting it on fire. No Argentinians appeared and so the platoon turned to a smaller building which was already ablaze. At that moment heavy artillery fire started to fall on the area at the edge of the creek, preventing the company aid post from coming forward to tend the wounded. 11 Platoon then began to engage the enemy in the schoolhouse itself. Taking two GPMGs and five men with him, 2nd Lieutenant Chris Waddington moved forward along the side of the inlet while the rest of the platoon provided covering fire. At the bottom of the inlet Waddington and his men met Captain Paul Farrar and his group from the Patrols Platoon.

The schoolhouse and surrounding area were under fire from enemy positions at Goose Green to the south-east, artillery and mortar rounds falling on the northern bank of the inlet. From his position Captain Farrar spotted several enemy troops in the upper storey of the main school building and others in the smaller building towards the shoreline. As far as he could discern there were no white flags being waved. Company Sergeant Major Greenhalgh's group took up positions in a line along the edge of the crest north of the school and opened fire with 66mm LAWs and 40mm grenades. Meanwhile Captain Farrar and his men moved round on a small track to the east side of the building. At this point Corporal Bishop's fire support group joined 11 Platoon to increase its firepower.

A joint attack then took place with the assault groups of both platoons charging the building under heavy covering fire. Greenhalgh's group attacked the main building, throwing grenades through the ground floor windows while the fire support groups concentrated on the upper storey. As the grenades exploded, the building caught fire. In the meantime Captain Farrar and his men were crawling towards the smaller building to the east where they cleared a number of bunkers with grenades. As the area was still under heavy fire from enemy positions on Goose Green Point, they did not move up to the building itself. Suddenly a heavy anti-aircraft gun opened fire on the schoolhouse while at the same time artillery and mortar fire intensified. Much of it landed in the inlet, although several bombs bounced off the crest line between the school and the inlet, ricocheting on to the beach or into the water.

During the battle for the schoolhouse 12 Platoon had been tasked with providing supporting fire. Looking up the hill Lieutenant Barry spotted what he thought was a white flag. He told his platoon sergeant that he was going to take a surrender and set off, accompanied by his runner, Private Jerry Godfrey. Sergeant John Meredith sent the platoon's signaller, Private Geordie Knight, after him and told Corporal Sullivan to follow behind. When he was told of this over the company radio net, Neame replied that Barry was not to make any such move; unfortunately, this order never reached Barry. Accounts of the events that followed differ but in essence it appears that as Barry approached the enemy position with Private Godfrey following behind, a small group of Argentinians appeared. He was in conversation with them when a long burst of fire, thought to be from the Machine-Gun Platoon, went overhead. The enemy retaliated by opening fire and killing Barry. Private Godfrey withdrew hastily and took cover as two Argentinians skirmished towards him – the remainder took shelter in a bunker. Both were killed by the signaller, Private Knight, who then reported the incident to D Company headquarters on his radio. Having brought forward a GPMG group to engage the bunkers and a group of Argentinians hiding behind a large pile of ammunition, Sergeant Meredith advanced along the track with Corporal Tom Kinchen's section to retrieve Lieutenant Barry's body.

Meanwhile Lieutenant Peter Kennedy, the second-in-command of C (Patrols) Company, had come under fire. Together with Lance Corporal Cole, he took cover in a shellhole before crawling down the side of the track where he met two NCOs, Corporals Ian Raynor and Tony Pearson. Passing the Reconnaissance Platoon by the bridge, Kennedy pressed on up the track. With Lieutenant Barry, he took over command of the troops in the immediate area and, taking two GPMG groups with him, continued along the track. As he approached the two bunkers where the enemy had earlier attempted to surrender, it became apparent that all had either fled or been killed. One of the GPMG groups was ordered to return to its platoon and Kennedy continued on with the other, subsequently moving into a position in a hedgerow from which he and his two companions could observe the enemy artillery almost 400 yards away behind a barn in Goose Green. Unfortunately Kennedy had no radio and could not pass on the location of the enemy guns. Had he been able to do so, they could have been put out of action by counter-battery fire from 8 Commando Battery or an air strike.

By this time the Machine-Gun Platoon had fired over 6,000 rounds and was running low on ammunition. Its sections were assembling belts from abandoned enemy 7.62mm ammunition. As the platoon came under heavier and more accurate mortar fire, Lieutenant Hugo Lister decided to move his men forward under cover of smoke.

The tiny hamlet of Goose Green and Darwin. It was to the west of the Brigade's route and not regarded as vital to Thompson's advance. Thompson had also planned to leave 40 Commando at San Carlos to protect the Brigade's rear flank.

However, when they advanced, they came under fire from Goose Green and were forced back.

Meanwhile the Anti-Tank Platoon had been engaging the anti-aircraft guns on Goose Green airfield with its Milan missiles, but two had gone out of control and missed their targets. The platoon also attempted to engage the guns and positions at Goose Green Point but they were just beyond the maximum range of the missiles. Captain Ketley sent forward Corporal George 'Bernie' Bolt's section; it fired another missile which landed 12 feet short of its target. The three firing posts were assisted by the battalion's snipers who, equipped with laser rangefinders, indicated targets for them. The snipers subsequently proved their worth while engaging enemy troops inside Goose Green itself, causing panic with their accurate harassing fire.

While the battle raged around the airfield and schoolhouse, B Company was carrying out its long flanking move via dead ground to the south-west side of Goose Green. This had not passed without incident – the men came across stocks of anti-personnel mines. As the company approached the airfield 6 Platoon laid down covering fire while 4 and

5 Platoons continued their advance. Then 5 Platoon began to go forward into the attack while 4 Platoon was ordered by Major Crosland to occupy two large bunkers in the airfield's south-east corner. All the other bunkers along the perimeter had been abandoned, and a large group of enemy troops could be seen milling around, apparently in disorder. As it headed for the bunkers, 4 Platoon observed sixteen more enemy to the south; when approached, these men clearly showed their willingness to surrender and be disarmed while others further away indicated likewise. By this time D Company was in action on the airfield and B Company was ordered to hold its fire because there was a risk of a 'blue on blue' contact taking place. At that moment, however, 5 Platoon came under fire from enemy mortars.

The operation was now reaching its closing stages. 2 PARA was offered reinforcements by 3 Commando Brigade but turned them down. Just after 6pm, with less than thirty minutes of daylight left, the battalion requested an air strike on the enemy positions at Goose Green Point because of the heavy fire being put down by the anti-aircraft guns positioned there. Two aircraft soon appeared – but they were not Sea Harriers from HMS *Hermes*'s strike force. Instead, they were Argentinian Skyhawks, followed shortly afterwards by a Pucara, which proceeded to attack B and D Companies as they were in the process of regrouping after the attack on the airfield. The leading aircraft strafed the ground with cannon fire but caused no casualties. Seconds later, however, it exploded in mid-air as it was hit by a Sidewinder missile fired from one of three Sea Harriers which now appeared from the south. Meanwhile the Royal Marine Blowpipe detachment with 2 PARA positioned in the gorse line, engaged the Pucara and shot it down.

The three Harriers proceeded to attack Goose Green Point. The first aircraft carried out its run-in from the north-west but its cluster bombs fell harmlessly in the sea. The second also missed but the third, making its approach from the north-east, hit the target area. Despite several casualties, however, the Oerlikon guns continued to fire. It transpired later that the strike had had a considerable psychological effect on the enemy – many of the Argentinians were reported as having been reduced to abject terror.

Ordered by Major Keeble to halt and regroup, D Company moved to a reverse slope position north-west of a flagpole located by the track between the airfield and the schoolhouse. Just before last light the company was attacked by a Pucara which was met with a hail of fire, reinforced by another wave of firing from B Company, which succeeded in shooting down the aircraft. The pilot ejected and was subsequently taken prisoner by Corporal Kinchen and Private Spencer of 12 Platoon.

B Company had regrouped on the outskirts of Goose Green and was in the process of brewing up some much-needed tea when Lieutenant Weighell heard the sound of helicopters and observed an enemy Chinook, followed by six UH-1 'Hueys', landing troops to the south. Weighell and Sergeant Aird swiftly worked out the position of the helicopters and called down artillery fire. The attack was accurate but by the time a fifteen-round fire mission exploded on the LZ, the aircraft were taking off and an enemy company was advancing towards the settlement, which it reached without loss. Concerned that this might be the prelude to a counter-attack, Major Crosland pulled his men back to the edge of the airfield where they took up positions close to an abandoned anti-aircraft gun. The ground was littered with copious quantities of Argentinian 7.62mm ammunition, which meant the company could replenish its magazines and link up belts for its GPMGs. Lacking digging tools, which had been left at Camilla Creek House, the men were unable to dig in and were reduced to excavating shell scrapes as best they could with their bayonets, knives and mess tins. The weather was cold and wet; rations and drinking water were scarce.

Meanwhile C (Patrol) Company was regrouping near the gorse-filled gully. Major Jenner had been wounded and Major Keeble ordered him to be evacuated, but he could not be found; he was finally discovered the next morning and flown by helicopter to the main dressing station at Ajax Bay. His second-in-command, Lieutenant Kennedy, was unaccounted for and reported as missing. In fact, Kennedy and two men of the D Company GPMG group had remained forward. At last light Kennedy had decided to seek out and attack the enemy artillery they had observed earlier and which was still firing. Accompanied by Private Slough, and covered by Private Mark Sheepwash with the GPMG, he set off towards the barns behind which he had observed the guns. As darkness fell it became increasingly difficult to find the guns which had now ceased firing. Kennedy and Slough searched the barns but found nothing. After a while, they withdrew and returned to Private Sheepwash. Seeing and hearing no sign of 2 PARA, they retraced their steps back to the bridge near the schoolhouse before moving up to the gorse line. There they took up positions for the night.

It was bitterly cold. Lacking sleeping bags and dry clothing, men were forced to huddle together for warmth. A and C (Patrol) Companies, along with Tac HQ, had received a resupply of water, ammunition and rations but as B and D Companies could not be located in the darkness, they went hungry and thirsty. Thirty sleeping bags were also brought forward but they were for the wounded. Another welcome arrival, albeit too late, was the battalion's other six mortars which were brought in by helicopter from Sussex Mountain. The mortar baseplate position was resited.

2 PARA's casualties were a matter of great concern that night because the only available method of evacuation was helicopter. The Regimental Aid Post (RAP) was operating in two teams, one under Captain Rory Wagan at Boca House and the other led by Captain Steve Hughes in the gorse-filled gully. The unceasing rain hampered their work and the problem of evacuating the more serious casualties grew steadily worse. Evacuation from Boca House in particular was not going well; Captain Wagan

Senior members of 2 PARA. Left to right: the Adjutant, Captain Worsley-Tonks; the commanding officer Lieutenant Colonel Chaundler, who replaced Lieutenant Colonel Jones; the second-in-command Major Keeble; and the RSM, WO1 Simpson.

reported this to battalion headquarters by radio and shortly afterwards a Gazelle helicopter arrived to pick up the sitting wounded. This still left several stretcher cases, among them Captain John Young, B Company's second-in-command, who was suffering from his wounds and the effects of the cold.

These and other difficulties led some in the battalion, unaware of other pressing commitments, to conclude that the attitude of brigade headquarters was decidedly unhelpful. At 10.40pm brigade headquarters finally agreed to send a helicopter to collect the six men requiring urgent evacuation. A Sea King appeared briefly but flew away again; just before midnight brigade headquarters located the aircraft but then announced that it could not return. Battalion headquarters objected strongly and

Argentinian Pucaras dropped napalm at Goose Green but failed to hit their target. Later in the clear up operation more napalm bombs were discovered.

eventually a casualty flight was authorised. This comprised a Scout helicopter flown by Captain John Greenhalgh of 656 Squadron AAC, who had volunteered for the task. By this time two casualties were in dire need of medical treatment, having been lying in the darkness for five hours.

Captain Greenhalgh's aircraft eventually arrived, and Captain John Young and an Argentinian prisoner were evacuated. All that Captain Wagan and his medics could do for the remainder was to sleep as close to them as possible in an effort to keep them warm. They were not evacuated until after first light on the following day, twenty hours after being wounded.

Captain Simon Hughes's group experienced similar problems. His first priority had been the casualties from A Company's action. Most of them had been evacuated by helicopter early in the day despite the enemy artillery fire which increased with every appearance of the aircraft. Captain Mike Ford had been responsible for organising stretcher parties during the C (Patrols) Company action and had been told of one man, Private David Grey, who had suffered serious wounds to one of his legs, which had

Casualties being evacuated to Ajax Bay from Goose Green. Several Paras were injured at Goose Green and the intense fighting delayed evacuation.

been nearly severed. Captain Ford and a medic, Lance Corporal Bill Bentley, went forward and found Grey. His life was saved by Bentley who used minimal instruments to amputate his leg below the knee. Ford and Bentley then carried Grey back to safety and he was evacuated shortly afterwards.

Meanwhile Major Keeble was considering how to persuade the enemy to surrender. Initially his plan had been to launch a heavy bombardment of the Goose Green settlement with artillery and mortars before attacking it, but this idea was dropped after he learned of the presence of civilians. He then decided to establish contact with the Argentinian commander by sending two prisoners into the settlement with an ultimatum: surrender or face the consequences, including responsibility for the fate of the civilians. Having obtained approval from Brigadier Thompson via the radio, Keeble produced a plan. His intention was to spin out the period of negotiations over surrender sufficiently long for reinforcements, in the form of J Company 42 Commando, to be flown in, along with a resupply of ammunition and supplies. The one nagging question at the back of his mind was what action he could take if the Argentinians refused to negotiate and held the civilians as hostages.

Throughout the night Keeble, Captain Alan Coulson and Captain Rod Bell drafted and redrafted the text of the ultimatum which was eventually translated into Spanish by Bell. At 10 the following morning, 29 May, two prisoners were sent into Goose Green carrying the message. They were told that if they had not returned within an hour, it would be assumed that the Argentinians wished to resume the battle and 2 PARA would attack. A few minutes later they came back and arrangements were made for the negotiations to be held in a hut on the western side of the airfield. Meanwhile A and D Companies deployed standing patrols nearby.

Keeble made his way some 1,500 yards to the hut, above which a white flag had been hoisted. He was accompanied by Major Hector Gullan, Major Tony Rice, Captain Bell and two journalists: Robert Fox of the BBC and David Norris of the

An Argentinian rifle abandoned at Goose Green. The enemy force at Goose Green was approximately three times larger than that of 2 PARA – 1,250 compared with 450. Goose Green was the bloodiest battle of the conflict.

The sheds at Goose Green were used as temporary shelters for the hundreds of Argentinian prisoners of war captured by 2 PARA. After the fight at Goose Green the Paras moved to Fitzroy and Bluff Cove to reorganise.

Daily Mail. They were met by a group of three Argentinian officers: the commander of the Goose Green garrison, Air Vice-Commodore Wilson Dosio Pedroza; the commanding officer of the 12th Infantry Regiment, Lieutenant Colonel Italo Piaggi; and a coastguard officer, Lieutenant Canevari Gopevich.

During the negotiations the Argentinians agreed to the removal of the civilians. While Pedroza appeared willing to accept the terms of surrender immediately, Piaggi stated that he wished to consult General Menendez in Port Stanley by radio. Major Gullan stressed there was no time for prevarication and added that Menendez should know his men had fought well but were now in a very dangerous predicament. He also insisted that a Spanish-speaking British officer would have to be present during any such conversation, but the Argentinians would not agree to that condition. Gullan's remarks were reinforced by Bell who emphasised the consequences if there was no surrender. Considerable time was devoted to the question of the accommodation of prisoners following a surrender and it was agreed that repatriation would be effected as soon as was practical. The question of minefields proved to be a problem because the Argentinians had not kept detailed records of mines laid by their troops; all they could offer was that they would make available the NCO who had been responsible for the work.

The memorial to the men of 2 PARA and others killed at Goose Green.

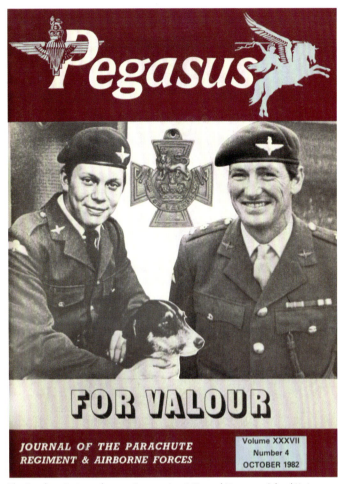

Pegasus

FOR VALOUR

JOURNAL OF THE PARACHUTE REGIMENT & AIRBORNE FORCES

Volume XXXVII
Number 4
OCTOBER 1982

The Parachute Regiment honours Sergeant Ian McKay and Lieutenant Colonel H. Jones who were both awarded the Victoria Cross and remembered on the cover of *Pegasus*, the regimental journal.

Eventually agreement was reached on all points and the Argentinians returned to the settlement, leaving Keeble and his companions at the hut awaiting developments. Thirty minutes later a column of 250 troops could be seen marching out of the settlement, heading to where Keeble and his group stood waiting. Having halted and formed a hollow square, they were addressed by Air Vice-Commodore Pedroza before singing the Argentinian national anthem and laying down their arms. Pedroza then approached Keeble and presented him with his pistol. Realising that the assembled men were all Argentinian Air Force personnel, Keeble asked what had happened to the remainder of the garrison. Pedroza pointed back to the settlement; a large body of troops, headed by Piaggi, were to be seen marching out. Numbering approximately a thousand in total, they halted beside the Air Force contingent. They were disarmed and then sent back down to the settlement to collect their personal belongings; this was later acknowledged as an error because the Argentinian troops looted and caused considerable damage before leaving the settlement for the last time. They were then placed under the watchful guard of D Company. Pedroza was collected by helicopter and flown to headquarters 3 Commando Brigade.

In due course Keeble, accompanied by Major Rice and Robert Fox, made his way down to the settlement. As they approached, the inhabitants began pouring out of the buildings, overwhelmed to be free, happy to be alive and full of gratitude to the men of 2 PARA for whom the battle of Goose Green was finally over.

During the battles at Darwin and Goose Green 2 PARA had suffered casualties totalling fifteen killed and thirty wounded. The Argentinians lost fifty-five killed and between eighty and a hundred wounded, with over a thousand taken prisoner.

The men of 2 PARA bury their comrades on the hillside above San Carlos Water. The battalion RSM, WO1 Malcolm Simpson, described it as a sight he would never forget.

Weapons and equipment captured by the battalion amounted to three 105mm pack howitzers, two 35mm and six 20mm anti-aircraft guns, six 120mm mortars, two Pucaras and large quantities of small arms, ammunition and stores.

On 31 May Major Keeble, accompanied by all six company commanders, Regimental Sergeant Major Malcolm Simpson and the padre, the Reverend Major David Cooper, flew by helicopter to Ajax Bay for the burial of 2 PARA's dead in a large grave dug by Royal Engineers on the hillside above San Carlos Water.

EIGHT

THE ADVANCE EAST

YOMP AND TAB ACROSS THE FALKLANDS

While 2 PARA was fighting hard at Darwin and Goose Green, the first stage of the advance east towards Port Stanley was taking place. 45 Commando and 3 PARA set off on 27 May for Douglas Settlement and Teal Inlet Settlement respectively. First to leave was 45 Commando, led by Lieutenant Colonel Andrew Whitehead. The unit had departed Ajax Bay before first light on the 27th aboard landing craft which took it to Port San Carlos. From there the men set off north-eastwards to march to Douglas Settlement, which lies at the western end of Teal Inlet on the northern coast of East Falkland. The first stage comprised some 12 miles' march to a location called New House. The weather was reasonable, but the terrain was as bad as ever for the heavily burdened marines, each of whom was carrying pack and equipment weighing approximately 120lb. The ankle-turning grass tussocks and the steep slopes combined to make the going difficult but at 10pm 45 Commando reached New House where it harboured up.

After a wet night the commando set off before first light on the remaining 7 mile journey to Douglas Settlement, the Reconnaissance and Surveillance Troops deployed forward as a screen and X Company leading the main body. They marched in fighting order, leaving their heavy rucksacks at New House. On reaching the settlement, Whitehead and his men discovered that the enemy had pulled out two days earlier. The inhabitants had been locked in the schoolhouse for four days. Evidence of the Argentinian occupation was plain to see: houses had been looted and damaged. 45 Commando took up defensive positions around the settlement and dug in, with the Mortar Troop setting up its baseplate position ready to provide supporting fire for the three rifle companies. On the following day, 29 May, the commando's rucksacks and a ration resupply were flown in by helicopter from New House, and the men put the settlement's sheepshearing sheds to good use for drying out clothing and sleeping bags which were soaking wet after two days of constant rain.

3 PARA was also on the march, having left the beachhead at 1.15pm on 27 May. Less D (Patrols) Company, commanded by Major Pat Butler, Battalion Main Headquarters and Echelon, it set off from Port San Carlos for Teal Inlet Settlement, which lies at the southern end of Teal Inlet, south-east of Douglas Settlement, approximately halfway between San Carlos and Port Stanley.

Royal Marines of 45 Commando start the long yomp across the Falklands. They carried backpacks weighing up to 100lb and their equipment included mortars, spare ammunition, Carl Gustav anti-tank weapons and 66mm anti-tank missiles.

During the following twenty-four hours the battalion carried out a gruelling march to a harbour position in the valley of the Arroyo Pedro River, approximately 5½ miles from Teal Inlet. A Company, led by Major David Collett and accompanied by the commanding officer and Tac HQ, took the lead. 3 PARA moved at a punishing pace despite appalling weather. Unlike 45 Commando, the battalion marched in light order; its packs, heavy weapons and equipment were carried on trailers towed by tractors driven by local farmers from Port San Carlos who had volunteered their services. Nevertheless, exposure and exhaustion resulted in a number of casualties who had to be evacuated by helicopter on the following morning.

Throughout 28 May the battalion lay up in the harbour area. After last light, at about 4.15pm, it set off for Teal Inlet Settlement. Meanwhile B Company, commanded by Major Mike Argue, carried out a flanking move to a position south-east of the settlement in order to cut off any enemy attempting to escape. During the afternoon a report had been received from the SBS that Teal Inlet was clear of enemy, but that

WO1 Pat Chapman, the Regimental Sergeant Major of 45 Commando, leads his boys across the Falklands. They yomped 50 miles from their landing at Ajax Bay to Stanley.

night a civilian reported it was possible that there were up to eleven wounded Argentinians in the settlement. At 2.30am on 29 May A Company, together with Lieutenant Colonel Pike and Tac HQ, advanced cautiously into the settlement and within thirty minutes had secured it. One enemy soldier had been taken prisoner but there were reports of stragglers in the area.

As the day wore on the rest of 3 PARA, which had remained at Port San Carlos, rejoined the battalion, the last to arrive being D (Patrols) Company. Unknown to the rest of the battalion, four of the company's patrols, under Operations Officer Captain Matt Selfridge and Company Sergeant Major Quinn, had been deployed on an operation. As 3 PARA prepared to set off from Port San Carlos, the patrols were dispatched in a Sea King helicopter for a parachute insertion on to Great Island, which lies at the southern end of Falkland Sound, for a surveillance task. However, bad weather resulted in the operation being aborted and subsequently the patrols were embarked on a frigate for a landing by boat. Having established two OPs, the patrols kept Fox Bay under observation, looking for movement by enemy aircraft and shipping, and giving early warning of air strikes or transfers of enemy troops by helicopter between East and West Falkland. After eight days the men were withdrawn and rejoined the rest of D (Patrols) Company.

The battalion was joined by 4 Troop of the Blues & Royals, commanded by Lieutenant Mark Coreth, which had been due to move with 3 PARA from Port San Carlos but had been delayed by a shortage of fuel. Coreth solved the problem the following morning by appropriating fuel for his two Scorpions and two Scimitars. The troop then set off in hot pursuit after 3 PARA, picking up a number of casualties along the way.

On the evening of 29 May 45 Commando and 3 PARA received warning orders to resume the advance eastwards, but there was to be no move before first light on the following day. The objective for both units was Estancia House, which 3 PARA would reach first and secure. 45 Commando would then pass through 3 PARA and press on to take Long Island Mount. Meanwhile during the night of 29/30 May, 42 Commando would be lifted forward from the beachhead to Mount Kent, the upper slopes of which had been occupied by D Squadron 22 SAS since the 27th. The enemy was reported to be holding the summit and it would be 42 Commando's task to attack and seize the feature. Unfortunately, bad weather prevented the helicopters from lifting the commando forward until the late afternoon of 30 May when Tac HQ, most of K Company and the Mortar Troop were flown the 40 miles from the beachhead to Mount Kent in two Sea Kings. They were accompanied by the commanding officer of 22 SAS, Lieutenant Colonel Michael Rose, and newspaper journalist Max Hastings. Just as the helicopters were approaching the LZ an enemy patrol of 601 Company appeared a mile to the north of the LZ and a firefight ensued. As Lieutenant Colonel Nick Vaux, the commanding officer of 42 Commando, and his men disembarked from the helicopters, they could see tracer and hear explosions. D Squadron was engaging members of the enemy patrol; some were killed but the remainder fled into the darkness.

While Vaux established his Tac HQ just a few hundred yards from the LZ, K Company, commanded by Captain Peter Babbington, carried out a night assault on the summit of Mount Kent which it found to be unoccupied. Two hours later three light guns of 7 Commando Battery RA and a quantity of ammunition were brought in by the Task Force's single surviving Chinook. The aircraft was due to bring in the rest of 42 Commando and more artillery ammunition that night but while flying at low level back to San Carlos it struck a lake. The pilot, blinded by a

The boots issued to the marines and paras could not cope with the wet terrain of the Falklands. Some soldiers suffered trench foot. Whenever they could they changed socks and attempted to dry their boots out, but there was little time for such activity.

THE BLUES & ROYALS

The Blues & Royals deployed two troops in support of the Commando Brigade. Their mobility, firepower and flexibility meant they could be used to ferry ammunition and casualties, and they proved to be an invaluable asset to the land forces during the Falklands campaign. Each troop had two Scorpions, two Scimitars and a Samson recovery vehicle. Many senior officers thought the light reconnaissance vehicles would get bogged down in the harsh terrain but they proved very effective and supported several key actions including Tumbledown and Wireless Ridge, and escorted troops in Stanley. The Scorpion was armed with a 76mm anti-tank gun firing high explosive (HE) or high explosive squash head (HESH) rounds. The HESH round impacts against the target and then detonates, showering the crew inside with steel. The Scimitar was armed with a 30mm Rarden cannon capable of firing similar rounds. Both were also fitted with a 7.62mm machine-gun.

The Blues & Royals were formed in 1969 through the amalgamation of two of the oldest and most famous cavalry regiments in the British Army, the Royal Horse Guards (the Blues) and the Royal Dragoons (1st Dragoons).

flurry of snow, had lost his vision. Fortunately, he was able to recover almost instantly and succeeded in returning to the beachhead. The helicopter, however, had been damaged and was unable to fly further that night.

The temperature plummeted that night and the men of K Commando spent miserable hours shivering on Mount Kent – their sleeping bags and packs were with the remainder of the commando waiting to be lifted forward as soon as weather conditions permitted. At first light on 31 May they were joined by their commanding officer and Lieutenant Colonel Rose, accompanied by a Blowpipe detachment which deployed on the feature. From their vantage point on Mount Kent K Company and the men with it could look to the south-east and observe the Royal Marine barracks at Moody Brook 12 miles away, which were believed to be occupied by enemy troops. At Rose's urging, the artillery FOO attached to K Company called down a fire mission from the three light guns of 7 Commando Battery on the barracks.

The remainder of 42 Commando were brought in by Sea Kings of 846 Naval Air Squadron on 31 May. As a result Mount Challenger was also taken and secured, the marines discovering abandoned trenches and equipment littering the ground.

3 PARA had continued its advance eastwards at first light on 30 May, led by D (Patrols) Company, and by that evening had crossed the bridge north of Lower Malo House. Continuing throughout the night, the battalion halted and lay up during the daylight, undetected by enemy in positions on Smoko Mountain to the south. After last light on 31 May it pressed on and, following a close reconnaissance carried out by D (Patrols)

Sergeant Bill Eades leads the marines of 42 Commando as they head off across the Falklands carrying their life support systems – food, ammunition and sleeping bags.

Company, seized the settlement at Estancia House, which lies at the south-eastern tip of Teal Inlet, a short distance north-west of Mount Kent. A Company was deployed on the high ground of Mount Estancia while Major Martin Osborne and C Company took up positions on Mount Vernet. B Company occupied the southern shoulders of the feature.

On 1 June D (Patrols) Company dispatched nine patrols and two sections of sappers from 9 Parachute Squadron RE to carry out 48-hour reconnaissance tasks on Mount Longdon. The following day one of the sapper sections discovered an abandoned enemy position comprising six sangars and seven tents which contained sleeping bags, personal equipment, a quantity of 2-inch mortar bombs and a 3.5-inch rocket launcher. After dark one of the patrols came under fire from an enemy mortar but suffered no casualties.

As 3 PARA established itself around Mount Estancia, it was assisted in the movement of its heavy weapons, equipment and stores by local farmers using tractors, trailers and Land Rovers. A screen of patrols deployed forward found evidence of an enemy company which had withdrawn prior to the battalion's arrival.

Meanwhile 31 May found Headquarters 3 Commando Brigade preparing to move forward from the beachhead. Major General Jeremy Moore and Brigadier Thompson were told that 2 PARA, recovering and reorganising at Goose Green, should be placed under the command of 5 Infantry Brigade which would advance on Port Stanley on a

42 Commando heads for Mount Kent. The lack of helicopters meant that the marines had to carry as much ammunition and food as they could across the Falklands, a distance of approximately 50 miles.

southern axis via Fitzroy and Bluff Cove, some 36 miles east of Goose Green. Initially it had been planned that the brigade would be flown from San Carlos to Goose Green but it soon became apparent that 3 Commando Brigade would need the support of all available helicopter resources – its lines of communication and supply were already extended, it depended entirely on resupply from the beachhead by helicopter, and needed to move its artillery forward with sufficient stocks of ammunition for the next stage of the advance on Stanley. 3 Commando Brigade's BMA would be transferred from Ajax Bay to Teal Inlet as soon as possible but in the meantime there would be no resources to transport 5 Infantry Brigade and so it would have to move on foot.

The leading element of the brigade, the 1st Battalion 7th Duke of Edinburgh's Own Gurkha Rifles (1/7GR), disembarked from *Canberra* in San Carlos Water on 1 June and immediately began the march to Goose Green. On the following day the brigade's other two units, the 2nd Battalion Scots Guards (2SG) and the 1st Battalion Welsh Guards (1WG), also landed at San Carlos.

The 35-strong Mountain & Arctic Warfare Cadre, commanded by Captain Rod Boswell, had initially based itself at San Carlos. Shortly after arriving the MAWC was deployed on an operation instigated by a report from a patrol which had been in OP positions on the route towards Teal Inlet Settlement and Port Stanley since 21 May. The patrol, commanded by Sergeant Chris 'Rocky' Stone, had observed two enemy helicopters approaching its location. To the dismay of the patrol, and those in the brigade headquarters listening to Stone on the radio net, the two aircraft had hovered low near the OP position before lifting off again and heading for Mount Simon. The summit of the feature was covered in cloud and Sergeant Stone thus assumed that troops had been dropped off on its lower slopes or on top of a nearby feature known as the Onion. The possible presence of enemy special forces on the high ground to the right of the approach to Teal Inlet was of major concern to Thompson, who realised that any enemy OPs would be able to report on the movement east by his brigade. The MAWC was instructed to deal with this threat. On 30 May one of the cadre's patrols was moving to Mount Challenger from Evelyn Hill, where it had been observing Teal Inlet Settlement, when its commander, Lieutenant Frazer Haddow, reported helicopters. Shortly afterwards he radioed to say he had seen a group of sixteen troops moving down a valley in the area of a deserted farm called Top Malo House, only 400 yards from his position. Boswell realised that the enemy group posed a serious threat and had to be eliminated swiftly. Ordering Haddow's patrol to maintain its position and continue observing, Boswell proceeded to assemble a small assault force. Atmospheric interference prevented him from contacting some of his other patrols and he had to turn to the men of the MAW Cadre's administrative section, his reserve patrol and his own small headquarters.

Boswell planned to insert his force by helicopter into an area some distance from Top Malo before first light on 31 May. Unfortunately, however, a delay in the arrival of a helicopter from 846 Naval Air Squadron meant he and his men did not take off until an hour after dawn. Flying at only a few feet above the ground, the Sea King moved from San Carlos to an area approximately 1½ miles south-west of Top Malo House. Boswell's force, comprising an assault team and a fire support group, disembarked. Corporal Steve Nicoll said: 'We landed relatively close to the house but had not had an update on the Argentinians since the initial sighting by Haddow's OP. We did not know if the enemy had been reinforced or had left the area altogether. Would they have sentries out? Were there other enemy groups in the area?'

A Royal Navy Sea King helicopter prepares to land on the *QE2*. Two helicopter decks were installed on the luxury liner by engineers from Vospers shipyard. The helidecks – big enough to take a Chinook – covered the ship's swimming pools.

The start chosen by Boswell for the assault was a ridgeline overlooking the house and three wooden outbuildings which comprised the settlement at Top Malo. His seven-man fire support group was armed with 7.62mm L1A1 self-loading rifles, M-16 5.56mm assault rifles, M-79 40mm grenade launchers and 66mm LAWs. On a signal from Boswell – a green miniflare – the marines would open fire with four LAWs, bring heavy automatic fire to bear on all buildings and then launch a further salvo of four LAWs. Corporal Nicoll was a member of the fire support group:

> We hurriedly extended and primed the rockets. Finally, I caught sight of the pale green flare as it arced over the buildings. I was forced to adopt a kneeling position. Taking aim, I lined the foresight up on the wooden outhouse and gently squeezed off the first rocket. I watched in disappointment as it crashed through the flimsy wall and exited at the far end without exploding. Throwing the empty launcher to one side, I snatched the second and concentrated on the main building; being two storeys high, it filled the foresight.

We were no more than 130 yards from the building, and I used a window as an aiming mark, before firing the second rocket. Other men in the group were firing 66mms and one fell short, bouncing off the turf 20 yards from the building before exploding harmlessly. Three other rockets hit the corrugated iron walls of the house and punched a hole through, before exploding inside. After two or three muffled bangs, the entire building erupted in one almighty explosion. The force of the blast sent the roof hurtling skyward and all four exterior walls peeled back like a banana skin. The only part of the house left standing was the brick chimney which refused to collapse into the surrounding debris.

The explosion had been caused by ammunition stored in the building. The Argentinians inside Top Malo House were not ordinary conscripts but members of 601 Company, an Army special forces unit formed at the time of the invasion. While one of its platoons had been deployed on Pebble Island to guard the airstrip and air force detachment there, the remainder of the unit had been deployed on anti-special forces operations, trying to track down and eliminate SAS and SBS patrols, but without success.

Despite the devastating firepower concentrated on the house, the 601 Company detachment came out fighting. Some of them headed for a gully with a stream about 50 yards in front of the building while the remainder made for dead ground forward and to the left of Captain Boswell's fire support group. From these positions they returned fire, one of them hitting an LAW.

The MAWC assault group charged downhill towards the house. As it did so, two of its number, Sergeants Terry Doyle and Chris Stone fell, wounded in the arms and chest respectively. Corporal Tim Holleran went to Sergeant Doyle's aid. The group closed on the house, Sergeant Derek Wilson, armed with an M79, firing 40mm grenades through the windows. The fire support group moved round to its left and began enfilading the enemy's right flank. At that point Corporal Steve Groves was hit in the chest. The Argentinians continued to put up a fierce resistance before eventually beginning to withdraw towards a nearby river.

Captain Boswell led the assault, during which the enemy commander attempted to escape and was killed by two M79 grenades fired by Sergeant Mac McLean and Corporal Barnacle. Shortly afterwards the second-in-command received four hits from Boswell's M-16 assault rifle before succumbing to his wounds. By the end of the action, which lasted only a few minutes, five Argentinians had been killed and seven wounded out of a total of seventeen men.

Boswell's force, together with their prisoners and the enemy dead, were extracted by helicopter to 3 Commando Brigade's headquarters at Teal Inlet Settlement. The wounded from both sides were flown to the main dressing station at Ajax Bay.

Two 601 Company OPs on Mount Simon and a feature called The Baby decided to avoid the same fate as their comrades. They both surrendered, one to 45 Commando at Teal Inlet and the other to 3 PARA.

The enemy OPs threatening 3 Commando Brigade's right flank had now been eliminated and Brigadier Thompson resumed the move east. On the night of 31 May/ 1 June L Company 42 Commando, elements of Support Company 45 Commando, 2 Troop 59 Independent Commando Squadron RE and the remainder of 7 Commando Battery RA were flown forward to Mount Kent. From there L Company, commanded by Captain Wheen, and 2 Troop were deployed to Mount Challenger to dominate the track leading from Fitzroy to Port Stanley. During the following two nights the remainder of 42 Commando was lifted forward to Mount Challenger.

Bad weather caused problems for 3 Commando Brigade on its move east; driving rain, mist and snow made flying conditions difficult. Nevertheless, 3 June saw 79 Commando Battery RA lifted forward to Mount Estancia. An added difficulty was that both Mount Estancia and Mount Challenger were within range of enemy artillery, and in particular three 155mm guns. Any visible movement on skylines or crest by day immediately attracted shell fire. In addition the night bombing raids carried out by an Argentinian Air Force Canberra were becoming increasingly accurate. The restricted availability of helicopters resulted in each commando battery being limited to 100 rounds for each fire mission and as a result counter-battery and harassing fire had to be strictly controlled. On a number of occasions targets could not be engaged.

On 3 June 45 Commando left Teal Inlet and marched to Bluff Cove Peak where it established a patrol base. On the same morning 3 PARA began preparing for a probing attack on Mount Longdon to the east. At 11am Lieutenant Colonel Hew Pike gave his orders at an 'O' group held on the top of Mount Estancia. The battalion would move out that afternoon supported by a fire base comprising the Mortar Platoon, Anti-Tank Platoon, Machine-Gun Platoon and the Scorpions and Scimitars of 4 Troop of the Blues & Royals. During phase one A Company would attack the north-east of Mount Longdon. In phase two C Company would take the western end, with B Company seizing the eastern end. While the 'O' group was in session, reconnaissance patrols of D (Patrols) Company returned with the information that the objective was held by approximately two companies of infantry and an independent platoon located to the north-east of the main feature. These troops were supported by two 81mm medium and two 120mm heavy mortars. In addition the patrols, who had worked their way to within 50 yards of the enemy positions, had also located three machine-gun sites and an administrative area at the base of the eastern end of the objective.

3 PARA began its advance at 4pm and subsequently encountered well-directed enemy artillery fire. At 6.24pm Brigadier Thompson, concerned that the battalion was

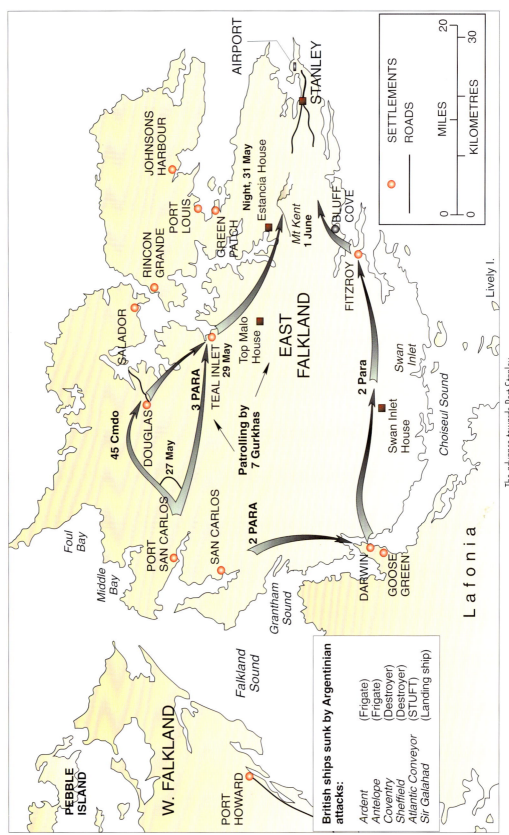

PEBBLE ISLAND

W. FALKLAND

PORT HOWARD

Falkland Sound

Middle Bay

Foul Bay

PORT SAN CARLOS

SAN CARLOS

2 PARA

Grantham Sound

Patrolling by 7 Gurkhas

Top Malo House

EAST FALKLAND

DARWIN

GOOSE GREEN

Swan Inlet House

Swan Inlet

Choiseul Sound

Lafonia

Lively I.

2 Para

FITZROY

BLUFF COVE

Mt Kent 1 June

Estancia House

Night, 31 May

TEAL INLET 29 May

3 PARA

SALADOR

RINCON GRANDE

PORT LOUIS

GREEN PATCH

JOHNSONS HARBOUR

STANLEY

AIRPORT

DOUGLAS

45 Cmdo

27 May

SAN CARLOS

British ships sunk by Argentinian attacks:

Ardent   (Frigate)
Antelope   (Frigate)
Coventry   (Destroyer)
Sheffield   (Destroyer)
Atlantic Conveyor (STUFT)
Sir Galahad   (Landing ship)

SETTLEMENTS
ROADS

MILES

KILOMETRES

0   20

0   30

The advance towards Port Stanley.

moving on too fast and could find itself in a position from which it could not retreat, ordered his men to halt. The battalion took up new positions with A Company forward, some 2 miles west of the Murrell Bridge and just to the north of the track leading from Estancia to Port Stanley; C Company remained on Mount Estancia. A standing patrol was deployed on Mount Vernet while a patrol base was established just west of the Murrell Bridge, from which patrols would carry out tasks on Mount Longdon.

On the night of 4/5 June two of 3 PARA's snipers, Corporal Phillips and Private Absolon, were dispatched to engage targets on the western end of Mount Longdon. In the early hours of 5 June, having worked their way to within 100 yards of the enemy positions, Corporal Phillips shot an Argentinian officer as he left a command bunker. Private Absolon destroyed the bunker itself with well-aimed 66mm LAW. Both then withdrew under fire.

One of D Company's reconnaissance patrols engaged an enemy mortar position and some OPs with artillery fire during the afternoon of 5 June. That night another patrol located two heavy machine-guns, two 82mm mortars and one 120mm heavy mortar. It also discovered a minefield with a frontage of some 550 yards.

On 6 June two patrols under Corporals Brown and Haddon rendezvoused 200 yards north of the Murrell Bridge and observed an enemy patrol crossing the skyline to the east of the river. As the men of 3 PARA watched, two enemy troops checked the bridge before being joined by the others. At that point the patrols opened fire, killing five Argentinians. As the remainder fled, they immediately came under mortar and artillery fire from an enemy base on Mount Tumbledown and were forced to beat a hasty retreat, abandoning their packs and radio but avoiding any casualties. The position was searched two days later by 3 PARA but there was no sign of the equipment.

On the evening of 8 June 3 PARA dispatched three large fighting patrols to Mount Longdon. Each comprised a half-platoon; one was accompanied by a guide from D (Patrols) Company and the other two by Falkland islanders Terry Peck and Vernon Steen. The patrols' mission was to locate suitable approaches to the objective and to test enemy reactions to probing. Unfortunately, however, the combination of a fine night and bright moonlight prevented them from penetrating enemy positions and only six Argentinians and an artillery piece were observed, the latter subsequently being engaged by one of the commando batteries.

While 3 PARA prepared for its operation on Mount Longdon, 2 PARA was once again on the move. Having reorganised and received its long-awaited resupply, the battalion pondered its next move. A Company's commander, Major Dair Farrar-Hockley, was engaged in a conversation with the manager of the Darwin settlement, Brooke Hardcastle, when the latter suggested that the quickest method of discovering the situation further to the east would be to telephone his counterparts at Bluff Cove and Fitzroy. However, the line from Burntside House was down. Major Chris Keeble ordered B Company to dispatch a small force to Swan Inlet to discover if a working telephone could be found there. Lieutenant Clyde Chapman and nine of his men, accompanied by Major John Crosland and 2 PARA's Intelligence Section NCO, Colour Sergeant Morris, took off in three Scout helicopters, accompanied by two more Scouts armed with SS-11 missiles.

Crosland's plan was to approach Swan Inlet at low level from the south. The two armed Scouts would launch their missiles while Crosland and his men, divided into three groups, would clear the settlement buildings. In the event, two of the missiles missed and the third destroyed a building. Crosland and Morris nevertheless succeeded in finding a telephone and made contact with the settlement manager at Fitzroy, Ron Binney, who said there were no Argentinians there. This information was passed to Brigadier Tony Wilson, the commander of 5 Infantry Brigade, who had been ordered to move his men 40 miles from Darwin to Fitzroy. Major Keeble requested the use of the Task Force's single Chinook, which was already in the process of moving Wilson's headquarters from the beachhead to Goose Green. Wilson agreed and that evening, with only two hours left before last light, the aircraft took off. The first lift comprised A Company and detachments of the Mortar and Anti-Tank Platoons which would be flown into Bluff Cove. The second lift involved B Company with Keeble and his 'R' Group to be landed at Fitzroy. Meanwhile Scout helicopters deployed two patrols of C (Patrols) Company into Bluff Cove and two others into Fitzroy to check for Argentinian troops and to mark the LZs for the battalion.

As the battalion moved forward an observation post manned by the MAWC on Smoko Mountain, some way from Mount Kent, saw a Chinook landing troops at Fitzroy. Unaware that a Chinook had survived the attack on *Atlantic Conveyor*, the men passed the message back to brigade headquarters at Teal. The gunners of 29 Commando Battery were in the process of laying on a fire mission using weapons in the Mount Kent area when their commander decided to check with headquarters. After a short delay he was told the Chinook was friendly. A disaster was averted.

That same day, 9 June, Lieutenant Colonel David Chaundler, 2 PARA's new commanding officer, arrived. He joined one of C (Patrols) Company's patrols as it was lifted into Fitzroy, leaving Major Keeble in command of the battalion until its move was complete.

Reconnaissance Platoon commander Lieutenant Colin Connor and his patrol were dropped off in Fitzroy, unaware that they had been inserted in the wrong place. They switched on the strobe beacon which would guide in the Chinook bringing B Company and Major Keeble. On arrival Keeble left B Company near the LZ and then took his

'R' Group and Connor to high ground to establish communications with A Company which he assumed had landed at Bluff Cove. It was only at this point that he and the men with him realised they were 2½ miles from their intended landing place.

Leaving B Company on the high ground, Keeble and his 'R' Group, together with the two C (Patrols) Company units, headed for Fitzroy which they reached without further mishap. There Ron Binney, the settlement manager, confirmed the absence of any Argentinians, although they had apparently attempted to destroy the bridge on the track to Bluff Cove. A check carried out by Connor and his men revealed that it had only been slightly damaged and could be repaired by sappers. The enemy had, however, laid a number of mines on the far side.

On the following day Lieutenant Colonel Chaundler assumed command, and the rest of the battalion was lifted forward to Bluff Cove and Fitzroy. At the same time Brigadier Wilson arrived by helicopter, followed by 29 Field Battery RA and sappers of 9 Parachute Squadron RE who began lifting the mines by the bridge soon afterwards. 5 Infantry Brigade followed during the next few days.

The Welsh Guards initially set off on foot from San Carlos but the going was difficult for the heavily burdened guardsmen, who had been employed on ceremonial duties in London before being embarked for the South Atlantic. They had not had a chance to prepare and were not as physically fit as they could have been. After twelve hours the attempt to march to San Carlos was abandoned and they were ordered to return to the beachhead. It was decided instead to move the battalion, together with the Scots Guards, to Fitzroy by sea. On the evening of 5 June the Scots Guards embarked on *Intrepid* and were 'floated out' of the ship's dock in LCUs to a position off Lively Island. They came ashore the following morning to relieve 2 PARA which was to concentrate at Fitzroy.

In the meantime the Welsh Guards embarked on *Fearless* and sailed to a point close to Fitzroy.* The deteriorating weather, combined with a shortage of landing craft, resulted in only two companies making the rest of the journey to Bluff Cove where they landed on the night of 6 June. The remainder of the battalion sailed for Goose Green where the Prince of Wales's Company, No. 3 Company, the Mortar Platoon and the battalion's Echelon, along with 16 Field Ambulance, were transferred to the LSL *Sir Galahad* which then sailed for Port Pleasant, Fitzroy's anchorage. On arrival the vessel could not use the channel leading to the disembarkation beach and so moved on to Fitzroy where she arrived before first light on 8 June. Already anchored there was

---

* It is worth noting that Port Pleasant is Fitzroy's anchorage and not to be confused with Port Fitzroy near Bluff Cove. The attacks on *Galahad* and *Tristram* took place at Port Pleasant.

A Welsh Guardsman checks his map board as he mans a sentry post. The Welsh Guards arrived in the South Atlantic on the *QE2* and cross-decked to *Canberra* in South Georgia.

her sister vessel *Sir Tristram*, which had arrived the day before bringing 2 PARA's 'B' Echelon and some brigade troops. The Welsh Guards were under orders to rejoin their battalion at Bluff Cove and when it was suggested that they would have to land at Fitzroy and march over 12 miles to reach their destination, their senior officer aboard *Sir Galahad* refused and requested that landing craft be made available.

The Royal Marine officer in command of the landing craft, Major Southby-Tailyour, was horrified when he saw the two LSLs moored at Fitzroy in broad daylight. Sailing out to *Sir Galahad* in a landing craft, he urged the Welsh Guards to disembark as quickly as possible, pointing out the danger from the air threat and emphasising that both the vessel and the men aboard were at great risk. Following a sometimes heated discussion, Southby-Tailyour returned to the shore and made his way to the headquarters of 5 Infantry Brigade, which did not know *Sir Galahad* and the Welsh Guards had arrived. The guardsmen were immediately ordered to disembark with all haste.

In the meantime, however, the commanding officer of 16 Field Ambulance had agreed with the Welsh Guards' senior officer that the field ambulance should disembark first because it had been given the priority task of setting up a field hospital at Fitzroy. When the Guards' turn came, the ramp of the landing craft to which they were to be transferred was jammed in the raised position. Disembarking would have to be carried out over the LSL's side rather than via her bow ramp.

It was too late. The enemy had learned of the LSLs' presence at Fitzroy and had dispatched aircraft to attack them. At 1.10pm an air raid warning was sounded and shortly afterwards two Skyhawks and two Mirages attacked *Sir Galahad* and *Sir Tristram*, both vessels receiving direct hits which set them on fire. All available helicopters were directed to the scene and, despite the danger from exploding ammunition and fuel aboard both vessels, succeeded in evacuating the casualties to 2 PARA's RAP from where, following emergency treatment, they were flown to the main dressing station at Ajax Bay. An hour later enemy aircraft reappeared and attacked Fitzroy. On this occasion, however, they flew into a hail of machine-gun fire which shot down the leading aircraft. A third raid took place later in the day: a landing craft en route to Goose Green was sunk by a Skyhawk on its way to Fitzroy, killing Colour Sergeant Johnstone and his crew.*

That night 2 PARA was transferred back to command of 3 Commando Brigade and on 10 June Lieutenant Colonel Chaundler was briefed by Brigadier Thompson on his battalion's role in the forthcoming assault on Port Stanley. The battalion would be in reserve, advancing on a northern axis and ready to support either 3 PARA, which would assault Mount Longdon, or 45 Commando whose objective would be the feature called Two Sisters.

Chaundler and his company commanders were flown to Mount Kent from where they studied the ground over which the battalion would move during the next phase of operations. The battalion was lifted from Fitzroy to a lying-up area a short distance to the west of Mount Kent and in the rear of 3 Commando Brigade, the redeployment being completed by last light. Chaundler then gave his orders for the following day.

* Colour Sergeant Johnstone's LCU was callsign Foxtrot Four. He had disobeyed orders and sailed in daylight because he judged, correctly, that bringing 5 Infantry Brigade's communications vehicles to Fitzroy was a high priority. Brigadier Thompson recalls this was the second time Johnstone had turned a Nelsonian blind eye to orders. The first was when he was evacuating HMS *Antelope*'s crew and the captain of *Fearless* ordered him to bear off because the frigate was burning fiercely and was about to blow up. Johnstone stayed and continued the rescue. His bravery and disregard for his own safety, and his initiative in getting important vehicles ashore at Fitzroy were marks of his outstanding determination. He was awarded the Queen's Gallantry Medal posthumously.

Above and opposite: Sir Galahad minutes after being hit by Argentinian bombs. The Welsh Guards were in the process of leaving the ship when the attack came. The explosion rippled through the landing ship, killing and maiming soldiers.

In the meantime 45 Commando had taken up a harbour area below Bluff Cove Peak to the south-west of Mount Kent. Lieutenant Colonel Whitehead deployed his Reconnaissance Troop, commanded by Lieutenant Fox, to reconnoitre Two Sisters, the commando's objective in the forthcoming operation. Accompanied by a section of 59 Independent Commando Squadron RE, Fox's patrol succeeded in reaching the western end of the Two Sisters and obtained a considerable amount of information. On the following night Fox and his men carried out a similar task, concealing themselves in a rocky outcrop on the end of the feature from which they were able to plot many of the enemy's positions. They had to take evasive action after being discovered by a force of some twenty enemy. A number of Argentinians were killed, the remainder fleeing the scene while Fox and his men withdrew under covering fire.

Lieutenant Colonel Whitehead established a patrol base on the northern side of Mount Kent. On successive nights thereafter 45 Commando dispatched fighting

patrols to the Two Sisters to carry out harassing operations. One such patrol, of 3 Troop X Company, commanded by Lieutenant Stewart, made its way undetected over 1,000 yards of open ground, killed two sentries, attacked enemy positions on the western slopes of the Two Sisters, killed several Argentinians and withdrew without incurring any casualties.

On 8 June the MAWC was tasked with reconnoitring a triangle formed by the eastern end of the Two Sisters, the eastern side of Mount Harriet, and Mount Tumbledown. Little was known of the area and there were no air photographs available. The task of reporting on enemy strengths and dispositions was given to two patrols commanded by Lieutenant Haddow and Sergeant Des Wassell respectively. Their job was to reconnoitre the north-eastern side of Mount Harriet and then the south-eastern side of the Two Sisters. After last light the two patrols moved from the eastern end of Mount Challenger together with a K Company 45 Commando fighting patrol commanded by Lieutenant Townsend. On reaching the western end of a feature called Goat Ridge, the reconnaissance patrols split from Townsend's men who headed

THE WELSH GUARDS

The youngest of the Foot Guards regiments, the Welsh Guards were raised in 1915 and have seen extensive service during their relatively short history. Since the Second World War there has only been one battalion of the regiment, distinguished by the two groups of five buttons on its scarlet tunics, the green and white plume worn on the left-hand side of its bearskins, and the leek cap badge in its forage caps and berets. Organised along the same lines as a standard infantry unit, the battalion has three rifle companies, the senior of which is the Prince of Wales's Company whose members are all 6 feet or over in height.

As they travelled south the Welsh Guards prepared themselves for combat with daily refreshers on weapons and fitness training. Here soldiers remind themselves about the operation of the heavy machine-gun.

Super Etendard aircraft and Exocet missiles (below) were the principal targets of the operation, along with their pilots, but the Argentinians had reinforced security and were expecting the British to launch a covert attack on the air base at Rio Grande.

A farmer helps Welsh Guardsmen ferry mortar bombs across open ground. The tough terrain meant that only the Royal Marines' (BV202s) tracked CVR-Ts and tractors were able to deal with the conditions.

40 yards away. It ran between Two Sisters and Mount Tumbledown, and was frequently used by the enemy. The patrols were also able to watch the Argentinian positions on the eastern slopes of Mount Harriet and the Two Sisters, as well as those on Mounts Tumbledown and William. Three hours after last light on 9 June the two patrols withdrew and made their way back to Mount Challenger and 42 Commando's Tac HQ before heading for brigade headquarters.

The information brought back by the two patrols completed the intelligence picture Brigadier Thompson needed in order to formulate his plans for the forthcoming operation. That morning he had received a visit from Major General Moore:

General Moore had come forward to 3 Commando Brigade headquarters and told me that he agreed with the plan to weight the attack on the north and west because Division now had intelligence that the Argentinians expected the main attack would come from the south-west and would be 'looking' in that

direction. Longdon would therefore be included in the first phase attacks and the Commando brigade would be reinforced, not by 40 Commando, who I had asked for yet again, but with 2 PARA and the Welsh Guards. The latter would have two companies of 40 Commando under command to replace two of their own companies, who had lost most of their equipment when *Sir Galahad* had been bombed at Fitzroy. Divisional Headquarters was about to issue an operation order which detailed 3 Commando Brigade to carry out Phase One (Harriet, Two Sisters and Longdon); 5 Brigade would capture Tumbledown and William in Phase Two, while 3 Commando Brigade captured Wireless Ridge; finally, in Phase Three, 3 Commando Brigade would capture all the high ground south of Stanley, starting with Sapper Hill.

Immediately after Major General Moore's departure, Thompson issued a warning order to his brigade. On the following day, 10 June, the commanding officers of all his units assembled at his headquarters. In essence, the outline of the operation, to take place on the night of the 11th, was as follows: 3 PARA was tasked with capturing Mount Longdon and would exploit forward on to Wireless Ridge if possible; 45 Commando would meanwhile capture Two Sisters and exploit forward on to Mount Tumbledown if possible; meantime, 42 Commando would capture Mount Harriet and be ready to follow up 45 Commando through Tumbledown on to Mount William. As Thompson made clear, the principal objectives were Mount Longdon, the Two Sisters and Mount Harriet, but he did not wish to place any limits on his men's initiative should the enemy give way with little resistance and opportunities for exploitation forward present themselves.

Following the 'O' group the commanding officers dispersed and returned to their respective units to prepare for the forthcoming operation.

Nine

Operation Mikado

SPECIAL FORCES PLAN TO STRIKE ARGENTINA

Before 3 Commando Brigade's landing at San Carlos on 21 May serious consideration had been given to the idea of carrying the war to the Argentinian mainland.

The Exocet attack on HMS *Sheffield* on 4 May had a devastating effect on the Task Force, and served to reinforce awareness among those aboard its vessels – and at the headquarters in Northwood – of the threat posed by such missiles. There were only three AM-39s left in the Argentinian inventory, but they still posed a very potent threat, in particular to the two aircraft carriers *Invincible* and *Hermes*, the loss of which would spell disaster for the operation to recover the Falkland Islands.

The French government had instituted a ban on exports to Argentina on 7 April. At that time Aerospatiale, the manufacturer of the Exocet, was in the middle of producing fifteen AM-39 missiles for Argentina, five of which had been delivered, for use with the fourteen Super Etendards supplied by Dassault-Breguet. The initial batch of five aircraft and five missiles had been delivered in November 1981 and the aircraft were due to be modified to carry the missile by a team of Aerospatiale technicians. They had been scheduled to arrive in Argentina in mid-April but their visit was cancelled following the French and EEC embargoes. Conversion of the Super Etendard to enable it to carry the Exocet required modification of the wing pylons to accommodate the missile and integration of both the aircraft's and the missile's avionics.

Eight technicians from Dassault-Breguet had accompanied the five aircraft to Argentina in November and were at a naval air base preparing them for commissioning and handing over to the Navy. The information about the five aircraft and five AM-39 Exocets already in the possession of the Argentinians was handed over to the SIS by its French counterpart, the Direction Générale de Sécurité Exteriéure (DGSE), which also provided details of the forty-eight MM-40 (a surface-to-surface version of the Exocet) missiles also ordered by Argentina; sixteen had already been delivered and fitted to four vessels in the Argentinian Navy's surface fleet. The remaining thirty-two were intended for four destroyers and six frigates under construction in West Germany.

All procurement of military equipment in France was handled by the Argentinian Military Commission, headed by a naval intelligence officer named Captain Carlos

Corti and located in Paris in the same building in the Avenue Marceau as the French government's defence aviation sales organisation, the Office Français d'Exportation de Matériel Aéronautique (OFEMA). The DGSE had learned that the Argentinian order had been placed much earlier with Aerospatiale but delivery had been delayed because of a large order for a hundred AM-39s placed by Iraq following the beginning of its war with Iraq in September 1980. This had been part of a huge purchase of arms from France by Saddam Hussein's regime; with a total value of $700 million, it resulted in priority being given to Iraq over all other customers, including Argentina.

Faced with the EEC and French embargoes, despite the fact that they had already paid for the aircraft and missiles, the Argentinians were forced to look elsewhere for an alternative source of supply for the Exocet. Captain Corti turned to the international arms industry and before long was in contact with an American dealer, Marcus Stone, who was offering four AM-39s for sale at the staggering price of just over $6 million dollars per missile – a highly inflated sum for a weapon costing $450,000 from the manufacturer. The Argentinians agreed to pay the price, transferring over $25 million to a bank in the Netherlands, but the deal fell through after it became apparent that no missiles would be forthcoming. However, Corti's telephone conversations with Stone in Los Angeles and other arms dealers elsewhere were being monitored by the French authorities who passed the transcripts to the DGSE. It informed SIS of their contents. At the same time SIS was provided with the details of Corti's telephone number in Paris so that his trans-Atlantic conversations could be monitored directly by GCHQ at Cheltenham.

Among those to whom the Argentinians turned next in their search for Exocets was the government of Peru, which approached the French with a request for an immediate purchase of AM-39s for fitting to its Sea King helicopters. The French soon saw through this ploy and played for time, demanding proof of funds available for the order. Payment for this type of transaction is invariably by letter of credit, which in this instance was supplied by Peru's Banco Central Riserva and supported by a deposit of $200 million provided by the Banco Andino. Investigations by the French revealed that the latter was a subsidiary of the Banco Ambrosiano, the largest bank in Italy, which was headed by a well-known figure in Italian financial circles, Roberto Calvi. The Banco Ambrosiano had collapsed during the previous year and was in the hands of administrators but the Banco Andino had escaped unscathed because of funding provided by two other Italian banks, one of them none other than the Vatican's own bank, the Instituto per di Religione.

The involvement of Calvi in the deal gave the French government the excuse to stall the Peruvians further. At the same time, while the DGSE and SIS continued their investigations into those involved in financing the order, efforts were under way in Britain to take direct measures against the five Super Etendards and the remaining three Exocets in Argentina.

In London the Current Intelligence Group (CIG) of the Joint Intelligence Committee (JIC) viewed the Exocet threat as a matter of priority and was considering how it might be neutralised. The first option was to insert SAS patrols by helicopter or submarine on the Argentinian coast to establish covert OPs. From these posts they could observe the Super Etendard base and provide sufficient warning of the aircraft taking off so that they could be intercepted shortly afterwards by Sea Harriers. The initial problem with this idea was that only three Royal Navy submarines were deployed in the area at that time – *Conqueror*, *Splendid* and *Spartan*. All were large SSNs and not capable of approaching inshore in depths of less than 300 feet. The most suitable boats for clandestine missions of this type were the diesel-powered 'O' class, one of which, HMS *Onyx*, was already en route to the South Atlantic but it would be another three weeks before she arrived in the TEZ. Furthermore, the Harriers were fitted with a radar which had proved to be unreliable over land rather than sea and so could not be guaranteed to intercept.

The CIG turned to a second option: carrying out a bombing raid on the Super Etendards' base. A strike by Sea Harriers was considered initially but ruled out because the aircraft's limited range would mean the Carrier Battle Group having to sail dangerously close to Argentinian shores, and the Harrier's limited payload of three 1,000lb bombs was such that seven aircraft would be required to carry out the attack. Also, the Harrier was the main fixed-wing asset of the Task Force and could not be risked in an operation of this type. A second air approach was then considered: an attack by a Vulcan bomber flying from Ascension Island. A Vulcan had already carried out a raid on Port Stanley airfield on 1 May in an effort to prevent the use of its runway by the Argentinians. Only one of its bombs had apparently hit the target – a failure later blamed on incorrect data fed into the aircraft's computer. In the case of an attack on the Super Etendard base, the bombing would have to be precise enough to hit five aircraft – which in all likelihood would be dispersed and under cover of some sort. This option was also discarded.

The third option was an assault by the SAS who would either be dropped by parachute or via a tactical air landing operation (TALO) from two RAF C-130 transports. Following insertion they would attack and destroy the five Super Etendards modified to carry the Exocet, while also locating and destroying the three missiles, and kill or capture the ten pilots trained to fly them. Thereafter the assault force, comprising a squadron of fifty-five men, would be extracted by the two C-130s.

At this time the commanding officer of 22 SAS, Lieutenant Colonel Michael Rose, together with his small Tac HQ element and D and G Squadrons, was already deployed to the South Atlantic. The regiment's main headquarters, including its intelligence cell, remained at its home base in Hereford and began considering the

various options for an operation to be carried out by B Squadron, the only remaining sabre squadron available, A Squadron being committed to providing the counter-terrorist force during that period.

The primary consideration was the location of the Super Etendards and the 2nd Fighter & Attack Squadron which flew them. There were a number of Argentinian Air Force and Navy bases along the coast and of these only five were considered possible locations. The first and northernmost was Trelew, now home to the Argentinian Air Force's 2nd Bomber Group, equipped with six Canberra bombers, which had been transferred from its home base further north. Next and further south was Comodoro Rivadavia from where Argentinian Air Force C-130 transports were ferrying men and supplies to Port Stanley. Further south still was the third possibility, San Julian, which was the closest to the Falkland Islands and the base of the Air Force's 4th and 6th Fighter Groups. Fourth was Rio Gallegos where the 5th and 8th Fighter Groups were based, along with the Air Force's two KC-130 tankers. Last and most likely was the naval air base at Rio Grande on the island of Tierra del Fuego, which lies off the southernmost tip of Argentina and Chile and is divided almost equally between the two countries. Located on the north-eastern coast of the island, some 50 miles to the east of the border with the Chilean half of the island, Rio Grande accommodated the 6th Fighter Group along with the 3rd Fighter & Attack Squadron. Not only was it relatively near to the TEZ but, as SIS revealed to 22 SAS, there was a great deal of hostility between the Argentinian Air Force and the Navy and thus it was highly unlikely that the latter would use an Air Force base from which to operate its Super Etendards.

With the assistance of the United States, in particular the CIA, Rio Grande was chosen and proved to be correct, the Super Etendards having been deployed there on 21 April. 22 SAS began planning an operation, codenamed Mikado, to attack it. In the absence of Lieutenant Colonel Rose, the regiment's operational planning and intelligence staff were overseen by the Director SAS.

The idea of a parachute insertion was ruled out early on by both 22 SAS and the RAF on the grounds that it would allow any defenders at Rio Grande sufficient time to stand-to and defend the base. As a result the second choice of a night TALO had been selected. The operation would be launched from the US air base at Wideawake on Ascension Island. The two C-130s would fly to Tierra del Fuego, having refuelled in mid-air en route, where they would land under cover of darkness after an approach from the west; the planners calculated that approaching from that direction would reduce the distance at which the aircraft would be detected by radar to 6 miles, giving the defenders just six minutes to react.

After swiftly disembarking from the two aircraft B Squadron would carry out its attack, with 5, 7 and 8 Troops seeking out and destroying the Super Etendards and

When the call came to join the Falklands Task Force, the battalion had just completed a tour of 'spearhead' duty and was in the process of preparing to lay up its old colours before receiving new ones from the Queen. At the same time it was due to provide two guards, each of seventy men, to take part in the Trooping the Colour on Her Majesty's official birthday.

On 12 May the battalion embarked on the *QE2* and sailed for the South Atlantic with other elements of 5 Infantry Brigade. The casualties suffered during the bombing at Fitzroy of the LSL *Sir Galahad* by Argentinian aircraft were a major blow but the battalion recovered and the courage of all ranks showed through when it supported the actions on Mount Tumbledown and Mount William as brigade reserve.

The men of 5 Brigade, including the Welsh Guards, had deployed to the South Atlantic on 12 May aboard the requisitioned liner *QE2*. Richard Spake was working aboard the ship at the time:

> We were heading for the US when we were told that we were turning back for Southampton and were to become a troop ship for the Task Force. Those who didn't want to take part came off and new crew replaced them.
>
> Within hours of being alongside dockyard workers from Vospers started cutting away parts of the ship. The cover on the swimming pools went and within a week we had helicopter decks fitted forward and aft. When the troops came aboard the atmosphere was very relaxed. It was almost a sort of holiday atmosphere, but when we got to Ascension everything changed. It became very serious. Every day the troops had been running around the decks to keep fit. Now they were firing rifles and missiles into the sea as they checked their weapons. When we left Ascension the atmosphere was warlike. Everyone knew they were going ashore and I don't think anyone really knew what to expect. We sailed for South Georgia where our troops were cross-decked to other ships of the Task Force and we took onboard survivors of some of the ships which had been hit.
>
> I remember saying goodbye and good luck to all the senior NCOs of the Welsh Guards who we had become very friendly with. They were excellent and as we shook hands I never thought that many of them might not come back. Sadly many were killed on the *Galahad*.

south and shortly afterwards engaged a enemy heavy-machine-gun position with a Carl Gustav 84mm MAW. The Argentinians responded with vigour, enabling the MAWC patrols to pinpoint their location. Lieutenant Haddow's patrol made its way along the northern side of Goat Ridge while Sergeant Wassell's travelled along the southern face. They then reconnoitred the eastern slopes of Mount Harriet and the Two Sisters, discovering strong enemy positions in both areas.

The two patrols rendezvoused at the eastern end of Goat Ridge before establishing an OP halfway along the ridge. From there they were able to observe a track some

Exocets while 6 Troop made its way to the officers mess and killed all those inside, among them the ten pilots trained to fly the Super Etendards. The squadron would then re-embark on the two C-130s, which would have repositioned themselves ready for take-off with their engines 'burning and turning'. Once airborne, the aircraft would head for the Chilean air base at Punta Arenas on the Chilean mainland, just across the Straits of Estrecho. They would land there before refuelling and returning to Ascension Island, refuelling again en route. However, should the two C-130s be damaged on landing or during the ensuing action, the squadron and both aircrews, having destroyed both aircraft, would withdraw and head 50 miles overland to the Chilean border on the island, seeking sanctuary before being evacuated via Chile itself.

Prior to the operation an SAS reconnaissance patrol of nine men of 6 Troop would be inserted to carry out a close reconnaissance of the objective. Its task was to confirm the presence of the Super Etendards and report on the numbers, dispositions and apparent state of alert of any defending forces. The plan involved the patrol being flown via Ascension Island and parachuted into the sea for a rendezvous with HMS *Hermes*. A Sea King helicopter would then fly them to Tierra del Fuego, approaching the island from the south before entering the Argentinian half from the west and inserting it at a location called Estancia Las Violetas, situated on the coast to the north-west of Rio Grande.

The aircraft would then fly back into the Chilean half of Tierra del Fuego where it would be crash-landed and abandoned, its Royal Navy crew claiming a 'navigational error' behind its sudden appearance on the island. The plan naturally required political approval, not only from the Prime Minister and her War Cabinet, and from the United States from whose air base on Ascension Island the operation would be launched, but also from Chile, whose assistance would be essential. Not only would the Chileans have to give their consent to the helicopter entering their airspace and being crash-landed on their half of Tierra del Fuego and to evacuating the crew, they would also have to provide assistance either through refuelling the two C-130s at Punta Arenas for the return flight to Ascension Island, or by providing sanctuary and ultimately evacuation for B Squadron should it have to exfiltrate on foot.

While approaches were made at the appropriate diplomatic levels, the men of B Squadron were training hard for the operation with two C-130s and their crews. Both aircraft practised low-level approaches at night, in each case landing on blacked-out airfields after a steep descent and halting as soon as possible afterwards to permit the troops aboard them to disembark and go into an immediate assault. On each occasion, however, the airfields reported that they had detected the incoming aircraft on their radar well beforehand.

Initially there was a degree of scepticism within the squadron as to whether political clearance would be given for the operation. When it appeared to be forthcoming, however, this was replaced by a certain amount of caution among the more experienced members and senior NCOs, who began to express serious doubts about the viability of the plan and eventually voiced them to the major.

In the meantime the commander and his reconnaissance patrol were dispatched to Ascension Island and duly made their rendezvous with HMS *Hermes*. Shortly afterwards Brigadier de la Billière received final clearance from the War Cabinet for the insertion of the patrol to proceed and on the night of 17/18 May the men lifted off in a Sea King helicopter of 846 Naval Air Squadron from HMS *Hermes*, escorted by HMS *Brilliant*, and flew west to a point as close as possible to Tierra del Fuego.

The helicopter, flown by Lieutenant Richard Hutchings RM and his co-pilot Lieutenant Alan Bennett, had been stripped of all non-essential equipment in an effort to reduce weight and increase its range. It had also been fitted with explosive charges, so that disposal would be easier. The men were well equipped for their mission: they had Arctic warfare clothing to enable them to cope with freezing temperatures, and satellite communications equipment with which they could make contact with the 22 SAS base at Hereford.

The flight to Tierra del Fuego passed without incident until the helicopter was detected as it approached the island. Hutchings saw his warning receiver indicate that a radar had locked on to his aircraft. Shortly afterwards a flare was observed being fired from the ground in the distance. Hutchings and the SAS commander both agreed that the operation should continue but just as the helicopter landed at Estancia Las Violetas, and the patrol was in the process of disembarking, another flare was observed, this time considerably closer.

Having discussed the situation briefly with the other members of his patrol, the captain decided to abort the operation: the reconnaissance mission had depended upon secrecy and avoidance of detection for its success and both were now in doubt. Accordingly the patrol climbed back aboard the Sea King, which had insufficient fuel to return to the Carrier Battle Group and HMS *Hermes*. It headed west for the Chilean mainland. Having landed the men in a remote area, Hutchings flew on to an area some 10 miles east of Punta Arenas. The operational plan called for the pilot to ditch into the sea and set the charges off in the event of being compromised. But the weather was very poor and the senior pilot was concerned that one mistake could cost a life, so he landed his aircraft on the beach and set it on fire. Then he and the other two members of his crew set off for the town.

Opposite: The Royal Navy Sea King that mounted the operation into Chile left the carrier group and flew off into the sunset. It had extra fuel tanks on board. The aircraft carried the call-sign Victor Charlie. *Inset*: The crew of the Sea King operation wore night vision equipment which enabled them to fly in pitch darkness.

The Sea King helicopter was abandoned in Chile. Its crew returned after addressing a press conference while the SAS team aboard made their way to the British Embassy.

At Hereford, the force commander, realising that the element of surprise had probably been lost, suggested that the alternative method of approach to the target – overland via Chile – should be adopted instead and that a second reconnaissance group should be inserted. Both these proposals were turned down and he was ordered to proceed with the operation. Assembling his squadron, he informed its members that the mission was to go ahead even without the assistance of the 6 Troop reconnaissance patrol. Such was the concern among senior members of the unit that one of them, a much-respected long-serving NCO, was driven to voice his disquiet. His concern was described in detail by Nigel West in his book *The Secret War for the Falklands*:

> How was the squadron to reach the target? Even with half-loads the Hercules aircraft would not have enough fuel to divert to anywhere else so, once over the Argentinian mainland, the SAS would be committed. There would not be enough time to circle and find Rio Grande, and if there was even the slightest error in navigating the first approach, the planes were likely to be shot out of the sky as they came round for a second attempt. The C-130 was renowned for its ability to take punishment and remain airborne, but this surely would be too great a test.

Indeed, if one Hercules was destroyed, which meant the loss of half of the squadron, the other could not abort and would have to carry on. In his judgement this amounted to needless and deliberate sacrifice. The sergeant reinforced his disapproval by withdrawing from the operation and submitting his resignation to the force commander, who was by this time harbouring similar doubts.

Flown to Ascension Island, B Squadron arrived to hear news of the Sea King crash in which twenty members of D and G Squadrons had died while being cross-decked from HMS *Hermes* to *Intrepid*. Shortly afterwards they received a signal announcing that Mikado had been postponed following the discovery of two Argentinian Navy radar picket vessels positioned off the coast to extend radar coverage of the approaches to the air base. Further postponements followed and the operation was eventually cancelled, some members of B Squadron being parachuted into the South Atlantic as reinforcements to replace those who had died in the Sea King crash.

Some of the SAS troops who were to mount the Chile operation were parachuted into the Falklands to meet up with the carrier force. When their operation was cancelled they replaced some of the troopers killed in the Sea King crash earlier in the conflict.

In the event the cancellation of Mikado was fortunate: the Argentinians had indeed guessed that a raid on the base at Rio Grande was afoot. The defence of the base was the responsibility of the 1st Marine Brigade, which had deployed to Tierra del Fuego within a week of the invasion of the Falkland Islands, reinforced by 2,600 Argentinian Navy air arm personnel. The entire force was commanded by the 1st Marine Brigade's commander, Captain Miguel Carlos Pita, who had received extensive training in unconventional warfare in Britain, including courses conducted by SIS at its special school in southern England. Pita was well aware of the capabilities of both the SAS and SBS and had appreciated only too fully that Rio Grande would be a prime target for them. Moreover, since the sinking of HMS *Sheffield*, the Argentinians were well aware that the Exocet was their prime weapon against the British Task Force and thus accorded high priority to the protection of their remaining small stock of missiles.

From 1 May onwards the five Super Etendards were moved from the airbase each night to the nearby town of Rio Grande where they were concealed under the protection of one of Pita's units. Around the base Pita set up two defensive perimeters and sowed minefields covering the ground approaches; areas not covered by mines had dummy minefields laid for the benefit of the US reconnaissance satellites which Pita was sure would be observing his activities. This part of his deception plan was reinforced via local radio with warnings of the presence of mines in those areas. Responsibility for local defence of the base was allocated to the 2nd Battalion of the 1st Marine Brigade which was equipped with a French ground surveillance radar. The 1st Battalion was deployed to the south while the 3rd Battalion, supported by a squadron of twelve armoured cars, was given the role of mobile reserve and positioned 4 miles away, ready to counter any threat.

As the threat of an attack on Rio Grande grew from the beginning of May, the defences were strengthened to incorporate anti-aircraft artillery consisting of an unknown number of Oerlikon 40mm guns, four Rheinmetall 30mm guns and six Bofors 40mm guns

Had Operation Mikado taken place, two C-130 Hercules aircraft would have landed on Tierra del Fuego. British troops were planning to destroy aircraft and kill the pilots living in the officers' mess.

SECRET SUBMARINE RAID

Following the cancellation of the mission to fly special forces troops into mainland Argentina on a search and destroy mission for the remaining Exocet missiles, British commanders opted to put a force ashore from a submarine.

The Exocet attacks that resulted in the sinking of HMS *Sheffield* and the *Atlantic Conveyor* made it clear that at least two French-built AM-39 missiles remained in the Argentinian arsenal. The Director of Special Forces was assigned the task of terminating the remaining missiles, destroying the fighter aircraft which could deliver the weapon and finally killing Argentina's frontline pilots.

The mission, part of the Operation Mikado plan, involved the insertion of twenty-four SAS men from 6 Troop of B Squadron on to the Argentinian mainland from a Royal Navy diesel-powered submarine. Carrying 66mm LAW missiles and explosive charges to destroy the aircraft and the pilots' living quarters, the SAS troops were to land at night. According to one of the SAS soldiers involved in the planned raid, the Navy submarine was to surface 7 miles off the coast and 6 Troop would make their way ashore in Gemini rubber boats which would be inflated on the casing deck of the submarine and loaded with equipment and men.

The soldier was one of the SAS's most experienced men, having seen action at the battle for Mirbat and at the Iranian embassy. He recalls that senior officers were seriously concerned about the possibility that the Argentinians might have procured more Exocets, even though intelligence indicated they hadn't.

> We carried out rehearsals in San Carlos aboard a diesel-powered submarine with advice from the SBS, but it was to be our operation. The objective was to get ashore to the base and then find and destroy the Exocets, the aircraft and the pilots. We carried 66mm rockets and planned to use them against aircraft and buildings.
>
> We were to be dropped off from the submarine several miles offshore at night and then make our way to the coast aboard rubber inflatables. There was a lot of equipment and weapons and the plan left nothing to chance, but we were all confident that we could have carried it through. Earlier ideas to land a Hercules at the Argentinian base were quite frankly suicidal, but this had a good chance of success. However, once the job was done that was it. There was no plan to get us out. We simply had to try to make our way to Chile and link up with our people there.
>
> However, as 6 Troop made their final preparations the Argentinians in the Falklands surrendered and the 'white flags over Stanley' resulted in the submarine raid being aborted.

covering an area of 10 square miles around the airfield. These were reinforced by a Westinghouse radar positioned at Cave Domingo and heavily defended; it had a range of 180 miles and would give early warning of the approach of hostile aircraft.

This was the strength of the opposition that the fifty-five members of B Squadron 22 SAS would have encountered if Operation Mikado had taken place.

Ten

The Push for Stanley

MOUNT LONGDON, TWO SISTERS AND HARRIET

During the first week of June 3 Commando Brigade prepared for the forthcoming operation against enemy positions on Mount Longdon, Two Sisters and Mount Harriet. 3 PARA was flown in by helicopter. The commanding officers of 3 PARA, 42 and 45 Commandos held their 'O' groups, their company commanders doing the same later in the day as they issued orders to their platoon and troop leaders. As last light came, companies, platoons and troops rehearsed their tactics and procedures, checked equipment and weapons and made other preparations for the coming night.

The first attack would be mounted by 3 PARA against Mount Longdon, with 45 and 42 Commandos attacking the Two Sisters and Mount Harriet respectively. Covered with rocks, Mount Longdon was a long feature running from east to west with two summits. It was so narrow that there was only sufficient room for one company to advance along it. Running north-east from the western summit was a spur. To the west of Longdon was a stream flowing north, and to the east lay Wireless Ridge which ran eastwards towards Moody Brook. To the south was Mount Tumbledown.

Enemy forces holding Mount Longdon were reported as comprising only B Company 7th Infantry Regiment and were not expected to cause serious problems for 3 PARA. In fact, 601 Company had also been deployed on Mount Longdon, along with a number of marines equipped with eight .50 heavy machine-guns. Moreover, the enemy was well dug in and supported by three 105mm pack howitzers sited at Moody Brook and a 155mm gun on Sapper Hill near Port Stanley.

Brigadier Thompson's plan required 3 PARA to attack Mount Longdon on 3 Commando Brigade's left flank:

> The battalion had been given an H-hour, the time at which its leading companies cross the start line, of 8.01pm. Because it was dark at about 4pm at that time of year, this should allow the approach to the objective to be made in darkness, but the moon should be up soon after 8pm giving some light for fighting through the objective. The timings for 42 Commando, 8.30pm, and 45 Commando, 9pm, were selected by me for the same reason. I planned that, by allowing three-quarters of the night for fighting through, the objectives

Soldiers of 2 PARA aboard a landing craft during their transit from Fitzroy to Bluff Cove.

would be secure by dawn. In this way, our assaulting troops would not be exposed to the fire of Argentinian machine-guns in the coverless terrain in daylight. Furthermore, it avoided the traditional dawn assault which I thought the Argentinians might expect. I expected that the superior training and quality of our troops would enable them to overcome the opposition in their well-prepared, mountain-top positions.

3 PARA would be directly supported by the 4.5-inch gun of the frigate HMS *Avenger* and the light guns of 79 Commando Battery RA, while 2 Troop 9 Parachute Squadron RE, commanded by Captain Robbie Burns, would provide engineer support. In addition, the battalion's Machine-Gun and Anti-Tank Platoons, with their GPMG SF and Milan missiles, would be grouped in fire support teams under the command of Major Peter Dennison; in the initial phase of the attack these platoons would be

3 PARA platoon and section commanders attend a mass briefing before the attack on Mount Longdon. A homemade model of the feature they were to fight for can be seen on the ground. This was used to give soldiers an idea of the ground they would be taking in the battle ahead.

deployed to a position nicknamed Free Kick, to the west of Mount Longdon, ready to be redeployed as required. Meanwhile the Mortar Platoon would move as part of another group, providing supporting fire where and when the assaulting companies required.

Lieutenant Colonel Hew Pike's plan was for Major Mike Argue's B Company to attack the two summits (nicknamed Fly Half and Full Back) while A Company, under Major David Collett, took the ridge (nicknamed Wing Forward) immediately to the north-east. C Company, commanded by Major Martin Osborne, would remain in reserve. Ammunition resupply and casualty evacuation teams, under Major Roger Patton, would bring up the rear.

After last light 3 PARA moved out of its positions and set off. A Company led the way, followed by the commanding officer and his Tac HQ, who were in turn followed by B and C Companies. Each company was led by guides from D (Patrols) Company. Eventually the battalion came to the Murrell River, which had been spanned earlier by a bridge of ladders constructed by the sappers of 9 Parachute Squadron RE troop. The crossing was slow, each man gingerly making his way over the bridge, and Lieutenant

Lieutenant Colonel Hew Pike, commanding officer of 3 PARA, and Lieutenant Colonel H. Jones, commanding officer of 2 PARA, on the way south.

Colonel Pike urged A Company to speed up. A further delay was caused by elements of Support Company cutting across and disrupting the rifle company columns, with the result that 5 and 6 Platoons became separated from the rest of B Company for approximately 30 minutes. Major Argue then changed the direction of his advance to approach the objective from the west, thus moving well south of the intended route and well to the right of A Company.

Eventually the entire battalion arrived at the start line, having bypassed the intended assembly area on Pike's orders. A and B Companies crossed the start line – a stream running south from Furze Bush Pass – fifteen minutes late. To the east a mist was rising while ahead of the battalion lay Mount Longdon, silhouetted in moonlight which revealed the degree to which the feature dominated the surrounding area. The moonlight, and the ground visibility, caused Major Argue to change his plan slightly. He ordered his platoons to move closer to the rocks to seek cover for subsequent fighting through on the objective. 6 Platoon, under Lieutenant Jonathan Shaw, had been given the task of clearing the southern slopes of Longdon where an enemy command post was known to be located. 4 and 5 Platoons, along with Company Headquarters, would clear the northern slopes.

After crossing the start line 6 Platoon advanced to the south-west corner of Fly Half while 4 and 5 Platoons shook out into extended line, with the latter on the right. Company Headquarters followed behind. All went well as the men crossed the open terrain. As they reached the rocks at the foot of the mountain, 5 Platoon began to file out and upwards into better cover while 4 Platoon remained on the low ground which was not quite dead to the enemy on the feature. At that point, however, the advantage of surprise was lost: Corporal Brian Milne, a section commander in 4 Platoon of B Company, trod on an anti-personnel mine, alerting the enemy. They opened fire on 5 Platoon, which was protected by the rocks. At the same time 6 Platoon also reported contact and heavy machine-gun fire from the southern part of the objective. Lieutenant Mark Cox, commanding 5 Platoon, deployed one of his GPMGs higher up on the rock face and this engaged the enemy position holding up the advance. Meanwhile one of the forward sections put an enemy machine-gun out of action with a 66mm LAW and the platoon's Carl Gustav 84mm MAW. The Argentinians responded by bringing down further fire with a heavy machine-gun sited further east along the ridge.

By this time some of 5 Platoon were on the ridge and they made contact with 6 Platoon to confirm the latter's location. Under covering fire from Lance Corporal Leonard Carver, Privates Gary Juliff, Darren Gough and Dominic Gray attacked an enemy position with a 66mm LAW but it misfired twice. Resorting to grenades they assaulted and cleared the position. At that point they came under fire from enemy snipers positioned to the rear of the platoon but these Argentinians were not dealt with because of the proximity of 6 Platoon.

6 Platoon had in the meantime gained a foothold on the southern side of Fly Half and had advanced for some distance without making contact with the enemy. Then, as the men moved through an unoccupied sangar, snipers opened fire, fatally wounding four members of the platoon in quick succession. Seven enemy troops now opened fire from a position bypassed earlier. Eight more members of the platoon were wounded before the position was cleared. The platoon's position became even more precarious as it strayed into 5 Platoon's field of fire. By this time Lieutenant Shaw was becoming increasingly concerned that any further attempt to advance would result in further casualties and thus, over the radio, he asked Major Argue for permission to regroup and recover his casualties to give them first aid. Argue agreed but informed Shaw of the increasingly serious situation to his front, warning him that he might be called upon to provide assistance for 4 and 5 Platoons.

On the northern half of the objective, meanwhile, 4 Platoon was advancing to the left of 5 Platoon, its right-hand forward section becoming intermingled with the latter's

A member of 3 PARA armed with a general purpose machine-gun (GPMG) during the battle for Mount Longdon. Every member of the platoon carried 200 rounds of link ammunition for the GPMG, adding to the weight of their equipment.

left-hand forward section, which was in ground that was partly dead to the enemy. Both platoons had arrived at an area forward of the summit of Fly Half where the rocky bridges began breaking up and the ground sloped away eastwards. Full Back, the eastern summit of Mount Longdon, could be seen in the distance. At that point both platoons came under fire from what turned out to be the western end of a company defensive position. Their immediate problem was how to deal with the nearest enemy platoon, whose positions were well sited and supported by a recoilless rifle, a heavy machine-gun and at least two GPMGs. In addition, the position contained a number of snipers whose accurate fire indicated they were equipped with image intensifiers.

The commander of 4 Platoon, Lieutenant Andrew Bickerdike, decided to carry out a quick reconnaissance. Accompanied by his platoon sergeant, Ian McKay, and his signaller, he moved forward cautiously but was spotted. Coming under fire, he and his signaller were both wounded, as were Privates Neil Gross, Gordon Parry, Jeffrey Logan and Kempster. Sergeant McKay immediately assumed command of 4 Platoon and decided to attack the heavy machine-gun position which was located in a sangar and protected by several riflemen. Together with the section commanded by Corporal Ian Bailey, Sergeant McKay went forward, but Corporal Bailey and Private Jason Burt were soon seriously wounded. McKay nevertheless continued forward and pressed home the attack on his own, clearing the enemy position with grenades. While doing so he was killed; his body was later found inside a sangar.

Hearing that Lieutenant Bickerdike had been wounded, Major Argue went forward to see the situation for himself. After observing the volume of fire confronting his two forward platoons, he ordered Sergeant Desmond Fuller to take command of 4 Platoon. Fuller found some of the platoon uncommitted and regrouped them. He also acquired a section of 5 Platoon and then began advancing up to and behind the enemy machine-gun position. Unfortunately, he and his men were spotted by the Argentinians, who showered them with grenades, causing a number of severe casualties. However, a section under Corporal Stewart McLaughlin succeeded in reaching the top of the ridge and crawled to within grenade-throwing range of the machine-gun. Several attempts to knock it out with grenades and 66mm LAWs failed, and McLaughlin and his men were forced to withdraw under heavy fire.

At this point Major Argue decided to withdraw his platoons and call for artillery support because it seemed there was little more that B Company could do to deal with such heavy opposition. Fortunately, the naval gunfire support officer from 148 Commando Forward Observation Battery RA, Captain Willie McCracken, had already laid the guns of 79 Commando Battery RA on Full Back and after Corporal Milne stepped on the mine Argue had called for fire on the target. Since then shells had been falling steadily on the feature, hitting the areas suspected of concealing enemy positions and falling only 50 yards in front of 4 and 5 Platoons as they withdrew.

Above: 3 PARA wounded being evacuated from Mount Longdon. The intense firefight of the battle prevented some soldiers from being treated until the assault was over. *Below*: Paratroopers being evacuated by Scout helicopters from Mount Longdon. They were taken to the hospital at Ajax Bay manned by commando and airborne medics.

79 Commando Battery then brought down fire on the enemy to the front of B Company, bombarding the heavy machine-gun position and others further to the east. Meanwhile HMS *Avenger* also brought down fire with her 4.5-inch gun, as did the Machine-Gun Platoon with its GPMG (SF).

4 and 5 Platoons were now amalgamated into a composite force under Lieutenant Mark Cox and were given the task of carrying out a left-flanking attack on the heavy machine-gun position. Accompanied by Major Argue, they moved off the ridge to the north and headed for their objective, pausing for supporting fire to begin from 79 Commando Battery, the battalion's mortars and the Machine-Gun Platoon, and then continuing the advance as Captain McCracken lifted the artillery fire and adjusted it to the east.

Suddenly, at a range of only some 30 yards, the enemy opened fire, killing Private Stewart Burt and wounding Lance Corporal Carver. Further casualties were avoided because much of the fire passed over and along the line of march. On an order from Argue, Captain McCracken fired a 66mm LAW from the rear of the platoon to indicate the enemy position. However, Lieutenant Cox remained uncertain of its exact location and ordered his rear section to throw grenades so that he could extricate himself and his signaller. Withdrawing to a position from which they could observe the enemy, who had ceased firing, he and one of his men fired two 66mm LAWs before charging the position and clearing it. Three Argentinians were found dead inside, and it was assumed that they had moved off the ridge to seek shelter from the shelling.

The advance now continued and, after breaking cover near where 4 Platoon had previously come under fire, 5 Platoon was attacked from two flanks. Major Argue decided to move back up on to the ridge and then round behind the enemy but as the platoon attempted to do so, the Argentinians opened fire again and wounded three men. Almost immediately 5 Platoon was subjected to a heavy bombardment by enemy artillery; one man was killed and four wounded.

In the meantime Lieutenant Colonel Hew Pike had joined B Company:

> By now I had got forward with my signaller, Lance Corporal Alan 'Jock' Begg, to the forward groups of B Company and had linked up with Major Argue. The company had been seriously reduced in strength, but was firmly in possession of the western end of the mountain, Fly Half. Every attempt to make further progress by outflanking was now being beaten back, with growing loss. It was at about this time, too, that we got news on the brigade net of enemy Huey helicopters taking off from Stanley and heading our way – perhaps some kind of counter-attack. But this seemed unlikely to make things any more difficult than they already were, and, in the event, the helicopters never arrived.
>
> It was clear to me that I must use A Company, now closer than C, to take the fight through to Full Back and to maintain the pressure of the attack. I reported

all this to the Brigadier as I crouched next to three bayoneted enemy corpses, telling him of our situation, but leaving him in no doubt that we would succeed in the end. There were, however, moments when I wondered, almost desperately, what more we had to do to force the Argentinians to give up the fight: positions thought to have been suppressed burst into life again with fire as heavy as ever. There was only one thing to do, of course – to battle on until the will of the enemy was totally broken.

Pike decided to move A Company through to take Full Back by first light. He was informed by the battalion headquarters command post that there would be reinforcements at daybreak in the form of 2 PARA which would reinforce the northern flank. A patrol from D (Patrols) Company was dispatched to rendezvous with 2 PARA and guide them up and through C Company.

Having crossed its start line, A Company had pushed on as the battle on Mount Longdon began. However, as it came out of dead ground and broke the top of the ridge, it came under fire from the eastern end of Longdon. It then moved forward to a series of peat banks but the enemy's fire grew heavier. 1 Platoon, commanded by Lieutenant Ian Moore, was in a good covered position along a peat bank, and soon spotted some enemy snipers which were engaged by Private Stephen Evans of No. 2 Section and the GPMG gunner of No. 3, Private Edward Dennis. 2 Platoon, under 2nd Lieutenant John Kearton, enjoyed less cover from only one small peat bank. During the first few minutes Private Timothy Jenkins was shot in the head and killed. The platoon succeeded in identifying some enemy positions and engaged them with its GPMGs but had to cease fire because it was endangering B Company. A Company was now under increasingly heavy and accurate fire. Initially the enemy artillery had concentrated on its DF tasks but then began to adjust its fire. Private Brebner, of No. 1 Section in 3 Platoon, was hit in the leg by shrapnel and was evacuated to the rear after being given first aid.

Unable to advance any further over the open ground without incurring heavy casualties from the machine-guns and snipers on the high ground above, the company was pulled back and ordered to move round the western end of Mount Longdon to come up behind B Company. It would then move through B Company to take Full Back. 2 Platoon moved up into the rocks while 1 Platoon halted at the base of the feature. 3 Platoon and the Company Headquarters Support Group, under Captain Adrian Freer, came under fire and were forced to take cover before they reached the main feature. Meanwhile Major David Collett, accompanied by Sergeant Malcolm French, had gone forward to B Company's position for a briefing from Lieutenant Colonel Pike and to carry out a quick reconnaissance. Shortly afterwards A Company moved forward by platoons and took up positions under cover among rocks on the northern slope, ready to advance.

It was obvious now that any attempt to outflank the northern side of the feature would only incur further losses, so the Company Headquarters Support Group moved forward to site its two GPMGs so that they could provide covering fire for the advance eastwards along the ridge. The FOO attached to A Company, Lieutenant John Lee, began bringing down fire on the enemy positions. As soon as the first shells began to fall – joined by fire from the GPMGs – No. 2 Section of 1 Platoon, led by Corporal Sturge, advanced over the ridge and began working its way forward, the lack of cover restricting all movement to crawling. Behind No. 2 Section came 2nd Lieutenant Ian Moore, followed by Corporal Lawrence Bland and No. 1 Section.

Progress was slow: B Company's earlier experiences had highlighted the importance of systematically clearing all enemy positions to minimise the threat of sniping from the rear. Moreover, the fire directed at 2 Platoon and the Company Headquarters Support Group was heavy and accurate. In spite of the covering fire from two GPMGs, the artillery and the Machine-Gun Platoon's GPMGs (SF), the leading section of 2 Platoon was forced to use all its grenades and 66mm LAWs and those belonging to the following section to clear positions as it moved forward.

As the last members of No. 3 Section of 1 Platoon crossed the ridge, some Argentinians were seen beginning to withdraw. Supporting fire had to be lifted as 1 Platoon followed 2 Platoon over the crest because it would otherwise have posed a threat to them. The two platoons then proceeded to clear numerous positions with fixed bayonets, 1 Platoon taking the southern slopes and 2 Platoon the northern. During the British advance more enemy troops were engaged as they withdrew towards positions to the east. Once Full Back had been secured, 3 Platoon moved forward to take over and hold the extreme eastern end of Mount Longdon, which consisted of a long narrow forward slope running towards Wireless Ridge.

The work of the Support Company fire support base had played a crucial role during the attack. Commanded by Major Peter Dennison, it comprised two elements: a manpack group and a vehicle-borne group. The former, led by Dennison and divided into four fire support teams, consisted of six GPMG (SF) detachments of the Machine-Gun Platoon with eighteen ammunition carriers (each with 600 rounds of 7.62mm linked ball ammunition), five Milan firing posts of the Anti-Tank Platoon with fifteen missiles, and a group of medics from the Regimental Aid Post (RAP). The vehicle-borne group, under Major Roger Patton, the second-in-command of 3 PARA, comprised the Mortar Platoon, a resupply of Milan missiles and GPMG ammunition, the remainder of the RAP, a Blowpipe air defence section, and 2 Troop 9 Parachute Squadron RE less its reconnaissance sections which were attached to the rifle companies. While the manpack group accompanied the battalion, the vehicle-borne group remained to the north of Mount Kent – it would advance when Two Sisters had been taken by 45 Commando.

As B Company started taking casualties, one of the fire support teams, commanded by Colour Sergeant Stephen Knights, moved to the western end of Mount Longdon with the RAP group and some stretcher-bearers. Dennison's team, accompanied by Sergeant Graham Colbeck's men, followed soon afterwards with the remainder of the stretcher-bearers. Knights's team joined 6 Platoon on the ridge dominating the western end of the objective and engaged some snipers firing from the centre of the ridge. In the meantime Captain Anthony Mason's team supported A Company's assault by firing two Milan missiles at enemy positions. Colbeck's men now helped 6 Platoon engage snipers on the forward slopes, while others were attacked by Knights's team with 66mm LAWs, Carl Gustav 84mm MAWs, GPMG (SF) and ultimately with Milan.

At this point Lieutenant Colonel Pike instructed Major Dennison to reform the fire support base. Major Patton's vehicle-borne group had been ordered forward and was crossing the Murrell Bridge and moving through 45 Commando's start line. On arriving at 3 PARA's start line, the Mortar Platoon bedded in its baseplates and began providing support for A and B Companies. Meanwhile the manpack group gave supporting fire for A Company's attack, during which an enemy recoilless rifle fired a round along the ridge, killing Private Peter John Heddicker and wounding Corporal Keith McCarthy, Lance Corporal Gary Cripps and Privates Philip West and Clive Sinclair. McCarthy and West died before they could be evacuated for medical treatment.

It was during this final stage of the battle that the enemy artillery brought down fire on the eastern end of Mount Longdon while A Company was reorganising. Throughout the shelling the already exhausted stretcher-bearers continued to recover and evacuate the wounded.

Lieutenant Colonel Pike vividly described the scene on Mount Longdon at the end of the battle:

> The misty scene as dawn broke will perhaps be the most haunting memory of this long, cold fight. The debris of battles was scattered along the length of the mountain, encountered round every turn in the rocks, in every gully. Weapons, clothing, rations, blankets, boots, tents, ammunition, sleeping bags, blood-soaked medical dressings, web equipment, packs – all abandoned, along with the 105mm recoilless rifles, 120mm mortars and .50 Brownings that had given us so much trouble during darkness. The enemy dead lay everywhere, victims of shell, bullet and bayonet. The sour odour of death lingered in the nostrils long after many of these corpses had been buried, for this was a slow job, which eventually had to be abandoned when their artillery and mortars started again. The enemy bunkers provided an Aladdin's Cave of Camel cigarettes, bottles of brandy, huge cakes of solid cheese and, of course, bully beef! Standing amongst the shell holes and shambles of battle watching the determined, triumphant but

Daybreak after the battle for Mount Longdon.

shocked, saddened faces of those who had lost their friends on this mountain, the Iron Duke's comment was never more apt 'There is nothing half so melancholy as a battle won . . . unless it be a battle lost!'

And then – more artillery – and once again the urgent cry from down a re-entrant, 'Medic!' . . . Yes, we had all lost friends, and the battalion some of its finest, most devoted soldiers.

The battle of Mount Longdon cost 3 PARA twenty-three killed and forty-seven wounded. Between then and the afternoon of 14 June, when it would head east for Stanley, it suffered six more killed and several more wounded. Enemy casualties amounted to over fifty killed, ten wounded and forty taken prisoner. In addition, two 120mm mortars, fifty FN rifles, several GPMGs and heavy machine-guns, a recoilless rifle and a Soviet-manufactured SA-7 Grail shoulder-fired SAM were among the weapons captured by the battalion.

While the battalion was fighting hard on Mount Longdon, 45 Commando was likewise heavily engaged on Two Sisters in the central part of 3 Commando Brigade's three-pronged attack. The feature comprises two peaks and five ridges. The north-eastern peak has a 500-yard spinal ridge along its crest and another of approximately equal length to the east. The slightly taller south-western peak has three ridges running east to west in a line over a total distance of some 1,500 yards. The entire feature is protected by rock runs and the main approach, a 250-yard climb from the valley below, could easily be covered by fire.

Enemy forces on Two Sisters comprised B Company 6th Infantry Regiment and the reinforced C Company 4th Infantry Regiment. Lieutenant Colonel Andrew Whitehead's plan was for X Company to attack the south-western peak and its three ridges, nicknamed Long Toenail, at 9pm on 11 June. Two hours later Z Company would begin its assault on the western ridge and the north-eastern peak, nicknamed Summer Days, while Y Company did the same on the eastern ridge. The attack was to be a silent one with fire support, in the form of artillery and mortars, on call but not to be used until the enemy had opened fire. The commando's Anti-Tank Troop armed with Carl Gustav 84mm MAWs and GPMGs would be attached to X Company to provide supporting fire for its attack and thereafter for the other two companies. The company had also been resupplied with Milan missiles and 66mm LAWs.

The commando, less X Company, left its positions between Bluff Cove Peak and Mount Kent at 10am on 11 June and marched to an assembly area north of Mount Kent. At 5pm, following last light, X Company, commanded by Captain Ian Gardiner, set off to the east, crossing over the saddle between Mount Kent and Mount Challenger, heading for its start line which was along a stream flowing due north from Wall Mountain to the Murrell Bridge. Whitehead's intention was that X Company's attack on Long Toenail would divert the enemy's attention as the remainder of the commando approached its objective.

X Company's approach march to its start line took almost double the allotted time of three hours. The terrain was difficult for the heavily burdened marines, especially those carrying the GPMGs and Carl Gustav and 66mm LAWs. One man fell down a cliff and was knocked unconscious; resuscitated by the company second-in-command, he continued the march. By the time the company reached its forming-up place (FUP), it was 2¼ hours behind schedule. Despite the order imposing radio silence, Captain Gardiner contacted Whitehead on the radio and advised him that he had been badly delayed. By this time the rest of 45 Commando was on its start line 800 yards south-east of the Murrell Bridge. Lieutenant Colonel Whitehead later recalled:

> As we arrived at our start line at 0255 hours, I was in an agony of uncertainty about the progress of X-Ray's attack. I did not want to run out of darkness for the second and bigger assault, but I had to be certain that X-Ray was secure before I launched Yankee and Zulu. Fortunately for me, the X-Ray Company commander disobeyed the rules on radio silence to inform me that he had been badly delayed negotiating the rocky terrain towards his objective. Down in our position, 2km away, I allowed the time for H-hour Phase 2 to come and go,

knowing that I must wait until I was sure that X-Ray was well on the way to capturing its objective. As we waited, lying among the rocks, an Argentinian artillery bombardment came down about 100 metres ahead of us. Had we started our attack on time, we would have been right in the middle of it.

By 3.50am Whitehead could delay his main attack no longer and gave the order for Y and Z Companies to advance. Moving in extended formation across the difficult terrain, which was interspersed with bogs, rock and the ever-present grass tussocks, the two companies succeeded in advancing unnoticed. At this point Whitehead told his men to halt and take cover while they waited for X Company to launch its attack on Long Toenail.

X Company had set off from its start line with 1 Troop, commanded by Lieutenant Kelly, in the lead and headed for its objective which was the western third of the spinal ridge on Long Toenail. On 1 Troop's left, and moving parallel to it 200 yards to the north, was a fire support section under the company sergeant major. It was armed with seven light machine-guns (LMGs) and a quantity of 66mm LAWs. Having reached his objective, Kelly informed Captain Gardiner that it was unoccupied and shortly afterwards the latter dispatched 3 Troop, under Lieutenant Stewart, which moved through 1 Troop. It also found its objective clear and having obtained permission to exploit forward, continued its advance. Approximately halfway up the 1,500-yard feature, however, it encountered two machine-guns, one a .50 HMG, which opened fire. This attracted an attack from a number of other positions on the right of the spinal ridge, so Lieutenant Stewart led his troop up the left side, only to come under fire from Summer Days, the north-eastern peak.

Gardiner pulled 3 Troop back under covering fire from the Anti-Tank Troop's GPMGs and Garl Gustav MAWs. He then called for fire from 45 Commando's Mortar Troop to support 2 Troop, under command of Lieutenant Caroe, as it began its advance up the feature. Unfortunately, however, the ground was so soft that after only a few rounds, the mortars' baseplates and the lower half of their barrels had sunk below ground level – they could not continue firing. To make matters worse, no artillery cover was available because the supporting battery was already fully committed to firing on other targets. Nevertheless, 2 Troop advanced on its objective, clambering up the hill towards the enemy positions. Working their way between the rocks, some of which were the size of houses, the men fought their way to the top, but were forced off shortly afterwards by enemy artillery. Undaunted, Caroe and his men fought their way back on to the ridge and secured it, killing several enemy machine-gunners in the process.

Meanwhile Y and Z Companies had also joined battle with the enemy. They remained unseen as the commander of Z Company's 8 Troop, Lieutenant Dytor, crawled forward following a report from one of his section commanders, Corporal Hunt, that he had observed enemy on the skyline above them through his individual weapon sight. Dytor and Hunt succeeded in pinpointing several positions, one of which was occupied by a .50 heavy machine-gun. Just as Dytor had dispatched his troop sergeant to inform Z Company's commander, Captain Cole, the Argentinians became suspicious and threw a flare on to the ground in front of the company's leading troops. 8 Troop opened fire, the enemy responding with rifles, GPMGs and heavy machine-guns, although most of the fire whistled harmlessly over the heads of Y and Z companies who were prone on the ground.

As the artillery FOO called for fire on the pre-registered targets on the western end of Z Company's objective, enemy 60mm light mortars began bringing down shells on the rear of Z Company, causing casualties among members of 9 Troop. At that point Lieutenant Dytor led 8 Troop forward, skirmishing into dead ground where he and his men were out of the line of fire. When the mortar fire controller (MFC) called for shelling, Captain Cole ordered 7 Troop, commanded by Lieutenant Mansell, to advance. As Z Company advanced, it brought to bear the full firepower of its GPMGs, 66mm LAWs and Carl Gustav 84mm MAWs.

Meanwhile to the right Y Company had remained prone in its position, unable to advance without becoming entangled with Z Company and prevented from providing supporting fire because of the terrain. It was subjected to fire by enemy mortars and sustained several casualties. Lieutenant Colonel Whitehead, who was moving on Z Company's right, now ordered Y Company to move up alongside him. No sooner had it done so than one of its 84mm MAW teams engaged and knocked out at least one heavy machine-gun position.

8 Troop then charged the crest of the objective, clearing Argentinian positions as it did so. Reaching the ridge the men came under fire from a machine-gun to the south and responded until told to cease for fear of firing towards X Company on its objective. Acting on an order from the commanding officer, who was by this time well forward, Lieutenant Dytor then led his troop to clear the southern side of Z Company's objective. Skirmishing forward, taking with it a captured heavy machine-gun, the troop continued clearing enemy positions until it reached the limit of the objective. 7 Troop did the same on the northern side while 9 Troop, weakened by casualties from mortar and artillery fire, remained in reserve.

Y Company was now advancing along the southern side of the eastern spinal ridge. At the eastern end it encountered some opposition from a machine-gun position but this was quickly dealt with by an accurately placed 66mm LAW rocket. Major Davis then dispatched a section, commanded by Corporal Siddall, to reconnoitre a suspected mortar position 500 yards east of the ridge; no mortar was found but the section did come upon four enemy, one of whom was killed and the other three taken prisoner. By now 45 Commando had taken its objective but, as it reorganised, enemy 155mm guns began shelling Two Sisters, forcing the marines to take cover among the rocks.

Dawn on 12 June saw patrols clearing Two Sisters and bringing in a number of prisoners. Earlier, at 4.30am, Whitehead had reported to Brigadier Thompson by radio, informing him that the feature had been captured and that he was preparing to move forward on to Mount Tumbledown. Thompson, however, ordered him to 'go firm':

> There were several reasons for making this decision. By the time 45 Commando had reorganised for the next attack, daylight would be only two or so hours off and it would take the remaining hours of darkness to cover the 5,000 metres from the Two Sisters to Tumbledown via Goat Ridge, the best route. Daylight would find the Commando starting its attack over open ground against a well prepared position where the heavy machine-guns would inflict many casualties. In any case, 42 Commando had not yet secured Goat Ridge, a prerequisite to 45 Commando moving on to Tumbledown. Finally, the 105 gun batteries were running low on ammunition and no naval gunfire support would be available in daylight. Indeed, HMS *Glamorgan*, who had bravely remained later than ordered to support 45 Commando, had paid the penalty for overstaying the time – she was hit by a land-based Exocet missile when she cut across the Exocet danger area in a bid to get away to the east before daylight. An attempt at Tumbledown, in daylight and without proper support, would be unnecessarily expensive in casualties.

The battle for the Two Sisters had cost 45 Commando four killed and eight wounded. The most serious losses, however, were sustained by HMS *Glamorgan* which had been providing naval gunfire support for 45 Commando. At 2.35am the destroyer had broken off its bombardment of enemy positions on Two Sisters and had headed out to sea to rejoin the Carrier Battle Group. As she did so a shore-based missile battery equipped with Exocets launched an attack on the vessel which was then at a range of 18 miles. Initially those on board the destroyer thought they were under fire from a 155mm gun but seconds later realised that a missile was approaching them. *Glamorgan* immediately turned herself stern-on to reduce her profile while chaff was fired and a Sea Cat SAM launched. Unfortunately, these measures proved ineffective and the missile struck the destroyer on her upper deck abreast of her helicopter hangar, penetrating into the galley below. It exploded in a massive ball of flame. The ship's Wessex helicopter then blew up, killing six of the nine men in the hangar at the time. A total of thirteen men were killed and many more wounded, some of them severely burned as a result of the attack.

During the next 2½ hours *Glamorgan*'s damage control parties fought the fires. Despite having two engines out of action, she was able to steam to a rendezvous with the heavy repair vessel *Stena Seaspread* which carried out the work essential to enable *Glamorgan* to sail for Britain and Portsmouth.

On the right of 3 Commando Brigade, 42 Commando, commanded by Lieutenant Colonel Nick Vaux, had been engaged in capturing its objective, Mount Harriet.

Rising some 975 feet above the plateau skirting Harriet Sound, the mountain was the southernmost feature dominating Port Stanley and was separated from Mount Challenger by a rocky chasm. Straddling this was a feature called Wall Mountain, which comprised a number of crags occupied by a group of FOOs, NGSOs and FACs who directed harassing fire on Argentinian positions. Around the base of Mount Harriet ran the track linking Stanley with Goose Green. The Argentinian forces on Mount Harriet were reported as comprising the 4th Infantry Regiment, less its C Company on Two Sisters. This force consisted of two up-to-strength rifle companies, a reconnaissance platoon, a platoon of 120mm heavy mortars, the regimental headquarters and an administrative element.

Prior to mounting its operation, 42 Commando had carried out a number of close reconnaissance patrols in the area, as Lieutenant Colonel Vaux described:

By now I knew that a frontal assault would be suicidal because this was clearly what the Argentinians expected. Apart from minefields, heavy machine-guns covered the forward slopes of Mount Harriet and the track below. To the south, the ground was ominously open, so 'right flanking' did not appear particularly feasible either.

North, towards Two Sisters, seemed to offer a covered approach around Goat Ridge, but 45 Commando's objective was Two Sisters and we might be dangerously restricted with two major units manoeuvring in the dark. Something original was clearly called for, so we decided to see if the enemy could be surprised from the rear.

Led by the resourceful Sergeant Collins of K Company, a patrol moved out one night to seek a route looping south across the plateau, then approaching the enemy from behind. Not long after crossing the track, however, they hit an unmarked minefield and Marine Patterson lost a leg. A light helicopter, flown by Captain Nick Pounds RM, surmounted appalling weather to meet the patrol back at the track and Patterson lived to tell his tale.

In the meantime Sergeant Collins resolutely continued with his task until his small group suddenly observed a large Argentinian patrol approaching from Mount Harriet. He and his men quickly went to ground in a water-filled depression, causing the enemy to seek cover as well. It was a desperate situation as Collins' patrol was heavily outnumbered and totally unsupported. He recognised, however, that his men's training and discipline might prevail in this 'Mexican stand-off' and he was absolutely right. An hour or so later, the disgruntled enemy succumbed to cold and impatience by withdrawing back to

SERGEANT GEORGE HUNT MM

On Two Sisters mountain Sergeant George Hunt's action saved many marines from injury or even death. Despite being seriously wounded himself, George, then a corporal, continued to lead his men until the battle was over. Just 50 yards from Argentinian trenches he directed fire against a machine-gun post and relayed vital information to his company commander as the ground around was pickled with enemy fire.

George was the point man in the first section of Zulu Company to take part in 45's assault. The Argentinians were heavily dug in and the marines had planned to get as close to their positions as possible before launching a surprise attack. As he led his men through a minefield, marking the way for others, George fell into a bog and was soaked from head to foot. He recalls: 'We had no spare kit on us and all I could think was that I would be freezing cold. The fact that I might be killed didn't enter my head.'

With bayonets fixed the marines advanced still closer to the enemy, stopping every few yards to scan the Argentinian positions through night sights. Suddenly a diversion attack began. Shaken by the close battle the Argentinians started firing down the mountain. Now within sight of the enemy George noted their positions and radioed them back to companies following on behind in the main commando attack.

The steep rocky terrain of Two Sisters gave the advantage to the Argentinians, and as the battle began George launched an attack on a machine-gun post. A section nearby was hit and two Marines were killed instantly. As George and his men went forward he was blinded by the flash of an explosion. His left arm was shattered, but despite the pain he got up and led his men in an assault – using his damaged limb to support his rifle as he returned fire. For the next two hours he fought with total disregard for his own safety and only stopped for treatment when the battle was over and Two Sisters was completely controlled by 45 Commando. After the Falklands War George trained as a helicopter pilot and served at Yeovilton with the Commando Air Squadron. He later recalled:

> There was a lot of heavy fire. I can remember the drone of the Browning machine-gun beating at us all the time. But you don't have time to think. The young guys in my section were brilliant. They worked really hard and it paid off in the end.
>
> I remember a flash and the shrapnel ripped into my arm, but the training took over and I simply moved forward using the skills I had learnt. When the Argentinians realised we were not going to stop until we had Two Sisters they started to run away – there was a lot of dead bodies.

He was awarded the Military Medal.

After Two Sisters 45 Commando moved towards Sapper Hill before getting the signal to move into Stanley. They later returned home aboard the *Stromness* and the *Canberra*. The names of those who died in the Falklands during 45's operations are carved in stone at the entrance to the group's base at Arbroath in Scotland.

Royal Marines of 42 Commando yomp across the Falklands carrying with them everything that they had loaded on to ships back in the UK.

their positions. These were all plotted by the patrol incidentally, and savagely shelled by our guns the next day. The following night, with an outstanding display of courage and determination for which he was subsequently awarded the Military Medal, Sergeant Collins finally established a route to the south which led to the fence east of Mount Harriet that we had earmarked as our start line.

However, Vaux was concerned about the open terrain which would have to be crossed by his commando, possibly in full moonlight. He obtained agreement from Brigadier Thompson that, unlike 3 PARA and 45 Commando, 42 Commando could make use of diversionary fire if necessary. In order to accustom the Argentinians to this, he instituted a programme of harassing artillery and mortar fire each night prior to the operation. At the same time he dispatched fighting patrols to probe the enemy positions and goad them into betraying their locations by opening fire. This allowed 42 Commando to pinpoint the positions that posed the greatest threat and plan pre-emptive strikes using the Anti-Tank Troop's Milan missiles. The targets were illuminated by the Mortar Troop with parachute bombs.

Mortars were vital in providing protection for units and where possible teams and their baseplates were flown ahead. Here 42 Commando's Mortar Troop loads aboard a Wessex.

By now Vaux had produced his plan for the attack. K and L Companies would march south from the western end of Wall Mountain, cross over a track leading from Fitzroy to Port Stanley and then head south-east until they reached a location 1,000 yards to the south of the track. From there they would turn north-east and cross the track again to an FUP on the south-east shoulder of Mount Harriet. From the start line, which was along the line of the fence running north-east of the track, K Company would attack the eastern end of Mount Harriet, nicknamed Zoya. It would be followed an hour later by L Company which would seize the western end of the feature. Once Zoya had been secured, K Company would then take Goat Ridge, nicknamed Katrina. J Company, which would be in reserve, would create a diversion on Mount Challenger with the aim of drawing the enemy's attention from K and L Companies as they made their outflanking move. As a further distraction the Argentinians would be shelled for an hour before H-hour.

On the morning of 11 June J Company took up its positions on the eastern slopes of Wall Mountain while the rest of the commando made its way to the assembly area at the western end of the feature. Tac HQ took up a position among the crags at the eastern end of Wall Mountain, nicknamed Tara.

As last light approached, K and L Companies – each led by guides from the Reconnaissance Troop and accompanied by FOO parties, sappers, medics, signallers and snipers – began to move from Mount Challenger to the assembly area. An hour after last light they began their flanking move. Not long afterwards, however, enemy artillery brought down fire on the Mortar Troop's baseplate area, killing a corporal and wounding several marines.

Preceding K and L Companies was J Company's 12 Troop under Lieutenant Colin Beedon and Sergeant Collins. Their task was to mark the previously reconnoitred route leading between two minefields and thereafter to position two sections of the Anti-Tank Troop with their Milan firing posts – one to the south of Zoya, from which it would provide supporting fire for K and L Companies, and the other on a track junction to the south-east to counter any attempt by the Argentinians to send in their Panhard armoured cars based at Stanley. Thereafter 12 Troop was to move to the start line to rendezvous with a patrol of the Welsh Guards.

The two companies plus supporting elements made their way carefully along the marked route between the minefields. Whenever the moon made an appearance, the artillery FOOs swiftly called down fire from the supporting commando battery. On two occasions the Argentinians fired parachute illuminating flares from their 120mm mortars but failed to see the two commando companies who froze or went to ground.

As K and L carried out the flanking move, 12 Troop reached the area of the start line and attempted to locate the Welsh Guards patrol. However, in the darkness the two groups missed each other and it was not until an hour had passed that they succeeded in linking up. This resulted in H-hour being delayed by sixty minutes, by which time the moon had risen fully and was illuminating the area.

Vaux was thus relieved to hear the voice of K Company's commander, Captain Peter Babbington, informing him over the radio that his men were on the start line. The order was given for J Company to begin its diversion and within seconds the area forward of Tac HQ's position erupted in gunfire, reinforced by the Anti-Tank Troop launching several Milan missiles at enemy machine-gun positions illuminated by the Mortar Troop with parachute flares.

At 10pm K Company crossed the start line and began advancing towards its objective, the eastern end of Zoya, which lay 800 yards away. Meanwhile L Company was moving into its FUP, followed by a 34-strong force of Headquarters Company carrying K and L's six GPMG (SF) kits of tripods and dial sights, plus 10,000 rounds of ammunition.

K Company succeeded in advancing 700 yards before 1 Troop, observing enemy moving in the rocks ahead, opened fire. Captain Babbington immediately ordered

2 Troop to clear the right-hand side of the objective. During the next forty-five minutes it captured a command post, several heavy machine-guns and four 120mm mortars. A section commander, Corporal Lawrence Watts, was killed at point-blank range while clearing a position which would have caused major problems if it had not been neutralised swiftly.

Once 2 Troop had secured its objective, 3 Troop moved through on to the ridge and, with 1 Troop advancing parallel and clearing the low ground to the south, began working its way towards the west. Both troops encountered enemy in well-sited bunkers, machine-guns and snipers among them. Many of these were cleared using 66mm LAWs and Carl Gustav 84mm MAWs which proved devastatingly effective among the rocks. Part of 3 Troop, led by Corporal Ward, was held up by snipers and machine-guns. A section commander in 1 Troop, Corporal Steve Newland, came to its aid by climbing a rock slab some 20 feet high and observing the Argentinian position which contained approximately half a platoon. Throwing two grenades into the position, Newland then charged and single-handedly accounted for the remaining survivors. At that point Ward shouted that he was about to launch a 66mm LAW and Newland took cover behind a nearby rock, the rocket slamming into the position immediately afterwards. He then went forward to clear the position but as he did so he was hit by a burst of fire which wounded him in the legs. Despite his injuries, Newland finished off the Argentinian soldier who had fired at him and thereafter, having propped himself against a rock, used his radio to direct 3 Troop towards another machine-gun position.

After further fierce fighting, K Company succeeded in seizing and securing its objective, the eastern end of Zoya. Vaux then ordered L Company, commanded by Captain David Wheen, to advance the 600 yards to its objective, the western end of Zoya. Within 200 yards of crossing its start line, however, L Company came under heavy and accurate fire which wounded the second-in-command, Lieutenant Ian Stafford (an officer of the Argyll & Sutherland Highlanders serving on secondment to the Royal Marines), and several other men.

Wheen called for supporting fire from the Anti-Tank Troop section positioned forward and left of his line of advance. It responded with some well-aimed Milan missiles which neutralised some machine-guns, enabling the company to skirmish forward and close with other positions containing snipers and more machine-guns. Six heavy machine-gun positions and at least four more occupied by sniper teams were cleared during the following five hours. As it reached the western end of Mount Harriet, its two leading troops encountered fifty Argentinians who were making it plain that they wished to surrender.

Having secured its objective, L Company regrouped and reorganised. The prisoners were dispatched to the rear, escorted by the Headquarters Company composite troop. The latter had delivered sustained fire kits to the two companies which immediately set

The 105mm guns of 29 Commando Regiment RA played a key role in destroying Argentinian morale. As the battle neared its end the regiment came close to running out of ammunition.

up their GPMG (SF) to deal with any enemy counter-attack. Meanwhile 5 Troop was dispatched forward to L Company's next objective, a known Argentinian position located in an outcrop some 500 yards to the north of the western end of the mountain. Captain Wheen concentrated the company's GPMGs, less 5 Troop's, on the ridge in order to provide supporting fire. However, as the men advanced down a slope towards the enemy position they came under heavy fire and were forced to withdraw. The position was then engaged by the company's GPMGs while Captain Wheen called down artillery and mortar fire. Shortly afterwards 5 Troop put in an assault, accounting for six of the Argentinians – the remainder escaped into the mist.

While K Company remained on Mount Harriet, L Company was ordered by Vaux to head for Goat Ridge. Vaux was on his way to Mount Harriet with his Tac HQ and J Company, moving via the most direct route in his haste to concentrate 42 Commando on its objective so that it was prepared as soon as possible for any enemy counter-attack. This route took him through a minefield, he and those with him sprinting through 'with fingers crossed'. Meanwhile L Company found Goat Ridge unoccupied but observed some fifty Argentinians running up the side of Mount Tumbledown, and called for artillery fire on them.

42 Commando now regrouped and reorganised with L Company on Goat Ridge, K Company on the western end of Mount Harriet and J Company on the eastern end. Despite the fierce fighting, 42 Commando had suffered extremely light casualties – two killed and thirteen wounded. Many enemy troops were littered across the mountain, with others still in their foxholes. Over 300 prisoners were taken by 42 Commando, including the commanding officer of the 4th Infantry Regiment, in an attack that was a classic example of inflicting the maximum damage to the enemy at minimum cost. The meticulous approach to battle had paid off.

Lieutenant Colonel Vaux later recalled that he would always remember the sight of 42 Commando's padre as he went over to speak to the prisoners. To the CO's amazement, as the padre went forward the Argentinians all blessed themselves and lay on the ground. It was clear they thought this man of the cloth was about to give them the last rites before they were executed. The prisoners were, of course, in no danger and while the incident raised a few smiles, there was also shock that the Argentinians expected to die. What might have happened to the men of 42 Commando if they had been taken prisoner?

First light on 12 June found 3 Commando Brigade secure on its three objectives. However, shortly afterwards Argentinian artillery began shelling all three locations, particularly Mount Longdon which was overlooked by enemy positions on Mount Tumbledown. The shelling continued throughout 12 June and the following day. By last light on the 13th however, it had become apparent that the Argentinians were not intending to mount a counter-attack. Brigadier Thompson was able to concentrate on his next move.

Eleven

Final Assault

TUMBLEDOWN, WIRELESS RIDGE AND MOUNT WILLIAM

The next stage in the advance on Port Stanley was an attack on the inner ring of hills overlooking the town by 5 Infantry Brigade, which moved up to a concentration area on 12 June. The attack had originally been scheduled to take place on the night of 12/13 June but a shortage of helicopters to move artillery ammunition forced Brigadier Tony Wilson to ask Major General Jeremy Moore for a further twenty-four hours. The extra time would give his men more time to prepare for a night attack over ground which they had not had the opportunity to reconnoitre. Moore agreed to this request and Thompson offered elements of the Mountain & Arctic Warfare Cadre, who was familiar with the terrain to be covered by 5 Brigade's battalions, to act as guides and 42 Commando to secure the start line for the Scots Guards.

The key objective was Mount Tumbledown, which dominated the surrounding area, its rock-clad slopes providing the enemy with good positions for well-sited bunkers and trenches while the exposed slopes below offered excellent arcs of fire. To the north of Tumbledown lay Mount Longdon, occupied by 3 PARA, while to the west was the Two Sisters, taken by 45 Commando. Goat Ridge and Mount Harriet were held by 42 Commando. To the east lay Wireless Ridge, Sapper Hill, and ultimately Port Stanley itself. Enemy forces on Mount Tumbledown comprised an approximately 100-strong company of the best unit deployed by the Argentinians to the Falkland Islands, the 5th Marine Infantry Battalion, which was well supported by mortars and ten SF machine-guns.

Brigadier Wilson's plan was for a three-phase attack with the 2nd Battalion Scots Guards, commanded by Lieutenant Colonel Mike Scott, attacking and seizing Mount Tumbledown on the night of 13/14 June. The 1st Battalion 7th DEO Gurkha Rifles (1/7GR) would then advance east from Mount Harriet and take Mount William. Thereafter the 1st Battalion Welsh Guards would move through and take Sapper Hill. In the meantime, while the Scots Guards were seizing Mount Tumbledown, 3 Commando Brigade would take Wireless Ridge while 2 PARA mounted a night attack; during this operation a diversionary attack by a composite force of elements of D and G Squadrons 22 SAS and an SBS team, landed to the north-east by 1 Raiding Squadron RM, would be mounted against the eastern end of the feature. Once secured by 2 PARA, Wireless Ridge would form a start line for the final phase which would

The Scots Guards land in the Falklands. They were the lead troops of 5 Brigade and sailed south aboard the *QE2* to support Brigadier Thompson's 3 Commando Brigade.

comprise a night attack by the whole of 3 Commando Brigade on Port Stanley itself on 14 June.

The Scots Guards' assault on Mount Tumbledown would be a flanking attack, launched from the west of the feature and supported by five artillery batteries and the 4.5-inch guns of HMS *Active* and *Yarmouth*. Further support would be provided by the battalion's Mortar Platoon, and the mortars of 42 Commando and the 1/7GR.

On 13 June the battalion was flown forward to an assembly area west of Goat Ridge where it dug in. Lieutenant Colonel Scott and his officers surveyed their objective, and the terrain which they would have to cross to reach it that night, from the vantage point of Goat Ridge. The rest of the day was taken up with 'O' groups, and checking radios, weapons and personal equipment as the battalion prepared for battle.

Scott's plan was for the battalion's three rifle companies – G Company, Left Flank and Right Flank – to make their approach down Goat Ridge for a three-phase attack. Thirty minutes before H-hour, the start of phase one, which was set for 9pm, a diversionary attack on enemy positions south-east of Mount Harriet would be mounted by a force commanded by Major Richard Bethell. This would comprise the Reconnaissance Platoon, a fire support group made up of members of Headquarters Company, and a troop of the Blues & Royals with their two Scorpion and two Scimitar CVR-Ts. In phase one G Company would take the western end of the feature; Phase two would see Left Flank, commanded by Major John Kiszely, moving through and attacking the main part of the mountain; and in phase three Right Flank, under Major Simon Price, would move round Left Flank and seize the eastern part of Tumbledown.

The night was clear but bitterly cold as the diversionary attack force under Major Bethell advanced on Argentinian positions to the south-east of Mount Harriet. The Blues & Royals troop moved slowly along the track to Stanley, hoping to draw the Argentinians' fire and thus discover their positions. By 8.30pm no contact had been made with the enemy, but shortly afterwards one of the Blues & Royals' Scorpions hit a mine; it incapacitated the vehicle but did not injure the crew. As the other CVR-Ts halted, Bethell and his men continued their advance under cover of the three GPMGs of the fire support group, and soon spotted a group of sangars.

Moving in silently for the attack, they found the positions apparently deserted but then heard snoring. At that moment they were spotted by an enemy soldier who opened fire. A battle ensued as the other Argentinians in the area, which held eleven trenches or sangars, brought fire to bear. As they did so, the fire support group came forward to join Major Bethell and his men. Two guardsmen were killed and four wounded in the initial exchange of fire, but the battle continued for two hours. Because of the threat of mines, the Blues & Royals were unable to move up to provide direct support as Bethell requested by radio. Eventually, however, the tremendous firepower of Bethell's force resulted in Argentinian resistance dying away.

Major Bethell now decided to withdraw his force which had completed its mission. While he was discussing how to move his wounded with one of the four medics in the unit, an injured Argentinian suddenly appeared over the edge of the trench and tossed in a grenade. Bethell immediately shot him dead but the grenade exploded, wounding the major in the legs and the medic in the lung. Under artillery and mortar fire Bethell withdrew his force but shortly afterwards he and his men found themselves in a minefield. Minutes later Lance Sergeant Miller trod on a mine which wounded him severely and injured three others. With four further casualties, Bethell's men now had to abandon the bodies of the two dead guardsmen. Slowly but surely, with Bethell leading the way, using his torch to find a route through the minefield, the guardsmen reached the Blues & Royals troop which was waiting for them. Just after midnight Bethell and his men succeeded in returning to their start line.

By now the attack on Mount Tumbledown was well under way. G Company had crossed its start line at the appointed H-hour of 9pm. It succeeded in reaching and

THE SCOTS GUARDS

The Scots Guards were formed in 1661 as the Scots Regiment of Foot Guards, and have also been known as the King's Regiment, the King's Foot Guards or the Scotch Guards. In 1713 Queen Anne changed their name to the Third Regiment of Foot Guards and in 1831 the regiment was again renamed to become the Scots Fusilier Guards. This title endured until 1877 when the regiment was redesignated the Scots Guards. Distinguished by the three groups of three buttons on their scarlet tunics and with no plume in their bearskins, Scots Guardsmen wear the star of St Andrew in their forage caps and berets.

Like all the regiments of the Household Division, the Scots Guards are first and foremost combat troops. This was entirely apparent when the 2nd Battalion faced the Argentinian 5th Marine Infantry Battalion on Mount Tumbledown in a battle which saw some of the fiercest fighting of the campaign. Having been engaged on ceremonial duties prior to its departure for the South Atlantic, the battalion switched to its operational role with ease.

The Scots Guards celebrate after the battle for Tumbledown. With bayonets fixed, they had fought a tough battle and suffered many casualties in the assault.

Scots Guardsmen escorting Argentinian prisoners after the battle for Tumbledown. The prisoners were taken away and interrogated before being confined with hundreds of others.

securing its objective – the western end of the mountain – unobserved, although there was sporadic artillery and mortar fire as it crossed the open terrain towards the mountain. As soon as G Company had secured the area, which had been abandoned by the enemy, Left Flank duly moved through and began heading up the steep slopes towards the main part of the mountain. However, at a range of some 300 yards it encountered heavy fire from two machine-guns, and snipers, equipped with image intensifiers on their rifles, killed three guardsmen and wounded two others.

As soon as the Argentinians opened fire 15 Platoon attempted to mount a section attack but this was beaten back. With supporting fire from G Company, Left Flank resorted to 66mm LAWs and Carl Gustav 84mm MAWs in its attempts to blast the enemy troops out of their bunkers and trenches, but the weapons seemed to have little effect because of the protection afforded by rocks. The battalion found itself pinned down on the lower slopes of the mountain and during the following three hours was unable to penetrate the well-sited enemy defences. Moreover, there were difficulties in bringing the supporting artillery, mortars and naval gunfire to bear. At 2.30am, however, shells began falling on the area in front of Left Flank's two forward platoons and Major John Kiszely ordered 15 Platoon to mount a platoon attack. With bayonets fixed, Lieutenant Mitchell and his guardsmen charged up the slope; Major Kiszely and his company headquarters followed behind. Reaching the crest of the ridge, they then engaged the enemy in a series of actions. Slowly but surely Left Flank headed for its objective, the summit of the mountain, forced to fight for every yard of ground by the well-trained Argentinian marines who opposed them. At one point Kiszely found himself apparently alone in the darkness, although he knew his men were scattered among the rocks around him. Calling out to 15 Platoon, he was answered by a shout of 'Aye, sir! I'm with with you!', followed by another of 'Aye, Sir! And I'm fockin' with you as well!'

Left Flank headed on for the next ridge, attacking enemy positions with great force and clearing them with grenades and bayonets. Kiszely shot two enemy dead and bayoneted a third. Pressing on, he led his company to the summit of the mountain. By the time he reached it, however, only six guardsmen were with him; the remainder were still clearing bunkers or rounding up prisoners. As Kiszely and his men looked down towards Port Stanley, they were suddenly reminded that the rest of the feature was still in Argentinian hands when a machine-gun opened fire, seriously wounding three guardsmen. Shortly afterwards, other members of the company succeeded in reaching the area of the summit and they held it until the arrival of reinforcements in the form of Right Flank.

As planned, the two leading platoons of Right Flank moved to the left around Left Flank. Their 66mm LAWs, M79 40mm grenade launchers and Carl Gustav 84mm MAWs were brought to bear as the two platoons attempted to blast the enemy out of their bunkers and trenches. Like Left Flank, however, they found that the Argentinian marines were so determined to hang on that in the end the only way to oust them was to do so with grenade and bayonet. One enemy position proved particularly troublesome and succeeded in pinning down a platoon. Under covering fire from some of his guardsmen, Lieutenant Robert Lawrence crawled towards the position and, taking cover nearby, threw a white phosphorous grenade into it. As the grenade exploded, Lawrence's platoon charged and overran the position which contained three machine-guns.

Yard by yard Right Flank forced the enemy off its objective and by 8.30am the Scots Guards were in possession of the entire mountain. It had been a hard-fought battle, during which the battalion had suffered nine killed and forty-one wounded.

At midnight on 11 June, two days before the attack on Mount Tumbledown, 2 PARA had set off for an assembly area north of Mount Kent. It would wait there in reserve while 3 PARA and 45 Commando attacked Mount Longdon and Two Sisters, and 42 Commando took Mount Harriet. Travelling in battle order, having left its packs with its A Echelon, the battalion made its way through the darkness guided by members of C (Patrols) Company. Ahead of it and to the right were the flashes and sounds of gunfire and explosions coming from 3 PARA's and 45 Commando's objectives. Shells howled overhead as the light guns of the commando batteries laid down supporting fire on Mount Longdon and Two Sisters.

On reaching the assembly area, situated below the feature between Mount Kent and Mount Estancia, the three rifle companies settled down to wait. Despite the quilted clothing and waterproofs which they carried in bundles on their webbing, men soon began to feel the bitter cold.

After a long wait 2 PARA received orders to move. It quickly became apparent that 3 PARA was still heavily engaged on Mount Longdon and many in 2 PARA assumed they were moving up in support. As first light approached, the battalion neared the

A Scots Guardsman armed with an L42 sniper rifle escorts Argentinian prisoners after the battle of Tumbledown.

Murrell Bridge where it was due to rendezvous with 3 PARA, which had secured 2 PARA's assembly area. However, a minefield en route meant it had to change direction northwards and follow the line of the valley along the western side of Mount Longdon.

At first light the battalion swung east and pushed on along the Murrell River. At that point the commander of B Company, Major John Crosland, went forward to reconnoitre the Furze Bush Pass, a large gully with a rocky escarpment which offered good protection against artillery fire and which had been designated as 2 PARA's assembly area. There he met a group of 3 PARA's D (Patrols) Company under the company commander, Major Pat Butler, who briefed him on the action on Mount Longdon during the night. 2 PARA moved into the area and dug in and later that day it was joined by 3 Troop of the Blues & Royals, commanded by Lieutenant Lord Robin Innes-Kerr, which would provide support for the battalion in its forthcoming operations.

At 6pm orders arrived for 2 PARA to carry out an attack on Wireless Ridge that night. The commanding officer, Lieutenant Colonel David Chaundler, later recalled:

> Three hours before last light, a Scout helicopter arrived. The brigade liaison officer, Major Hector Gullan, climbed out and, running towards me, shouted, 'Wireless Ridge tonight, chaps', surely the shortest set of orders ever given for a battalion attack. I quickly devised a plan and summoned my officers. Half-way through our conference the boundaries of attack were changed, and when I got to the point of asking 'Any questions?', we heard that the assault had been postponed for 24 hours.

This postponement resulted from 5 Infantry Brigade's request for a further day to prepare for its impending operation against Mount Tumbledown. In the event it gave Chaundler much-needed time to draw up a proper plan and orders, as well as allowing his battalion to prepare for battle. On the following day he flew by helicopter with Major Tony Rice of 8 Battery to 3 PARA's position on Mount Longdon; from there they could observe Wireless Ridge. They met Lieutenant Colonel Hew Pike and Captain Willie McCracken of 148 Commando Forward Observation Battery RA. Chaundler and Rice were briefed on the enemy's positions on Wireless Ridge, which were stronger than previously thought, and on a hitherto unknown position to the north-east – a feature on a small headland at the mouth of the Murrell River.

Lying to the east of Mount Longdon, Wireless Ridge ran eastwards towards Moody Brook. At its western end was a 300-feet high feature from which a spur ran northwards. As it ran east, the ridgeline narrowed and towards the eastern end it was crossed by a line of telegraph poles that ran due south to the barracks occupied by the Royal Marine garrison before the Argentinian invasion. A track from the north also crossed the ridge to the west of the telegraph poles and led south to the road running from below Two Sisters to Port Stanley. Unlike Mount Longdon and the other features in the area, the terrain around Wireless Ridge was flat and open – it offered plenty of room for 2 PARA to manoeuvre. Enemy forces on Wireless Ridge were now believed to comprise four companies of the 7th Infantry Regiment and a platoon. Chaundler decided to mount a four-phase attack:

> My plan called for an attack in four phases, with each axis of attack coming from a different direction. The battalion's experience at Goose Green had taught us the importance of fire support. Up to this point of the campaign, all our attacks had been launched in silence in order to achieve surprise. Mortar and artillery fire had been held back until contact was made. I decided upon a noisy attack with an extensive preliminary bombardment, believing that the Argentinians, essentially a conscript army, would crack under a heavy barrage. It was hardly surprising that the impact of fire support was generally underestimated. Before the campaign none of us had either seen or experienced the effects of a bombardment with large quantities of high explosives. On Wireless Ridge we were to do both. We asked for, and got, two batteries of artillery (twelve 105mm light guns), fire support from a frigate (HMS *Ambuscade*) and 3 PARA's mortars, in addition to our own mortar and machine-gun platoons. But perhaps the most significant support weapons were Lieutenant Lord Robin Innes-Kerr's four Scorpions and Scimitars from the Blues & Royals, which up to this stage of the campaign had not seen action. They made a remarkable journey from Fitzroy through the mountains to join us in our assembly area and, though normally classed as reconnaissance vehicles, were used as light tanks and their fire was to prove devastating.

In addition, D and G Squadrons 22 SAS, together with an SBS team, would carry out a diversionary attack on enemy positions at the eastern end of Wireless Ridge, having been landed earlier on the coast to the north-east by assault craft of 1 Raiding Squadron RM.

In phase one of the operation D Company would attack the enemy position west of the northern spur of Wireless Ridge, nicknamed Rough Diamond. During phase two A and B Companies would take the northern spur itself, nicknamed Apple Pie, and in phase three C (Patrols) Company would capture the feature on the headland at the mouth of the Murrell River. In phase four D Company would advance down Wireless Ridge, nicknamed Blueberry Pie, from west to east as far as the telegraph poles, taking out two enemy positions from their flank. The Anti-Tank Platoon would move with the battalion, as would 3 Troop of the Blues & Royals.

Before last light the Mortar Platoon, the Blues & Royals troop and the Reconnaissance Platoon, whose task was to secure the start line, moved off. The weather was deteriorating, with intermittent snow and sleet making visibility very poor. Without their sleeping bags, few in 2 PARA had slept during the previous two nights and there had been no ration resupply for twenty-four hours. Compounding the battalion's problems was the fact that the Argentinians were aware an attack was in the offing and were shelling the most likely approaches, including those leading to the battalion's FUPs.

No sooner had the battalion reached its FUPs than Lieutenant Colonel Chaundler was called to his main headquarters, located three-quarters of a mile to the rear, where the second-in-command, Major Keeble, showed him a map found on a captured enemy officer: it revealed that a minefield had been laid across 2 PARA's main axis of attack. However, it was now too late for Chaundler to change his plan and the battalion would have to advance through the minefield.

At 9.15pm artillery fire began falling on the battalion's objectives. Thirty minutes later Major Phil Neame's D Company crossed its start line with supporting fire from a commando battery, the battalion's mortars, the Machine-Gun Platoon, and the Scorpions and Scimitars of the Blues & Royals Troop. Meanwhile suppressive fire came from HMS *Ambuscade* and another commando battery. On reaching its objective, D Company observed enemy troops fleeing into the night. The position was empty apart from a number of dead. However, as the company reorganised it came under fire from 105mm and 155mm guns launching airburst shells. Major Neame pushed forward another 300 yards to get clear of the enemy DF before halting and consolidating while A and B Companies began their advance south towards Apple Pie, one on either side of the track. Colour Sergeant Findlay, moving in the rear of A Company, was killed by shellfire and some men of Headquarters and Support Companies were wounded.

As the two companies reached the edge of their objective, a position occupied by the Argentinians' regimental headquarters and a company, heavy supporting fire from the commando batteries, mortars, machine-guns and CVR-Ts lifted to allow them to put in their assault. The paratroopers skirmished forward, and the enemy broke and fled into the darkness while the Blues & Royals' CVR-Ts, equipped with image intensifiers, turned their guns on enemy troops on the ridge and drove them off. Having cleared all the enemy positions and taken thirty-seven prisoners, both companies swiftly reorganised and began to dig in under increasingly heavy artillery fire.

2 PARA now prepared for the next phase: the attack by C (Patrols) Company on the enemy platoon position on the Murrell River headland. As the men approached the Argentinian position, they heard weapons being cocked, but shortly afterwards the enemy troops' courage failed them and they fled, several leaving their boots behind them.

With the first three objectives secured, D Company moved towards its start line for phase four. Meanwhile the Blues & Royals and the Machine-Gun Platoon joined A and B Companies, ready to provide D Company with supporting fire. As they did so, they came under fire from artillery and anti-tank weapons on Wireless Ridge further to the south. D Company reached the western end of the ridge unobserved, clearing a number of bunkers and trenches it found on the reverse slope, all of which were abandoned. D Company then came under fire from machine-guns in well-sited bunkers. As it continued its advance 12 Platoon reached a gap in the ridgeline. It moved through, past some ponds, and then came under fire from a machine-gun to the front. At that point the leading section, under Corporal Barton, spotted what appeared to be a minefield marker, but the platoon pressed on regardless. Meanwhile 11 Platoon had also encountered a suspected minefield after one of its section commanders, Corporal Harley, tripped on what appeared to be a tripwire. Pushing on, the platoon encountered barbed wire obstacles. Sappers of 9 Parachute Squadron RE troop came forward and quickly reconnoitred safe paths between the obstacles.

While 11 Platoon was negotiating the minefield, 12 Platoon continued to advance with 10 Platoon now deployed on its left. Suddenly there was a heavy burst of fire and a brief but fierce firefight took place. 12 Platoon pushed on, however, and could soon see the lights of Moody Brook below. 10 Platoon also moved up and both units kept up the pressure on the Argentinians. The enemy troops withdrew eastwards along the ridgeline under fire from the Blues & Royals whose guns were being directed by Major Neame.

Eventually D Company reached the limit of its advance – the line of telegraph poles. 12 Platoon reorganised there while 10 and 11 Platoons consolidated further to the rear. At this point, however, enemy artillery fire grew heavier and snipers began to shoot from positions further to the east. For the next two hours D Company was under constant bombardment and small arms fire as it sheltered in abandoned enemy positions. Lieutenant John Page, who had taken over command of 12 Platoon following the death of Lieutenant Jim Barry, had a very narrow escape when a bullet passed between two grenades fastened to his webbing and hit a magazine in one of his pouches. Although he was knocked over by the force of the round, he was unharmed. Even more miraculously, as he lay on the ground, a 7.62mm round exploded in the magazine without setting off his grenades.

Lieutenant Colonel Chaundler attempted to contact Major Neame by radio to obtain a report on his situation. However, Lieutenant Shaun Webster of 10 Platoon was the only officer near Company Headquarters. As he was briefing the commanding officer, Argentinians could be heard talking below. 10 Platoon opened fire and a group of enemy, estimated at between ten and fifteen strong, responded with automatic weapons. 11 Platoon immediately moved up in support and joined the firefight, at which point Major Neame appeared and advised Chaundler that he suspected an enemy counter-attack was imminent. At the same time D Company came under fire from enemy troops on Mount Tumbledown, which had not yet been cleared by the Scots Guards. Neame reorganised D Company, leaving a standing patrol forward while 10 and 11 Platoons moved on to the reverse slope where they made use of some abandoned enemy positions. 12 Platoon remained near the telegraph poles.

A and B companies were still in their positions on Apple Pie where they had been joined by the Mortar Platoon which had established a new baseplate position on the side of the feature. Its main problem, which was encountered by all mortar teams and artillery gun crews during the Falklands campaign, was the nature of the terrain – either soft peat or hard rock. During the action at Wireless Ridge 2 PARA's mortars fired on supercharge for extra range and the teams had been forced to improvise to prevent the baseplates from sinking into the peat. Another problem was that the tubes would occasionally jump out of the baseplates on recoil. To prevent this, team members took it in turns to stand on the baseplates, but the shock was so great that four of them had suffered broken ankles by the end of the battle. Despite these problems, the mortars continued to provide effective supporting fire, as did those of 3 PARA.

Throughout the battle men of the battalion's A Echelon continued to bring forward ammunition and evacuate the wounded. It was assisted by the Assault Pioneer Platoon under WO2 Grace who ensured a steady supply of ammunition for the Machine-Gun Platoon whose six GPMGs (SF) were constantly in action. The command element of 2 PARA also saw action when a Canberra flew in low and dropped a stick of bombs in the area of the battalion main headquarters, wounding Private Steele, a member of the Defence Platoon. Meanwhile a signaller in the commanding officer's 'R' group, Private McLoughlin, was struck by a bullet which penetrated his helmet but caused no injury.

At first light on 14 June a small force of Argentinians mounted a counter-attack on a section of 10 Platoon led by Corporal Owen, which had been deployed forward as a standing patrol. The section opened fire, Owen engaging the enemy with his M79 40mm grenade launcher. The rest of the platoon came forward in support. One member of the section, Private Lambert, heard an enemy soldier shouting close to his position and threw a grenade in the direction of the voice, which stopped abruptly as the weapon exploded. 11 Platoon then observed another small group which ignored a challenge from 2nd Lieutenant Chris Waddington. The platoon opened fire and the enemy withdrew swiftly.

Artillery fire was then brought down to discourage any further attempts at counter-attacks on D Company. Enemy guns responded by bringing down very accurate fire on 11 Platoon and Major Neame, anxious that the muzzle flashes of his company's weapons were enabling the enemy to pinpoint his positions, ordered his men to cease

Artillery shells pound Stanley. The final bombardment unsettled the Argentinians and shortly afterwards they agreed to surrender.

fire. He then spotted a large force of Argentinian troops moving up towards Sapper Hill to the south-east and called for artillery fire, but the two supporting commando batteries were fully engaged on other tasks. Twenty minutes later the Argentinians had reached the top of the feature and support became available. The British guns opened fire.

Chaundler arrived at D Company's positions and ordered it to engage the enemy who were now in full flight towards Port Stanley. To the south-west other troops were running down the slopes of Mount Tumbledown, driven off it by the Scots Guards. As D Company opened fire with its machine-guns, three armed Scout helicopters of 656 Squadron Army Air Corps, led by Captain John Greenhalgh, appeared and engaged an Argentinian artillery battery with SS-11 missiles. The enemy rapidly responded with anti-aircraft fire and the three helicopters were forced to take swift evasive action and withdraw.

THE 7TH DUKE OF EDINBURGH'S OWN GURKHA RIFLES

Gurkhas have served in the British Army since 1815 and have earned a distinguished reputation. The 7th Gurkha Rifles were formed in 1907 as part of the Indian Army, subsequently seeing service on the North-West Frontier and during the First and Second World Wars. On the departure of the British from India in 1947, the regiment was one of four Gurkha units transferred to the British Army. Later renamed the 7th Duke of Edinburgh's Own Gurkha Rifles, its battalions saw service in Malaya and Borneo during the Malayan Emergency and Borneo Confrontation campaigns, thereafter serving in Hong Kong, Brunei and Britain.

In 1982 1/7GR was hastily recalled from jungle training in Belize and embarked on the *QE2* along with the rest of 5 Infantry Brigade. Numbering 720 all ranks organised in four rifle companies, a support company and headquarters company, it was the largest of the infantry and commando units in the Task Force. The Gurkhas spearheaded the assault on Mount William, but were disappointed to find that the enemy had already fled. This was largely the result of lurid accounts of the 'devils with knives' (a reference to the razor-sharp kukri carried by each man) which had been put around earlier, instilling considerable fear among the Argentinian forces on the islands.

Gurkha soldiers keep fit aboard the *QE2*. The news that the Gurkhas were deploying was used as a psychological weapon against the Argentinians who were fed horrific stories about the troops and their kukri fighting knives.

Much to their annoyance the Gurkhas did not see a lot of action on the Falklands. Mount William was their big battle but there were few enemy troops and by then the war was almost over. It was claimed the Gurkhas complained that the Argentinians on William ran away and refused to fight.

Meanwhile the commanding officer had ordered A and B Companies, along with the Blues & Royals troop, to move forward on to Wireless Ridge with all haste. It was vital to reach Port Stanley before the Argentinians had a chance to reorganise. By this time Brigadier Thompson had joined 2 PARA and had been told by Lieutenant Colonel Chaundler of the enemy troops seen fleeing in large numbers from Moody Brook, Mount William, Tumbledown and Sapper Hill. Thompson was well aware that the Argentinian artillery was still effective, having just observed it bringing down fire on to the northern side of Mount Tumbledown. After discussing the next move with Chaundler, he told him to move 2 PARA forward as far as the spur above the Esro building on the very edge of Stanley. The battalion was to consolidate there and wait while 3 Commando Brigade moved up.

Gurkha soldiers on Mount William. This was their first and only battle in the Falklands. Like the Guards, the Gurkhas had sailed south aboard the *QE2*.

Paratroopers make the final tab for Port Stanley. When they arrived in the town they couldn't believe that the Argentinians had garrisoned troops in the port and not moved more units across the island.

Returning to his Tac HQ, Thompson received a message from the Divisional Headquarters that he was to take personal charge of the advance into Stanley. Thompson issued quick orders to all his commanding officers, but shortly afterwards came the news that the Argentinians were surrendering.

2 PARA led the advance towards Stanley, followed by 42 Commando and 3 PARA. 45 Commando headed for Sapper Hill. B Company reached the ridgeline and was ordered to move down to Moody Brook. 5 Platoon led the way and quickly cleared the ruined barracks before pushing on and taking the area of the bridge over the Murrell River. The platoon was moving cautiously, keeping a sharp eye out for booby traps and mines, while being continually exhorted to keep advancing by Major John Crosland. The company then moved south on to high ground on the other side of the valley, covering A Company as it advanced down the road towards Stanley with

Above: Men of 2 PARA write themselves into the history books as the first troops to enter Stanley. The streets were full of rubbish after Argentinian commanders allowed their soldiers to go on the rampage. *Below*: It's all over. Marines of 45 Commando watch over hundreds of Argentinians in Stanley.

The recovery of enemy dead from Wireless Ridge after 2 PARA's second major battle.

C (Patrols) and D Companies following behind. Meanwhile the Blues & Royals troop moved east along Wireless Ridge, ready to give covering fire if necessary. News of a ceasefire was then received over the battalion radio net. At 1.30pm on 14 June A Company, led by 2nd Lieutenant Mark Coe's 2 Platoon, entered Port Stanley, the rest of the battalion arriving shortly afterwards.

In the early stages of the battle four Rigid Raider fast assault craft embarked sixteen SBS and twenty members of 22 SAS. The men were ferried round the coast and landed for the diversionary attack on enemy positions at the eastern end of Wireless Ridge. This was intended to distract the Argentinians from 2 PARA's approach from the west. The attack group was supported by sixty men of D and G Squadrons who gave covering fire with 81mm mortars, Milan missiles and GPMGs from positions on the northern shore of the harbour inlet. Unfortunately, as it landed the attack group encountered heavy fire from enemy anti-aircraft guns which hit and damaged all four Rigid Raiders. At the same time an Argentinian hospital ship switched on all her lights, illuminating the entire area. The attack group was forced to carry out a fighting withdrawal and seek cover in dead ground, suffering two wounded in the process. In

Above: The men of 3 PARA celebrate victory in Stanley after they had tabbed across the islands and helped defeat the enemy to restore British rule. *Below*: Bent under the weight of their backpacks, 45 Commando march into Stanley. The conflict illustrated the benefits of the marines' tough training, which includes marching across Dartmoor in darkness and surviving for days without resupply.

due course the group linked up with 2 PARA and remained with the battalion until it could be evacuated.

During the battle of Wireless Ridge 2 PARA had suffered light casualties – three killed and eleven wounded. The enemy, later estimated as numbering 500 in total, lost ten killed, an unknown number wounded and seventeen taken prisoner.

As the men of 2 PARA, followed soon afterwards by 3 PARA, arrived in Stanley, 45 Commando was making its way to Sapper Hill. It found the 1st Battalion Welsh Guards there, together with A and C Companies of 40 Commando. They had arrived there on the orders of 5 Infantry Brigade which had not informed either 3 Commando Brigade or the Divisional Headquarters. 45 Commando proceeded to occupy Sapper Hill while the Welsh Guards took up a position on a key feature overlooking Stanley.

Despite the Argentinians' announcement that they wanted to surrender, Brigadier Thompson was taking no chances. His units were positioned to cope with any unexpected show of force and all the batteries of 29 Commando Regiment RA had their guns laid on targets at the eastern end of Port Stanley and the narrow part of the airport isthmus.

Meanwhile 42 Commando had secured the western end of Stanley, installing itself in an old sea-plane hangar and a large building nearby. 2 and 3 PARA moved into requisitioned houses in their respective areas of the town while Thompson and his brigade headquarters installed themselves in the upper storey of a house occupied by members of B Company 2 PARA. There they shared a huge stew of 'liberated' enemy rations with members of B Company's headquarters, and washed it down with bottles of Argentinian red wine found by Major Hector Gullan. For most of them it was the first food they had eaten in twenty-four hours.

Twelve

Victory

L ate in the afternoon of 14 June, as 3 Commando Brigade was still in the process of entering Port Stanley, a Gazelle light helicopter arrived over the town with a white parachute trailing below it. Aboard the aircraft were the commanding officer of 22 SAS, Lieutenant Colonel Michael Rose, Captain Rod Bell RM and an SAS signaller. The aircraft landed some distance away and the three men made their way towards the town on foot.

Since the break-out from the beachhead at San Carlos, the British had maintained a series of daily radio broadcasts aimed at weakening the resolve of the Argentinian forces on the Falkland Islands, in particular the senior commanders based in Port Stanley. The messages were transmitted by the Spanish-speaking Captain Bell using the civilian radio frequency operated by the Falkland Islanders under Argentinian supervision for the provision of medical aid to outlying settlements. At noon on the 14th, Bell had broadcast: 'The position of the Argentinian forces is now hopeless. You are surrounded by British forces on all sides. . . . If you fail to respond to this message and there is unnecessary bloodshed in Port Stanley, the world will judge you accordingly.'

Bell's messages had been reinforced by Dr Alison Bleaney, the senior medical officer at Stanley Hospital, with whom he and Lieutenant Colonel Rose had previously made contact. Bleaney had made her own approaches to the Argentinian military hierarchy in Port Stanley, in particular to a senior naval officer with the British-sounding name of Captain Melbourne Hussey. She begged Hussey to respond to the British appeals for surrender for the sake of the civilian population as well as his own troops. The captain referred the matter to his commander-in-chief, General Mario Menendez, who previously had expressed his determination that the British would have to fight for Port Stanley. He had convinced himself and his superiors in Buenos Aires that the town was impregnable. Menendez's forces were plentifully supplied with arms and their performance at Goose Green, Mount Longdon, Two Sisters, Mount Harriet, Mount Tumbledown and Wireless Ridge had shown they were capable of putting up stout resistance when attacked. However, with the exception of one or two units, such as the 5th Marine Infantry Battalion on Mount Tumbledown, they suffered from poor morale. This became clear later from accounts given by soldiers of the 7th Infantry Regiment, attacked by 2 PARA on Wireless Ridge:

Until 1 May no one had really believed that we were going to fight. But when the British started attacking, everyone started getting more worried. Some of our boys complained about the weapons they had. They were told that they had enough ammunition for two or three days, but when the time came to fight they ran out in two or three hours. . . . No one told us where we were going. . . . We were not prepared psychologically. I felt like a machine. In my company we all had secondary education at least, but in A, B and C Companies, who were all the ones in the front line, there were boys with whom I talked who didn't even know what the Malvinas were.

By 14 June Menendez had obviously changed his mind because at 1pm Captain Hussey transmitted a radio message to the British that his superior had agreed to discuss the matter of surrender. Lieutenant Colonel Rose and Captain Bell arrived to negotiate with the Argentinian commander-in-chief who was also military governor of the Falkland Islands. The talks took place in Government House and it soon became clear to Rose and Bell that Menendez no longer wished to continue hostilities. Initially Menendez claimed that he only had power to surrender the forces on East Falkland but under pressure from Rose he capitulated and agreed that the troops on both islands would lay down their arms. Using the portable satellite communications system carried by his signaller, Rose was in constant communication with London and so was able to clear and confirm every aspect of the conditions of surrender as they were negotiated.

Eventually the terms of the surrender were agreed by both sides and all that remained was for Major General Jeremy Moore to arrive to sign the surrender document with General Menendez. However, bad weather made flying impossible and did not clear until late evening. At 9pm on Monday 14 June the surrender document was signed by the commanders of the British and Argentinian forces. The Falklands Conflict was at an end. In London at 10.15pm Prime Minister Margaret Thatcher made an announcement to a packed House of Commons: 'Our forces reached the outskirts of Port Stanley. Large numbers of Argentinian soldiers threw down their weapons. They are reported to be flying white flags over Port Stanley.'

As Britain celebrated, the rest of 3 Commando Brigade and 5 Infantry Brigade made their way to Stanley. On arrival they observed with astonishment the regiments of enemy troops that had never been deployed outside the town and its surrounding area, and the huge stocks of arms which should have been distributed to the units facing the two British brigades. Among these were several artillery pieces and anti-aircraft guns, as well as large numbers of small arms ammunition, shells and even Exocet missiles for shore batteries.

Royal Marines raise the Union flag at Government House — a moment of history. Many of the men pictured are from J Company, the unit formed from men who were in the Falklands at the time of the invasion.

An armoured vehicle of the Blues & Royals pictured outside the Globe, one of the Falklands' drinking holes.

During the last few hours of their occupation of Port Stanley, the Argentinian troops had wreaked havoc over much of the town by looting, wrecking and fouling houses. As Lieutenant Colonel Hew Pike, the commanding officer of 3 PARA, later wrote in a letter to his family: 'We almost ran into Stanley, down the moorland to be greeted with scenes of destruction, chaos, shambles. It is such a merciful relief that it now seems over, I am terribly sad about the people we lost. The Duke of Wellington was indeed right about the "melancholy nature of victory".' During the days that followed over 11,300 prisoners-of-war were rounded up. The total number of casualties suffered by the Argentinians is unknown but the government in Buenos Aires later announced that 652 men had been declared killed or missing presumed dead as a result of the war. British losses were 255 men killed and 777 wounded.

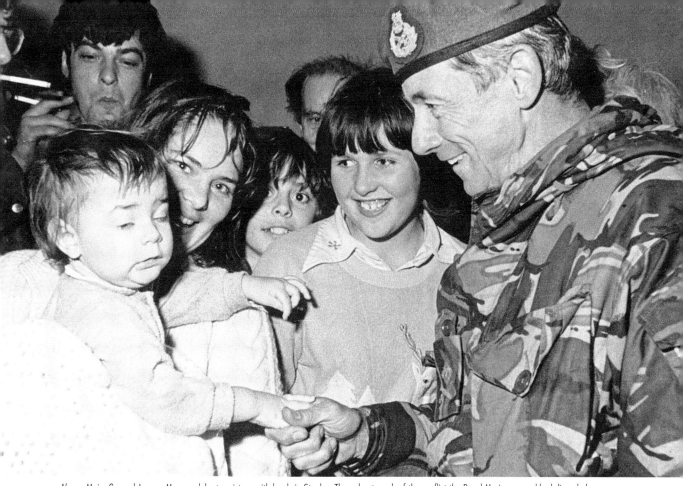

Above: Major General Jeremy Moore celebrates victory with locals in Stanley. Throughout much of the conflict the Royal Marine general had discarded his green beret and worn a cap in order to appear impartial to the units under his command. With the war over he adopted his beret again.

Below: Victory celebrations on the journey home. Brigadier Julian Thompson (left) lets his hair down with his men aboard *Canberra*.

Above: Hundreds of small boats filled Southampton Water as *Canberra* arrived back in the UK. During the war *Canberra* had been dubbed the 'white whale' by the Task Force. *Below*: The Prince of Wales meets marines aboard *Canberra*. His brother Prince Andrew returned on the carrier *Invincible* where he had served in the front line as a helicopter pilot.

Above: Royal Marine Al Gibson comes close to losing his patience as he direct prisoners in Stanley. *Below*: Injured Argentinian soldiers are searched in Stanley by Military Police after British troops moved back into town to take the surrender.

The last words of this history of the Falklands War belong to Brigadier Julian Thompson, commander of 3 Commando Brigade, who was later named 'Man of the Match' by Major General Jeremy Moore. He said:

So it was all over. There were prisoners to be collected, disarmed and guarded until they could be returned to Argentina. There were minefields and booby traps to clear which would cost two more lives and several more men a foot. But there would be no more fighting and no need to re-embark in ships to assault West Falkland, which would have been necessary if Menendez had not been persuaded to order the capitulation of all Argentinian troops on the islands of the group.

So with luck all of the young men now alive in my Brigade would go home alive, the soldiers of B Company 2 PARA lying asleep in heaps all over the house we shared, so that every square inch of space was covered in bodies, still clutching rifle or machine-gun, only sentries alert: the gunners of 29 Commando Regiment Royal Artillery, asleep beside their now silent guns, only the gun sentries awake, one at each gun, ready to fire the loaded pieces on to the targets on which they were laid; 45 Commando shivering with cold on Sapper Hill; 42 Commando among the rats and debris of the sea-plane hangar; 40 Commando about to go to West Falkland; 2 PARA and 3 PARA in deserted houses, sheds and the racecourse grandstand in the west end of the town; the sappers who had taken part in every attack; my logisticians working through the night, as always, preparing loads at Teal and Ajax Bay for the morrow; Major Armitage missing and with a broken back being kept warm by his driver, Gunner Inch, lying out in the dark and snow all night by the wreck of their Bandwagon, destroyed on a mine when it became separated from my Tactical Headquarters in a snowstorm; Corporal Lockyer my staff car driver who came south at his insistence, without his staff car, but with his rifle, who should have been in the back of Major Armitage's Bandwagon and dead, but at the last moment had replaced another Bandwagon driver. He, and about five thousand others like him in my Brigade, had done what we had come 8,000 miles to do.

Chronology

19 March	Scrap metal merchants land at the disused whaling station at Leith in South Georgia and raise the Argentinian flag
21 March	HMS *Endurance*, the ice patrol ship, re-embarks her Lynx helicopter at Port Stanley along with a Royal Marine detachment and nine members of NP 8901 and sails for South Georgia
22 March	The Argentinian vessel *Bahia Buen Suceso* departs Leith harbour leaving behind a party of scrap metal merchants
23 March	NP 8901 provides security at Stanley airport
24 March	HMS *Endurance* lands Royal Marines to monitor Argentinian activity at Leith
25 March	*Bahia Paraiso* lands Argentinian marines at Leith
27 March	NP 8901 stands guard at Stanley airport
29 March	The new NP 8901 arrives in Stanley
31 March	*Endurance* lands marines at Grytviken, South Georgia
1 April	Bad weather delays Argentinian invasion. Operational command of RM detachment changes with the arrival of new NP 8901
2 April	Argentinian forces invade the Falklands. Royal Marines disperse around Stanley and put up a fierce fight. Governor Rex Hunt orders them to surrender. UN adopts Resolution 502 ordering Argentina to withdraw. Brigadier Julian Thompson and 3 Commando Brigade alerted for operations

Paratroopers of 2 PARA take the opportunity to cook a meal after the battle for Goose Green.

3 April	Special forces units and 148 Battery prepare to depart. Argentinians overrun Royal Marines at Grytviken. South Georgia captured by Argentinian infantry. UN passes Resolution 502 calling for withdrawal of Argentinian forces
4 April	HMS *Conqueror* departs Faslane with 6 Section SBS aboard. Rear Admiral Sandy Woodward transfers flag from *Antrim* to *Glamorgan*. Brigadier Thompson briefs his officers at Plymouth
5 April	Lord Carrington, Foreign Secretary, resigns. The Carrier Group of the Task Force sails from Portsmouth with HQ 3 Commando Brigade on board as well as elements of 40 and 42 Commando units. First Nimrods reach Ascension. NP 8901, which was captured on 2 April and flown to Uruguay, arrives at Brize Norton
6 April	Royal Navy warships at Portsmouth and Plymouth prepare to depart for Falklands
7 April	HMS *Antrim*, *Plymouth* and RFA *Tidespring* refuel from *Fort Austin*. President Ronald Reagan approves Haig peace mission
8 April	*Broadsword* and *Yarmouth* sail from Gibraltar. Haig arrives in the UK
9 April	*Canberra* sails from Portsmouth with 40 and 42 Commando and 3 PARA
10 April	*Antrim* group arrives off Ascension. Haig arrives in Buenos Aires
11 April	M Company 42 Commando embarks *Antrim* at Ascension and sails south under the command of Major Guy Sheridan
12 April	Britain declares 200-mile Maritime Exclusion Zone around the Falklands. Haig returns to London
13 April	Planning continues to establish the best area to land in Falklands
14 April	*Brilliant* group leaves Ascension. Rear Admiral Woodward leaves Ascension on *Glamorgan* with *Alacrity*, *Broadsword* and *Yarmouth*. Haig briefs Reagan in Washington

15 April   Haig returns to Buenos Aires

16 April   Admiral Woodward flies to *Fearless* for talks with Commodore
                     Michael Clapp and Brigadier Thompson. *Invincible* leaves Ascension.
                     Wideawake airfield is the busiest in the world that day

17 April   *Fearless*, RFA *Stromness* and two LSLs arrive at Ascension.
                     Commander-in-Chief of the Fleet Admiral Sir John Fieldhouse and
                     Major General Jeremy Moore fly to Ascension to brief Rear Admiral
                     Woodward, Commodore Clapp and Brigadier Thompson on board
                     Hermes. A Company of 40 Commando RM transfers to *Sir Tristram*

18 April   *Hermes*, *Invincible*, *Broadsword*, *Glamorgan*, *Yarmouth*, *Alacrity*
                     and RFAs *Olmeda* and *Resource* sail from Ascension. Six Victor
                     tankers arrive at Ascension. The Argentinian Navy carrier *Veintecinco
                     de Mayo* returns to port

19 April   NP 8901, re-formed as J Company, 42 Commando, leaves UK for Falklands

20 April   Government gives the go-ahead for Operation Paraquet. *Canberra*
                     and *Elk* arrive at Ascension. The marines captured in South Georgia
                     and thirteen members of British Antarctic Survey team arrive in UK

21 April   *Antrim*'s Wessex recces and drops SBS and SAS on South Georgia. Sea
                     Harrier intercepts snooping Boeing 707

22 April   SAS retrieved from Fortuna Glacier. Two helicopters crash. Foreign
                     Secretary Francis Pym goes to Washington

23 April   Argentinian submarine *Santa Fe* is sunk. M Company 42 Commando
                     lands on South Georgia. Petty Officer B. Casey is killed in Sea King
                     helicopter crash. He is the first casualty of Operation Corporate

24 April   *Atlantic Conveyor* completes fitting of helicopter decks at Devonport.
                     Ships taken up from trade (STUFT) are now hurriedly prepared for sea

25 April   HMS *Intrepid* (which had been out of service), *Atlantic Conveyor*
                     and *Europic Ferry* leave UK. *Atlantic Causeway* is made ready at
                     Plymouth

26 April	Argentinian forces in South Georgia sign surrender agreement. RFA *Blue Rover* arrives at Ascension
27 April	War Cabinet approves the landing of forces in the Falklands. *Norland* and *Sir Bedivere* sail from the UK
28 April	Britain announces that it is to introduce a total exclusion zone to include ships and aircraft of all nations, the aim being to draw Argentinian aircraft out into the open
29 April	Major General Moore flies to Ascension to brief Commodore Clapp and Brigadier Thompson. *SS Uganda*, hospital ship, leaves Ascension for South Atlantic
30 April	President Reagan declares support for UK. At midnight TEZ comes into effect. Two RAF Vulcans and eleven Victor tankers take off from Ascension
1 May	First British special forces land on Falklands. General Haig's peace mission fails. A Vulcan bombs runway at Stanley; Sea Harriers bomb Stanley and Goose Green airfields. They engage and shoot down a Mirage and a Canberra. *QE2* requisitioned by government and returns from mid-Atlantic while heading for the USA
2 May	Argentinian warship *General Belgrano* sunk by submarine HMS *Conqueror*. The main Argentinian Navy returns to port and never puts to sea again
3 May	Helicopters from HMS *Glasgow* and *Coventry* sight and sink patrol vessel *Alferez Soral*
4 May	Sea Harrier shot down over Goose Green. Vulcan attack on Stanley airport. HMS *Sheffield* hit by Exocet missile
5 May	Eight RAF Harriers from No. 1 Squadron arrive at Ascension
6 May	Two Royal Navy Sea Harriers lost in fog. *Argonaut* group sails from Ascension. 2 PARA arrives at Ascension. No. 3 Wing RAF assumes control of Ascension

7 May	Secretary General of UN launches peace initiative
8 May	Extended TEZ enforced. First long-range air drops to Task Force in South Atlantic
9 May	Argentinian 'spy' trawler *Narwhal* strafed by Sea Harriers then boarded by SBS and sunk. *Sir Bedivere* leaves Ascension
10 May	First Nimrods of 206 Squadron RAF support the Task Force
11 May	Argentinian supply ship *Isla de los Estados* sunk by the Type 21 frigate HMS *Alacrity* in Falkland Sound
12 May	*QE2* sails from Southampton with 5 Infantry Brigade aboard. HMS *Glasgow* holed by Argentinian aircraft. Four Argentinian Skyhawks shot down. Sea King ditches. RAF Nimrod sights Boeing 707 spying. 3 Commando Brigade issues operational order for landings
13 May	Brigadier Thompson planning meeting aboard *Fearless*
14 May	SAS raids Pebble Island and destroys all aircraft
15 May	SBS lands in Grantham Sound
16 May	Peace negotiations continue
19 May	Cabinet approval given for landings. Amphibious force carries out cross-decking
20 May	Sea King helicopter lands in Chile
21 May	3 Commando Brigade lands at San Carlos. Diversionary attacks made at Goose Green and Darwin. *Ardent* sunk. Sixteen Argentinian aircraft shot down
22 May	3 Commando establishes a shore hospital at Ajax Bay
23 May	*Antelope* sunk after explosion

24 May   *Sir Lancelot*, *Sir Galahad* and *Sir Tristram* bombed in San Carlos Water

25 May   HMS *Coventry* and *Atlantic Conveyor* sunk

26 May   2 PARA advances on Goose Green

27 May   45 Commando and 3 PARA start yomp to Stanley. SAS to Mount Kent. *QE2*, *Canberra* and *Norland* in South Georgia

28 May   2 PARA battles for Goose Green and Darwin

29 May   Argentinians surrender: 1,300 prisoners taken; PARAs had just 450 men

Paratroopers man a machine-gun during the battle to retake the Falklands.

An Argentinian prisoner is escorted by a soldier of The Parachute Regiment. This Argentinian was a member of the special forces who captured Government House on 2 April. He is wearing a jumper taken from one of the Royal Marines of NP 8901.

30 May   Major General Moore lands in Falklands

31 May   42 Commando flown to Mount Kent. MAWC attacks Argentinian special forces unit. 45 Commando at Teal Inlet. 3 PARA reaches Douglas

1 June   RAF Vulcan attacks on Stanley airport. 5 Brigade disembarks at San Carlos. *Sir Percival* arrives at Teal Inlet

2 June   2 PARA flies to Bluff Cove. Surrender leaflets dropped on Stanley

3 June   RAF Vulcan raids Stanley airport, then lands in Brazil after refuelling problems

5 June   Scots Guards embark in *Fearless* for Fitzroy, where 5 Brigade is established

Gurkha soldiers pose alongside a captured anti-aircraft gun. The Argentinian forces were well equipped, although their personal combat clothing and motivation were poor compared to those of the British forces.

A sailor is welcomed home at Devonport, Plymouth. The naval ports of Plymouth, Portsmouth, Faslane and Rosyth held special celebrations to greet the returning sailors.

6 June	Welsh Guards embark in *Fearless* for Fitzroy
8 June	*Sir Galahad* and *Sir Tristram* bombed at Bluff Cove – fifty-one killed, the majority of casualties being from the Welsh Guards. LCU F4 sunk in Choiseul Sound, six dead. *Plymouth* damaged by bomb. Major General Moore finalises plans for attack on Stanley
9 June	Battle for Stanley begins. 42 Commando attacks Mount Harriet, 45 Commando attacks Two Sisters and 3 PARA is on Mount Longdon
12 June	All attacks successful by dawn. HMS *Glamorgan* hit by land-based Exocet. Final Vulcan attack on Stanley
13 June	2 PARA on Wireless Ridge, Scots Guards at Tumbledown and Gurkhas on Mount William
14 June	All objectives are taken. Argentinian forces surrender

Peter Holdgate's Falklands images have become part of military history. His shot of a Royal Marine yomping across the islands with the Union flag flying from his backpack has become famous across the world. But Peter, a Naval Commando, was part of a media team and remembers on more than one occasion having to take cover as he tried to get the best images. He said: 'I was at San Carlos when an Argentinian air raid was in progress and I heard someone shout "Get down, Pete, get down." The aircraft was coming straight at us and it all seemed to be happening in slow motion.' After the war Peter's famous picture of the yomper was used as the basis of a statue which now graces the entrance to the Royal Marines Museum in Portsmouth.

Acknowledgements

This book would not have been possible without the work of Peter Harclerode. Peter, a military historian and author of numerous books including *PARA!*, *Secret Soldiers* and *Fighting Dirty*, carried out much of the research and I thank him sincerely. I would like to thank Matthew Little at the historical records section of the Royal Marines Museum. Alan Brown at the Airborne Forces Museum also deserves special mention. The accounts lodged at the Royal Marines Museum by Major Ewen Southby-Tailyour, Lieutenant Colonel Whitehead and Lieutenant Colonel Nick Vaux were priceless. I must also thank Ana at the *Buenos Aires Herald* and the Argentinian Air Force. I am also in debt to my good friend Peter Holdgate who has made this book possible with his outstanding photographs from the Falklands War, many of which have become images of history; the Regimental Headquarters of the Welsh Guards and the Scots Guards; Patrick Allen for his knowledge of naval helicopter squadrons; Geoff Page-Bailey, better known as PB, for some of the dits that only PB could remember; Rob Boswell, the commanding officer of 40 Commando's Recce Troop in 1976 and the OC of the MAW Cadre at Top Malo House in the Falklands; and of course George Gill, an old room-mate and outstanding soldier who can truly say he has seen the film, read the book and starred in both. Finally, I thank Julian Thompson, my Commanding Officer in 40 Commando, who became brigadier and eventually major general and kindly wrote the foreword.

Picture Credits

Images were provided by: Andrew Chittock, Dil Banerjee, Richard Spake, Harry Steele, Patrick Allen, Paul Maher, Richard Cooke, Graham Bound and Tom Hannon of The Defence Picture Library; Teddy Neville of TRH Pictures; Tom Smith via the Airborne Forces Museum; Mike Critchley at Maritime Books; and the Royal Navy. Thanks are due to the Royal Navy, the RAF and the Army for their support in collating images. The majority of the pictures were collated by The Defence Picture Library, Sherwell House, 54 Staddiscombe Road, Plymouth, Devon PL9 9NB, www.defencepictures.com.

BIBLIOGRAPHY

History of the Commandos (The Commando Association, 1993)

Ballantyne, Ian, Brumwell, Steve and Reynolds, David, *The Falklands War* (Northcliffe, 1992)

Harclerode, Peter, *PARA! Fifty Years of the Parachute Regiment* (Arms & Armour, 1992)

Hastings, Max, *The Battle for the Falklands* (Michael Joseph, 1983)

Ladd, James, *By Land, By Sea, A History of the Royal Marines* (HarperCollins, 1998)

McManners, Hugh, *Falklands Commando* (William Kimber, 1984)

Oakley, Captain Derek, *The Royal Marines into the Nineties* (DNR, 1993)

Reynolds, David, *3 Commando Brigade RM* (Royal Navy, 1996)

Smith, John, *74 Days, An Islander's Diary of Falklands Occupation* (Century, 1984)

Thompson, Julian, *No Picnic* (Leo Cooper, 1985)

——, *The Royal Marines, From Sea Soldiers to a Special Force* (Sidgwick, 2000)

Underwood, Geoffrey, *Our Falklands War* (Maritime Books, 1983)

Vaux, Nick, *March to the South Atlantic* (Buchan & Enright, 1986)

Wells, Mike and Reynolds, David, *Across the Beach* (Newgate Press Limited, 1995)

West, Nigel, *The Secret War for the Falklands* (Little Brown, 1997)

INDEX